Higher Education at Risk

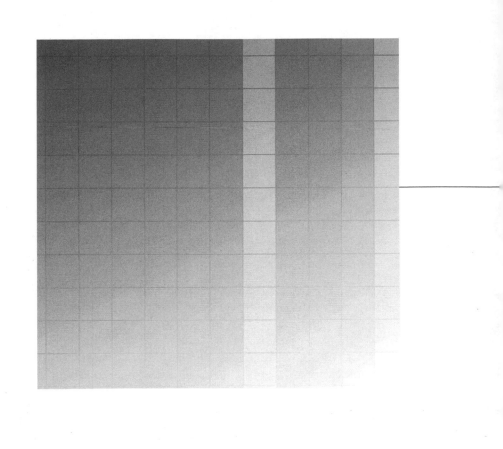

Higher
Education
at Risk

*Strategies to Improve Outcomes,
Reduce Tuition, and Stay Competitive
in a Disruptive Environment*

Sandra Featherman

Foreword by Stephen Joel Trachtenberg

Sty/us

STERLING, VIRGINIA

Sty/us

Published by Stylus Publishing, LLC.
22883 Quicksilver Drive
Sterling, Virginia 20166-2102

Library of Congress Cataloging-in-Publication Data
Featherman, Sandra.
Higher education at risk : strategies to improve outcomes, reduce
tuition, and stay competitive in a disruptive environment /
by Sandra Featherman.
    pages cm
Includes bibliographical references and index.
ISBN 978-1-62036-067-5 (cloth : alk. paper)
ISBN 978-1-62036-069-9 (library networkable e-edition)
ISBN 978-1-62036-070-5 (consumer e-edition)
1. College costs—United States. I. Title.
LB2342.F38 2014
378.3'8—dc23
                                                          2013044058

13-digit ISBN: 978-1-62036-067-5 (cloth)
13-digit ISBN: 978-1-62036-069-9 (library networkable e-edition)
13-digit ISBN: 978-1-62036-070-5 (consumer e-edition)

Printed in the United States of America

All first editions printed on acid-free paper
that meets the American National Standards Institute
Z39-48 Standard.

Bulk Purchases

Quantity discounts are available for use in workshops and for
staff development.
Call 1-800-232-0223

First Edition, 2014

10 9 8 7 6 5 4 3 2 1

CONTENTS

FOREWORD

The invitation to write the foreword to Sandra Featherman's important new book, *Higher Education at Risk*, came at the same time I was asked to address a leadership seminar on the state of American higher education in 2036 organized by the American Association of University Administrators: A splendid coincidence that allowed me to use the manuscript of this important and prescient book to inform my remarks on the future.

At the time of writing I was preparing to speak at the 55th reunion of my Columbia University college class. As I drafted this foreword and thought about my more than half-century career in higher education I came to realize that Columbia's core curriculum is a central part of my personal trinity of knowledge—the core of my core, so to speak.

Part I is the study of the Torah—the Five Books of Moses, revealing in a written and oral tradition the ethics and practices of the oldest of the Abrahamic religions. Part II is Columbia University's core curriculum—the accomplishments of Western civilization and, as amended, Eastern civilization, studied primarily through the humanities: history, literature, philosophy, and fine arts. And Part III is Mario Puzo's *The Godfather* (1969)—a practical guide to how to live life, outlined, more or less, in ten steps, two of which are: "Make him an offer he can't refuse;" and "Keep your friends close but your enemies closer."

Sandra Featherman has forced herself to think about the unthinkable, producing a book that candidly addresses the challenges to American higher education in the first quarter of the 21st century. And through the use of experience, diligent scholarship, case studies, and observations she provides prescriptions that may help to preserve the best of higher education as we know it and as we adapt it in the decades to come.

Obviously, as we know and as this book explains, in 20 years the rationale for the college experience will be very different from today's understanding. We will have adapted many, but probably not all, of the place based ivy-campus traditions to a world including virtual learning, which will combine Star Trek, Harry Potter, Google Glass, and other characteristics yet unrevealed.

For centuries, the bricks-and-mortar campus has served us in four primary ways:

First, it is the traditional *learning hub* for the transmission of knowledge from one generation to another; the place where students establish a broad-based intellectual underpinning and ultimately master a specific discipline. For most of the academy's history, these have been designed as a series of pedagogical silos—discipline A residing vertically next to discipline B next to discipline C, with only minor horizontal interchange. Both the learning hub and the silos will change by 2036. Disciplines will collide; the quad surrounded by academic buildings will continue to open its gates. Integration—not isolation—of knowledge will become more common.

Second, universities conduct *research*, applied and basic, in all fields of study: the sciences, social sciences, humanities, and fine arts. This research stretches the boundaries of known knowledge, and takes at least one day a week of the faculty's time. A good deal of this will remain in the domain of faculty members but more and more will move out of the academy and into less institutional settings. *The New York Times* recently profiled a group of "billionaires with big ideas [who] are privatizing American science" (Broad, 2014). Researchers at institutions are used to going out to find funding. Now the funders are going out to find the researchers. Often they build their own facilities, hire their own staff, and conduct their own work. This could significantly alter research on campus as research often leads the prestige parade in the rankings and perceptions of academic quality.

If you combine private research with open source collaboration, the research field will get broader and wider very quickly.

Third, a function of place-based education is *socialization*. College serves as a halfway house between adolescence and adulthood for millions of 18- to 22-year-olds; the four years spent on campus coincide with the transition from financial and emotional reliance on one's family to the establishment of individual independence. Parents are delighted their daughters and sons are out of the house as hormones rage and social behaviors are pushed to extremes. If children do not go off to college, parents will find some other place to export them. And frankly, for $50,000 (plus out of pocket expenses) there are a lot of options.

And last, but certainly not least, colleges and universities provide the *six skills* necessary to successfully compete in the work world: (1) critical thinking; (2) working as part of a team; (3) taking responsibility for one's actions, (4) punctuality, and (5 & 6) the ability to write cogently and speak persuasively. Colleges believe they are doing a fine job at this assignment; industry disputes that assumption. Teaching life skills isn't easy. In the years to come a middle ground will be found, keeping some tasks with colleges and moving others to the work place.

Featherman assists us in better understanding these four components and others. Will they occur on a traditional on-site college and university campus? Will the campus continue as a platform, but the methodology of instruction and research change? Should work-place skills be taught elsewhere?

In the pages that follow Featherman is clear-eyed about the direction that higher education needs to take, and in doing so offers some trenchant prescriptions around issues such as tenure, athletics, responsiveness to students' changing needs, and the "arms race" for improved facilities.

Change does not come easily to the academy. The transition from the Cambridge, England in the year 1200 to Cambridge, Massachusetts in the present day is pretty much a flat line. Lectures and tutorials from master to student are conducted in a format easily recognizable from one generation to the next. If Socrates walked into a typical law school classroom today he'd feel right at home. (Hmm. That sounds like the start of an old joke.)

Yes, there has been some tweaking of the old family recipe of higher education; the two most conspicuous changes are diversity and affordability. Women and other previously marginalized groups are now admitted to the once all-male student body; and scholarships and financial aid have seriously leveled the socio-economic playing field from the time when largely the rich went on to enroll in colleges and universities. Today, nearly anyone who wishes to attend a school of post-secondary education can find an affordable place to go. There is at least a community college in almost every congressional district.

In the past fifteen years, we have witnessed serious inroads to the traditional structure of colleges, most noticeably changes brought about by the information technology revolution and the rise of social media.

The answers to most of life's questions are now more easily accessible online than in the classroom. When I was a kid my parents would answer a question I asked with the response, "Look it up in the encyclopedia." Today, the phrase, "Google it" is a part of the daily lexicon.

Throughout the ages, each generation has used new technology to probe deeper, calculate faster, and make connections among more complicated and random factoids than previously considered. Let's look at the development of communications technology, a field that is evolutionary—like so many other human tools. It began in prehistoric times with sharp rocks, sticks, and pictograms on cave walls; then papyrus, moveable type, flags, and blinking lights to send messages from ship to ship, village to village; smoke rings to signal war, peace, and Papal elections; dots and dashes across the wires of the telegraph; and now apps on smartphones and tablets. We've moved from charcoal sticks to lead pencils to lasers beams; from fresco cycles to PowerPoint. Technology is an aid and a tool but not an end in and of itself.

What will be the technology du jour in 2036? We can only guess. But we can be assured something new will be on the horizon, something unfathomable to our current state of thinking; something "revolutionary," as were the inventions of the printing press and the home computer.

Bless technology for the aid it provides the learning process, but never succumb to the belief that it is THE ultimate panacea.

All of the following gadgets and processes, many considered "wonders of the world," were invented and developed by the human mind and hand—it takes imagination to move the world forward but it is the application of the technology that is the important factor, not the tool itself. Here are a few examples:

- The abacus, invented 2500 BCE, is the first calculating tool.
- Dutch lenses of the early 1600s perfected the telescope and microscope, to study things large and small, far and near.
- An Englishman gave us the slide rule in the 1650s—the second calculating tool.
- Mitch Kapor provided the world with Lotus 1-2-3 and Bill Gates created Office, software that calculates, writes, and edits in systematic order and then helps us rearrange our worksheets in a totally new format—a perfect system for those of us who are always saying, "On second thought…"
- And, of course, Steve Jobs taught us the power of a simple swipe of our fingers—how Zen!

Technology will continue to play a major component of the learning process—making connections faster than the human mind can process. Platforms will be open and collaboration will abound, sharing knowledge and pushing the boundaries faster than traditional silos. Software will provide more learning tools and management applications, redesigning how classes are taught, information gathered and analyzed.

When I was growing up in Brooklyn in the 1940s, a man who lived down the street from my house enjoyed a good game of chess. One of his favorite opponents was his adult son who lived in Boston. They sent chess moves to each other via postcards—long distance telephone calls were scarce and expensive in those days. The men learned tactics and patience.

The technology phrase of the year 2014 is "data analytics" —whether it is big, medium, or small, data is analyzed and applied to most aspects of university life: administrative, pedagogical, and accountability. Twenty years from now it will be something different, as yet unnamed, and twenty years after that, and so on.

MOOCs (Massive Open Online Courses) have proven themselves to be a grand experiment but not yet a learning panacea. But they will be reassessed, refined, and retested in the market place in the coming years. One chief information officer, John Unsworth at Brandeis University, calls MOOCs "marketing over other considerations." Soon we will move beyond the hype of MOOCs and find an interesting blend of place-based and electronic learning, giving students more choices—some traditional, many not-so-traditional—that will develop flexibility in what is learned and where it is learned. In the new lingo, students will find pathways suited to the individual, not only to the institution, and the colleges that help to provide those pathways will be on the cutting edge. In the 1970s we called this "defining one's own major" and it required the dean's approval.

Students will become more of an equal partner at the learning table than previously was the case. The professor at the front of the room of 200 students sitting politely in fixed seat rows is almost an extinct relic. Posted office hours are part of the past. Want to reach your professor, send her a text and wait for a speedy reply. Will this intellectual parity have a maturing effect on students? Endow them with a heavy does of responsibility? Hard to know.

Over the course of the last 10 years, we've increasingly read in the press that a college degree is transactional. People want to know how much their degrees will cost, what kind of a job will they get at the end, and how much will they be paid by their employers. This may be the current rhetoric but I find it terribly sad. Call me old fashioned but I believe a college education should put a little wonder into each student's mind each semester: I wonder what the Greeks were thinking when they sailed off to Troy; why did Michelangelo put those figures on the Sistine Chapel; and can the Founding Fathers and Mothers—God Bless Abigail Adams—be replicated to restore democracy to America?

The years of college should have a heavy dose of intellectual exploration and frankly, if that comes from books on paper, music on CDs or iTunes, iPads, and Kindles, I don't much care. I'll be disappointed if we replace the study of literature for a session on effective public speaking; or if we remove the foreign language requirement from the undergraduate curriculum and replace it with a class in social behavior.

I don't want to throw out the baby with the bath water. Disruptive change must be constructive as it reinvents the form and format of higher education and, in the end, we must all remember that education begins with a capital E. Teach me something I don't already know; connect it to the past and project it into the future. A good education transforms our lives by teaching us how to be discerning readers and astute thinkers; to analyze with judgment and listen with acuity. In sum, a master professor teaches her students how to care about learning and to learn with care.

And remember, evolution and revolution are two different things. Mixed together—shaken or stirred—you have a potent cocktail.

Whatever the format, whether delivered by a flash drive or a bolt from heaven, education should knock your socks off.

Those who read Sandra Featherman's book will need to buy new socks, but they will also be armed for the exciting and challenging agenda facing all of us who earn our livelihoods in the world of higher education. And because of this volume, higher education will be less at risk and more likely to not only survive but prevail.

Stephen Joel Trachtenberg

President Emeritus and Professor

The George Washington University

Washington, DC

and

Chairman of the Higher Education Practice

Korn Ferry International

References

Broach, W. J. (2014, March 15). Billionaires with big ideas are privatizing American science. *The New York Times*, p. A1.

Puzo, M. (1969). *The godfather*. New York, NY: Putnam.

Trachtenberg, S. (2014, April). Keynote presentation session. *Higher education in Transition: Looking Ahead to 2036*. Seminar conducted at the American Association of University Administrators 2014 Leadership Seminar, Washington, DC.

For about a decade, I have been thinking about how to control the rising costs of higher education. I had been speaking and occasionally writing about why costs rose faster than the rate of inflation, and suggesting to colleagues the ways in which our institutions could cope with declining revenues and increased cost pressures. At times I was partly an apologist for tuition increases and partly an advocate for tighter management controls, but increasingly I have become a critic of our cultural lack of capacity to make rapid and meaningful adaptations to the changes occurring in our external environment.

As a commissioner of the New England Association of Schools and Colleges (NEASC) Commission on Institutions of Higher Education, I was able to overview many different types of colleges and universities in our region, from small independent church-related colleges to nationally renowned liberal arts colleges and major research universities. One of the most stimulating experiences I had at NEASC was the opportunity to participate in a small-group private discussion with several leaders of for-profit education corporations. It was an eye-opener for me, changing my worldview of the potential of for-profit higher education possibilities. It made me realize that in spite of the issues concerning the lackluster academic performance of the for-profit sector, it had the motive, the intentionality, and the means to improve its act and grow.

As I watched states cut public college budgets and saw the investment portfolios of many colleges fall during the recession, I kept thinking about how the for-profit colleges were growing, and what useful lessons the non-profit sector could learn from the best of what the for-profits were doing.

What led me to start writing this book was the experience of a woman I met, Marianne, whose story of overwhelming college loan debts follows. I have made a number of efforts to contact her by phone and e-mail, to let her know I have told her story, all without success. I hope that she is in a good place with her career and is pleased that she was the catalyst for some of my ideas to help eventually lower federal college loan debts for future students.

Many people in academia will not agree with the recommendations I make. Some are drastic. All involve significant changes to the way business is usually done in higher education circles and institutions. I could have made less culture-changing suggestions, but they would not have helped American colleges survive, and I believe that institutional survival is at stake.

I have very little physical courage, but over the years I believe that I have demonstrated another type of courage by making difficult political decisions within the institutions at which I have served. You cannot move an institution forward without taking actions that will alienate some constituents.

Every decision to change the way an institution performs involves allocative determinations that, at the minimum, alter benefits and costs for people and programs within the institution. If nothing is altered, and no one gets angry, then generally nothing has been done.

When I came to the University of Minnesota Duluth as the vice chancellor for academic affairs, my life was threatened by a group that called itself "the Deer Hunters." For four years, they sent me letters claiming that I would be assassinated, because of my diversity efforts. It was also made clear that whoever sent the threats did not want a woman in such a senior position.

At first, I kept the threats quiet, sharing them only with the leadership of the university, because I did not want to be perceived as a victim. When I learned that the threatening environment had preceded me by several years, and been hushed up across the university system, I decided to go public. "Every time I am threatened for wanting to write all the invisible groups in American history back into the history we teach here, I am going to make another diversity effort," I told the press. "We will turn each lemon of a threat into lemonade."

While I was at the university I received the Administrator of the Year Award from Minnesota Women in Higher Education. It was a lovely award, but having regular anonymous threats against your life is not easy to tolerate. The FBI agent dealing with it told me that people who made such threats rarely carried them out, but I knew that men who threaten women often did fulfill their threats.

The threatening letters were not the only form of harassment I faced in Minnesota. In my final months there, on the eve of the anniversary of Kristallnacht (the night when Nazis shattered the windows of Jewish homes across Germany), someone spray painted "Gas Featherman and burn Levy" on a hallway wall in one of our buildings. Harold Levy is in fact not Jewish. He is African American and was the director of affirmative action at the university at the time.

Another time, because of my support for gay and lesbian issues, a reporter called to tell me that he had been told I was a lesbian. "Is it true?" he asked me. "I am not answering that question," I said. I told him it was homophobic to ask. When I told my husband about it, I was very proud of him for commending me for standing up for what was right.

Earlier in my career, I had served as president of the faculty senate at Temple University. When I was a candidate for the position, the faculty union leader came to see me to urge me to join the union. I told him that I was not opposed to the union but could not join because I could never participate in a strike that would cut off classes for students. He assured me that the faculty would never strike.

I got elected in spite of my position. Later, when I accepted an appointment as assistant to the university president, some faculty felt that I had sold my soul. During a faculty strike that did take place, some professors refused to speak to me. Some faculty who taught during the strike were shunned by colleagues for the rest of their careers. Fortunately for me, faculty leaders remembered my long-term commitment to never going on strike if it could negatively affect students.

Several years later, desiring to teach again, I let the president know that I wanted to return to faculty status. After he ignored my requests for a while, I sent him a formal notice of my intention. A few days later, he stopped by my office to tell me that someone had sent him a note about it and had signed my name to it.

When I became a university president, I undertook a number of acts that were controversial at the time, including a merger with another college, 30 miles away. During my tenure we redesigned our college structure, outsourced some functions that had previously been done in-house, dramatically increased both our enrollments and our income, and changed from a teaching to a research-oriented institution.

At one of my retirement parties, a lovely member of our staff, Andrew Golub, made a toast to me. "You are retiring as a beloved president," he said to me and the assembled group. My immediate response was one of true surprise. "Damn," I said. "I wish someone had told me that sooner." I had always feared that one day I would awaken to newspaper reports that the faculty had voted "no confidence" in me.

It says a lot about the quality of the faculty at the University of New England that it never did so, not because I was so good, but because most of our faculty were so good. They were willing to undergo change to help the institution move forward and thrive.

A lot of good people have helped me in almost every endeavor I have ever undertaken. For this book, a number of academic and business leaders shared their knowledge and their insights with me, helping me to understand what they were seeing and experiencing in their worlds. I am exceedingly grateful to them.

Most of the people I interviewed for this book received advance copies of the questions I was going to ask them. The questions were quite similar for most of those interviewed, with occasional questions that related to specific circumstances of the college or agency or business in which the interviewee was engaged.

The persons interviewed were selected because of their specific knowledge or experience. I made no effort to interview large numbers of colleagues. Rather, I limited the discussions to a set of leaders I knew and respected who, for the most part, were involved in leading or evaluating institutions undergoing important changes.

Three regional accreditation agency leaders provided an excellent overview of changes occurring among colleges in their regions: Barbara Brittingham, president of the Commission on Institutions of Higher Education, NEASC; Belle Wheelan, president of the Southern Association of Colleges and Schools Commission on Colleges; and Richard Winn, senior vice president of the Western Association of Schools and Colleges Senior College and University Commission. Winn also shared outstanding insights into the rapid changes occurring in the for-profit sector overseen by his agency.

Judith Eaton, president of the Council for Higher Education Accreditation, provided valuable information about challenges facing colleges and accrediting agencies nationally. Konrad Miskowicz-Retz of the Commission on Osteopathic College Accreditation forwarded numerous newsletters and reports on higher education and federal policies to me. Stephen Shannon, president of the American Association of Colleges of Osteopathic Medicine, shared thoughts about the future of academic medical training.

Chancellors, college presidents, and senior staff were extremely generous in providing information. They include Terrence MacTaggart, who served as chancellor of the University of Maine System, and before that as president of the Minnesota State College System; Neil Theobald, president of Temple University; Danielle Ripich, president of the University of New England; Ronnie B. Martin, dean of the College of Osteopathic Medicine at Liberty University; and especially Paul LeBlanc, president of Southern New Hampshire University, who generously gave me far more time answering questions than I had originally asked for. He also opened for me, and for all of higher education, a whole new way of thinking about how we account for what we offer and what our students learn.

Two business leaders of for-profit education corporations were extremely helpful. One was Richard Pattenaude, president of for-profit Ashford University, former president of the University of Southern Maine, and former chancellor of the University of Maine System. The other leader was John R. McKernan, Jr., governor of Maine from 1987 to 1995, who served as the chief executive officer of Education Management Corporation until 2012, and remains a member of its 11-member board. McKernan, who chairs the board of the Maine Community College System, was also recently named as president of the U.S. Chamber of Commerce Foundation.

Other academic leaders who provided information include William Strampel, dean of the College of Osteopathic Medicine at Michigan State University; several administrative leaders at Liberty University; and Donna Shalala, president of the University of Miami. Peter Mills, executive director of the Maine Turnpike Authority and former state senator, provided me with helpful information and insights.

Some of the individuals who provided very forthright observations said I could quote what they said but politely asked me in a few instances not to say that they were the ones who said it, especially when they were critical of colleagues or making remarks their boards might not sanction. I honored those requests. Several people asked me not to identify them at all, such as the person who still preferred to think of the college owner as a "founder."

My colleagues on the board and staff of Florida Polytechnic University also helped, without realizing it, by forcing me to focus on the issues they and I saw continually confronting a new public university.

I particularly want to thank Susan Slesinger, whose excellent and extensive reviews and suggestions helped to strengthen the book, and John von Knorring for his thoughtful editing suggestions. Alexandra Hartnett was always available to me for editing advice. I also want to thank my son John for doing an early and comprehensive review, and my son Andrew for his suggestions and review.

Finally, I must give a bucket load of thanks to my husband, Bernard, for his love and strong support. He not only read endless drafts, but nagged me day and night to finish my work on the book, especially on days when I despaired that what I was writing would ever be properly completed.

It is unlikely that any of those mentioned would agree with all or even most of my recipes for higher education. The information and ideas they provided grounded the book and offered windows into their worlds of both nonprofit and for-profit higher education.

The flaws are all my own. I hope that they are minimal, and that the ideas for changes they seek to accomplish will be deemed more important than the problems of either commission or omission.

Higher education offers us the chance to have a more perfect society, if we can sustain its best features and modify those that need change.

1 Higher Education at Risk

Several years ago, I met Marianne. A part-time housekeeper for a friend of mine, she had just enrolled in a local community college as a nursing student. As an older student, she told me that she was studying nursing so that she could eventually earn a decent living.

"You know, Marianne," I told her, after she had finished her first year of classes, "you might want to go back for your bachelor's degree after you work for a year or two. You would have improved job options."

Her response shocked me.

"Sandra, I have a bachelor's degree. In fact, I have a law degree."

She told me that after she graduated from law school, she could not get a job as a lawyer. She took low-wage jobs, to make a living, and ended up with a student loan debt of nearly a quarter of a million dollars. She was taking up nursing in order to earn enough to pay down some of that debt, which she believed would never be fully paid off because, as she reminded me, you cannot eliminate federal student loan obligations by declaring bankruptcy.

I told her story to another friend recently, who told me that her neighbor's housekeeper had two master's degrees and also had difficulty finding work in her degree fields.

Where Higher Education Is Going

Public higher education ought to be free in our country, just as public basic education is. Students should not have to go deeply into debt to get the kind of education that would not only give them secure futures, but also benefit the nation by supplying well-trained and educated graduates to fill the jobs that a good society requires.

It is not likely to become free for most students in the near future, though. Instead, it is likely to become more expensive as state governments grapple with significant budget problems competing for those higher education dollars.

There is much about American higher education that is wonderful. We have grand universities, some of the best in the world. College life on several thousand campuses across the nation so enriches the recipients of the programs in those schools that they bond with the colleges for a lifetime, giving and bequeathing generous gifts to their alma maters. They make friendships that last for years and often find homecoming events at their former colleges to be among their most anticipated trips.

Our colleges and universities are such good places to be that few of us would want to do much more than tweak them into modest improvements, year after year, the sum total of which would ensure their continued relevancy and excellence. Much as we would like to consign our colleges to such a smooth and pleasant future, two major issues have occurred that are disrupting that trajectory: the rising cost of a college degree, which is outstripping the ability of potential students to afford to invest in it; and the competition rearing up from more aggressive nonprofit colleges, online classes, and especially the for-profit college explosion of growth.

The number one problem facing higher education today is the student debt that upward spiraling costs have engendered. Although the average student debt is $26,600 for those with loans, many people are graduating with much higher debt, and even worse, many students, especially at for-profit colleges, are dropping out of programs of questionable value and accumulating high debts with no degrees to show for it.

Lured by advertisements promoting easy access and tantalizing job opportunities, too many people have signed on for college programs for which they are inadequately prepared, for methods of instruction that may not be appropriate for their learning needs, or for career training for fields that are either overcrowded with entrants or that offer compensation levels far below what those advertisements led prospects to believe.

The issue of student debt has been highlighted recently because of the economic problems facing the nation, but debt relative to what students can expect to be able to earn after graduation has been a growing problem for some time. Higher education costs have generally grown faster than inflation over the last 60 or so years, for a number of reasons that I will examine, but state and federal funding growth, along with institutionally provided scholarship funds, papered over the problem until the recession of 2008 propelled it into the public arena in the years that followed.

For example, a report from *Bloomberg News* indicated that "college tuition and fees have surged 1,120 percent since records began in 1978, four times faster than the increase in the consumer price index" (Jamrisko & Kolet,

2012). At my alma mater, the University of Pennsylvania, the yearly cost of liberal arts undergraduate education in 1950 was $600 tuition, a $25 general fee, and room and board costs of $690, a total of $1,315. Those costs increased to $58,328 in 2013–14 (Penn University Archives & Records Center, 2013).

As a result of the downturn in the economy, states faced huge budget shortfalls. To deal with their budget problems, many governors and legislatures gave flat or declining allocations to their state-funded colleges. At the same time, as the national economy went through a period of decline, followed by political divisiveness over the federal budget, businesses trimmed their employee rolls. Graduating students could not get jobs. Debts on student loans piled up.

Suddenly, the media was covering the issues of student debt, the tight job market, and rising tuition levels. Together, these stories have had a substantial impact on prospective student choices. Law schools have seen their applications decline dramatically, to almost half their previous high. Many undergraduate colleges with high tuition levels are facing continued steep declines in enrollments, or else the need to offer more internally funded financial aid, both of which are straining the resources of tuition-dependent institutions.

Competition is the other major issue that conventional colleges are facing. Competition from rapidly expanding for-profit colleges already has lured tens of thousands of students away from traditional colleges. For-profit colleges advertise more aggressively for students and are likely to continue to do so. Many prospective students do not really understand what the difference is between for-profit and nonprofit colleges. We can expect the for-profit sector to continue to grow, as new companies seek entry and as present ones seek to expand, even in the face of what are temporary cutbacks for some.

Higher education institutions are facing problems for which they are inadequately prepared, not because there are not smart enough minds at the helms of the colleges, but because their culture of consultation and respect for tradition makes them slow responders and slow adapters of change, at a time when major changes in the competitive marketplace are confronting the entire sector.

Colleges today must be prepared for and able to cope with new forms of competition for students, rising costs that many prospective students will no longer be able to afford, declining public support, greater use of technology in delivering content, potential separation of assessment from delivery of academic programming, job placement issues, and increased federal accountability demands.

Not all of our presently functioning colleges will be able to meet all these challenges successfully. Many people in higher education realize this. So do many observers. In *The American Interest,* Nathan Harden (2012) opens his article, "The End of the University as We Know It," with a powerful warning, by stating what has become a much repeated mantra by critics worried about the future of higher education. He claims that "in fifty years, if not much sooner, half of the roughly 4,500 colleges and universities now operating in the United States will have ceased to exist. The technology driving this change is already at work, and nothing can stop it."

Many higher education administrators and supporters know that financing their institutions is becoming more difficult, but they think that their own schools will ultimately manage to squeak by, or even be successful. Like ostriches, they are ignoring the telltale signs of massive change.

Just consider the vast number of elementary, middle, and high schools that have closed across the nation in recent years. For example, more than one of every four Catholic schools across the country was closed or consolidated between the 2000 and 2013 school years, the total being 2,090. The number of students enrolled declined by 651,298, a 24.5% loss. According to the National Catholic Educational Association (2013), elementary schools have been the most seriously impacted.

But it is not just religious schools that have been faced with closures, and potential closures. Public schools are closing, too, at least in large urban areas. The city of Chicago recently closed 54 public schools, and Philadelphia has proposed to close 37. A number of other cities across the country are also closing public schools, and citizen backlashes are taking place as complaints are filed in those cities, their states, and through the U.S. Department of Education's Office for Civil Rights.

Public schools are closing because there are too few students in many large city public schools for the school districts to be able to support keeping all their schools open. Families with young children have been moving out of the cities to the suburbs, but they have been doing that for more than 60 years, so while the trend continues, it is unlikely to be the only reason, or even the major reason, for the decline in numbers of children available to populate city schools.

Many of the students who have left public schools and Catholic schools appear to have moved to the new charter schools opening up across the country. Charter schools are publicly funded by their community school districts but enjoy substantial flexibility in their management, rather than being controlled by their school district boards.

The growth of charter schools has changed both public and private school enrollment patterns across the country. One study asserts that "while most students are drawn from traditional public schools, charter schools are pulling large numbers of students from the private education market and present a potentially devastating impact on the private education market, as well as a serious increase in the financial burden on taxpayers. Catholic schools seem particularly vulnerable, especially for elementary students in large metropolitan areas" (Buddin, 2012).

What happened to the public schools and Catholic schools was a game changer: the arrival of a different kind of entity that embodied a mix of public school funding with the smaller size and more personalized attention to students given by private schools at no cost to the parents. Higher education is also ripe for game changing. There are four potential game changers facing higher education right now. The first is the rise of for-profit competitors. The second is the development of technological innovations that are enabling high-quality online classes. The third is the establishment of consortia that can bring powerful institutions together to offer classes and degree programs that few smaller public or private colleges will be able to afford to invest in. And the fourth, of course, is higher education costs and debt, which have now spiraled almost out of control.

If our public and parochial schools at the elementary level are feeling the pain, even though our public schools are free, what is the prognosis for our nonprofit colleges, when most of them, even the public ones, now cost more than the average student can afford to pay?

Colleges That Will Not Succeed

Just as with the elementary through high school closings, many colleges will be closed or consolidated. There are no charter schools competing with them, of course. Instead, there are much more powerful economic and social forces that together are going to alter the fundamental way that we conceive of a college-going experience.

"There is a convergence of issues confronting higher education right now," Richard Winn, senior vice president of the Western Association of Schools and Colleges (WASC) Accrediting Commission for Senior Colleges and Universities, told me in an interview. "The days when colleges could just pass on their costs to their students are over. What is happening in some states, such as California, is that as the state colleges lose money, they offer fewer courses, and so students often can't get courses they need to fulfill their graduation requirements."

The response of students to changes in cost and availability of programs is going to lead them to explore multiple options, which many are in fact doing already. For-profit companies see an opportunity for business in higher education. In fact, more than half of the new schools seeking WASC accreditation are for-profit.

In response to a question about the likely impact of for-profit colleges on public and independent nonprofit colleges over the coming decade, Winn replied that the impact could be massive. He said that for-profit companies offering college courses are very agile. "They can turn things around in a matter of weeks," he said, whereas nonprofit higher education is not very nimble.

WASC is so concerned about colleges being prepared for the challenges they will be facing that it now requires every institution it accredits to do an essay identifying forces of change impacting the institution.

Many of the higher education leaders interviewed for this study agree overwhelmingly that some types of schools are at great risk for survival. Those schools can generally be described as less selective or nonselective colleges. These colleges are highly tuition dependent, needing to bring in enough students each year to meet their expenses. Most of them are small, private nonprofit colleges. Generally, colleges with fewer than 5,000 students are considered small. Many of those at greatest risk, however, have fewer than 2,500 students, and a number have under 1,000 students.

They are small colleges less by their choice than by market choice. Too few students select them each year to allow them to grow. Many would like nothing more than to admit many more students. The ceilings on their total enrollment are not determined by how many students they are willing to admit, but by how many are willing to enroll.

By contrast, elite colleges, with a healthy excess of applications over seats available, determine their class sizes by intention. Many of the elite small colleges have set the size of their student body at some institutionally agreed-upon target, often somewhere between 1,500 and 1,800 students. These colleges have decided on the numbers they will admit based on an assessment of the size they believe will yield them enough students to support a broad enough mix of courses, an appealing selection of clubs and activities, and a large enough group of students on campus to enable these activities to function, while allowing the college to maintain a small-community feeling.

They can succeed because even if application numbers drop in a given year, a school with a strong reputation can lower its admission criteria just a little, or dip into the applicants on its waiting list, to still meet its desired class size. Many of these colleges slightly expanded the size of their classes in the late 1990s, when some college consultants were claiming that smaller class sizes might not be sustainable, and that a majority of prospective students no longer thought of smallness as a desirable attribute they were seeking from a college. The additional enrollees also meant additional income for those colleges with application numbers deep enough to allow increases in incoming class sizes without significantly lowering the bar for admission.

Unfortunately, most American private colleges were not in a position to do this. They would gladly have taken in more students, if only they could.

However, for too many small schools, there is no waiting list, and most applicants are admitted, even if they are only minimally college-ready. Then, once admitted, students have to be wooed to enroll and pay their deposits. Today, most applicants apply to multiple colleges, so that when they receive admissions letters, they can compare what is being offered by each school that has accepted them.

For those colleges with no application piles to fall back on, a shortfall in enrolled students can lead to a shortfall in the institutional budget. These are tuition-dependent colleges, meaning that most of the income they derive each year comes from student tuition dollars. To get those dollars, in the competitive marketplace, they frequently cut the cost of tuition for many of their applicants, offering the cuts in the form of student aid. The trick for these colleges is to be sure that the reductions they offer are not too deep overall, and that they still enable the college to bring in enough dollars from the students who do enroll without cutting fees so much that the college ends up with its finances in the red and an inability to stay afloat.

Most of these small tuition-dependent colleges are decent places to get an undergraduate education, but because they are not perceived as exclusive, or lack large endowments, they have to hang on to life by their fingernails, by discounting the costs of admission, building athletic programs to lure students who might not make the teams of more competitive schools, and admitting more marginal students than they want to in order to balance the books.

Now some of them are in very serious trouble. One college president recently told me, "You would be shocked by the cocktail hour chatter I have been hearing at education conferences, where presidents are saying things like they hope their school can hang on five more years, until they reach retirement age."

An article in the *Boston Globe* about the closing of several private colleges that served the New England region speculated that more closings could be looming because these colleges are "heavily dependent" on New England recruits. Because the number of high school graduates in New England is facing a steep decline, colleges that are dependent on students from the region could face a convergence of problems, including "a steep drop in the number of high school graduates, increasing sensitivity to cost, and new competition from online higher education and other cheaper alternatives" (Marcus, 2013).

Several academic leaders who lead or have chaired accreditation commissions say that small, faith-based colleges are at real risk of closing. One leader said that many of those schools are experiencing a death rattle: "Their support is eroding, and support for their particular doctrines is eroding."

Liberty University, however, which calls itself a Christian university without designating a denomination, is thriving. It has been the fastest growing college in the nation, largely because of its strong embrace of technology and online degree programs.

While we can expect a number of small private colleges to close, merge, or be bought out by for-profit education firms, public colleges also will not be fully insulated from similar problems, just as some public elementary, middle, and high schools (K–12) were not exempt from being closed. Although local public demand and consequent public dollars will keep many of them afloat, branch campuses will close and small public colleges will undergo administrative mergers.

We can expect to see substantial changes over the next decade. As public dollars for higher education dwindle, not necessarily in absolute dollars, but in dollars provided per student, cutbacks are inevitable. Most states will not be able to fund higher education at the levels they did two decades ago. The impacts of the recession are not the sole factor in this decreased ability to provide funding. Even in an improved economy, financial problems for public higher education will remain.

The need for state funds for higher education competes with the need for funds for K–12 education, health care, and the criminal justice system, all major cost drivers putting increasing pressures on state budgets. Many states also face significant financial challenges because of underfunded public employee pension commitments.

An analysis of state pension funds found that while state unfunded pension liabilities vary greatly from state to state, the median state has set aside just 45 cents for every dollar it owes. The analysis suggests that the states are almost a trillion dollars short in their obligations to their pension funds, not including the additional obligations of local governments, such as school districts (Walsh, 2013). According to Moody's Investors Service (Moody's, 2013b), which released the findings, the ratios of adjusted net liabilities to state resources reflect pension burdens faced by the states, all of which have apparently underfunded their pension liabilities to some extent.

Yet, even as available dollars to support college budgets appear to be receding, college costs have been growing faster than the rate of inflation and are likely to continue to do so because the provision of higher education is extremely human resource intensive.

As a nation, going forward, we will need to provide college educations for more, not fewer, students. As our population continues to grow, more people than ever will need a college degree. A compounding issue is that the recession of 2008 demonstrated that persons without a college degree were far more likely to lose their jobs, not be able to get new jobs, or else only be competitive for new jobs at lower compensation rates.

For small and less prestigious public colleges, other than community colleges, the major changes likely to occur will be similar to those afflicting the private colleges, but not quite so severe. They will not close, but their programs will be reduced, their staffs will often be cut back, and many will find themselves merged with other public colleges or becoming branch campuses of larger universities. Even at the University of Southern Maine, the second largest higher education institution in that state (based on full-time equivalent students), budget reductions required the institution to trim the number of its collegiate units, which was done by reorganizing programs.

Many of the small colleges that may not succeed are good places where students can receive a decent education and have a wonderful college life. Almost all of our nonprofit colleges in this country are good schools with much to commend them. Their boards volunteer untold hours to governance issues, their administrators work long hours to position and improve the prospects for both their students and their institutions, the faculty is committed to providing interesting and meaningful learning, the alumni are loyal, and the students for the most part feel wanted and nourished.

Often, over the years, parents I have known have asked me what colleges their sons and daughters should select. I have always advised them that there are more than 3,000 good colleges offering undergraduate degrees, and that their child should visit several that offer courses of study in which he or she is interested, then pick the one that provides the most comfortable fit. I have always believed that the first step toward graduating from college is picking a college that "feels right." But that was before debt loads got completely out of hand. Now, the combination of total net cost and the debt that will build up has to be considered.

For colleges that are highly tuition dependent, the future looks scary. A tuition-dependent college is an institution whose annual income is largely supplied by student tuition. It has limited endowment funds; generates little investment income; does not raise enough dollars through gifts and grants to fund more than a few months of expenses, if any; and has limited other sources of revenue.

A great many private nonprofit colleges in America are in this category. Income comes in twice a year, as students pay their tuition and other bills for each semester. Prior to the due dates for these payments, the colleges are often cash shy and have to borrow money against open lines of credit at their banks until the new tuition dollars come in.

Many of these colleges have been struggling to maintain their student numbers, that is, to meet or exceed the number of students they brought in the previous year. That is the target number on which classes to be offered, rooms to be rented in the residence halls, meals provisions to be negotiated for, and coaching and other service contracts are all tied.

When we built a new building on my former campus, my chief financial officer used to remind me that even if we had raised the funds, or could meet the payments for a bond supporting the facility, we still needed new money to pay for the upkeep. At the time, when we were still struggling to both grow and meet our expanded payroll obligations, that often meant that we needed 20 or 40 or maybe even 100 additional students, at the net tuition levels we could anticipate receiving from them.

Lots of schools plan to bring in more students every year. For many community colleges, with their low tuition and public support, the damaged economy has sent them more students than they can handle, without larger state subsidies. They are experiencing students cascading into facilities that cannot absorb them all or cannot offer enough classes to meet their needs. But for other colleges, especially midlevel-tuition independent colleges, the effort to attract additional students in this down economy can feel like climbing an insurmountable wall.

High-tuition colleges are often elite institutions with established reputations for excellence, and substantial surpluses of applicants. More students want to come to them than can possibly be accepted. Midlevel-tuition colleges do not enjoy the luxury of having excess applicants. They are the colleges that still have seats available the first week in September that they may still be willing to fill. They want more students. They hire consultants to help them find ways to attract and yield more students. Sometimes, they succeed at raising their numbers slightly. But it is a hard game for them to play, and it is getting much harder, with the rise of for-profit colleges and other competitors for student tuition dollars.

Chester E. Finn Jr. (2013), a former assistant secretary of education and senior fellow at the Hoover Institution, recently wrote that private education, both K–12 and college level, was becoming "unaffordable, unnecessary, or both." He suggested three reasons why the problems confronting all but the most selective private institutions are not more universally visible. First, they are happening gradually. Second, the colleges do not want to create uncertainty about their futures with enrollment or donor prospects. Third, elite colleges are still enjoying surplus applications. He then asked and answered a potent question: "Can run-of-the-mill private schools and colleges reboot? Can they change themselves—including both their delivery systems and their cost structures—enough to brighten their own futures? I wouldn't bet a year's tuition on it."

Colleges That Will Succeed

There will always be people who want a traditional type of college education, with all of the trappings that we have come to associate with an idyllic college experience: on-campus life; small, engaged classes with outstanding professors; friendly, available faculty; clubs where lifetime friendships are formed; manicured lawns where students can stretch out in gab sessions with colleagues; and all the myriad other leisure cocurricular opportunities people fantasize about.

For those students who see traditional college life as an anticipated or expected rite of passage and can afford this type of institution, residential campuses will still hold a strong appeal. Colleges will compete more aggressively for these students, as they become a smaller proportion of the overall college student pool.

In much of the country, there will be more students in the pipeline to college due to population growth. However, that growth has been primarily fueled by minority group births. The White non-Hispanic share of the population is slipping and will fall below 50% in the near future. Already, fewer than half of all children in the nation 3 years old and younger are White and non-Hispanic (Frey, 2011).

The U.S. Census Bureau (2012) projects that by the year 2060, nearly one of every three people in the United States will be of Hispanic origin, up from one of six. Black Americans will represent almost 15% of the population, just a small gain, and Asians will rise from 5% to 8%. The Census Bureau also projects that the United States will become "a majority-minority nation" in 2043.

Nationally, high school populations are becoming more diverse, and more and more prospective applicants are low-income and first-generation students. Black Americans and Hispanic Americans have historically earned less than White non-Hispanics and Asian/Pacific Islanders. In 2009, the median household income for White non-Hispanic Americans was $51,861. For Black Americans it was just $32,584, and for Hispanic Americans it was $38,039. It was highest for those categorized as Asian/Pacific Islander, at $65,469 (U.S. Census Bureau, 2013). Within each of these groups there are substantial numbers of families at or below the poverty level.

White non-Hispanics and Asians have enrolled in and graduated from college at higher rates than other groups in our nation until now. Things are changing, though. African Americans and Hispanics, who historically had lower rates of attending college than non-Hispanic Whites, are experiencing growth in their college-going rates. Hispanic enrollment rates in 2013 exceeded the enrollment of White students from their same high school classes (Fry, 2013a). African American college-going rates currently are almost equal to White college-going rates.

Although enrollments have grown, there are still bifurcations among the groups in where students enroll, their graduation rates, and their income levels. For example, Hispanic high school graduates are still less likely than non-Hispanic Whites to enroll in a four-year school, attend full-time, or graduate with a bachelor's degree. They have a 56% likelihood of enrolling in a four-year college, compared with 72% for White graduates (Fry, 2013b).

A study by Georgetown University found that "Whites have captured most of the enrollment growth at the 468 most selective and well-funded four-year colleges, while African Americans and Hispanics have captured most of the enrollment growth at the increasingly overcrowded and under-resourced open-access two- and four-year colleges" (Carnavale & Strohl, 2013, p. 6).

According to a Century Foundation study (Kahlenberg, 2004), the low college completion rates of low-income students "reflect in significant measure lower levels of academic preparation. Low-income students are less likely on average to receive a high quality K–12 education, and the two federal programs that seek to improve the academic preparation and persistence of low-income students in secondary and tertiary education . . . receive little financial support" (p. 7).

For many colleges, these demographic shifts will require colleges to adapt their recruitment strategies to reach lower income students. As the senior director of higher education services in the College Board's New England office stated, "We have to meet them where they're at . . . . We can't just keep doing the same old things" (Hoover, 2013).

What we can see from this is that there will be more students needing a college education, but more of them will be coming from families with lower incomes, exacerbating the need to find ways to both hold down the costs of tuition and fees and increase the amount of financial support available to students with financial need.

Most independent nonprofit colleges that support high-quality programs and facilities charge high tuition. They may be able to fully meet the financial needs of some bright but less affluent students. However, the number of students most colleges will be able to admit with institutionally provided full financial aid, and still meet the college's costs, is likely to be small.

The top elite colleges in the nation will still be able to attract enough students to do well, of course, even students needing "a full ride" in aid. Nonetheless, as one college president said to me, even most of these top schools could face challenges, if their costs keep increasing, even though they will survive. "In the end, the elites will be fine. They have 10 applicants for every seat. Still, they lose money on every student they admit." He then added a stunning observation about one of the top 10 undergraduate colleges in the nation: "They charge about $50,000 a year for room and board, but it costs them $70,000 a year, per student. How long can they keep doing that?"

There are still a handful of colleges that are free, or near free, because of large endowments or holdings, but even they are facing tougher economic realities. Cooper Union was one of those free colleges, but it announced in 2013 that it needed to start charging tuition in 2014. Cooper Union was totally tuition free through 2013. Every student admitted received a full scholarship for all four years of study, which enabled the college to be highly selective. Cooper Union had a huge endowment, but through losses in its portfolio, it can no longer offer full aid. Although its students have protested the changes, Cooper Union still will be able to offer enough financial aid to stay highly desirable to many applicants.

So which colleges will succeed? Two kinds of colleges will be successful. One set will be those colleges that will continue to attract enough students to be viable because they will be the very best at what they have traditionally offered. They will provide their students with top-notch professors. They will offer opportunities for their students to work on research projects that engage them. They will offer the traditional college cocurricular life that their students value and can pay for. In this category, those colleges that can best provide a combination of top classroom and after-class offerings will continue to thrive, although their margins of income over costs may shrink.

The other set of successful colleges will be different. Some will be new colleges, formed to offer learning in new and competitive ways. Others will spring up from today's second-tier colleges and will grow and flourish by being great in other ways. In particular, they will grow because they will examine how they serve students, and how students can best learn. These colleges will change the things they are presently doing that constrain them, or fail to help them meet their missions. They will redesign their institutions, pare away what is unnecessary and not cost effective. They will adapt the best technologies and the tools that they will need to offer meaningful degree programs to students at affordable costs. They will focus on student-centered education and will continually assess what works for their students and their institution, measuring and documenting the achievements of their students, making necessary changes to tweak their offerings to provide continually improving outcomes for the students and their consequent careers. Much of what they offer will be a blending of online and face-to-face classes, where students can work at their own pace online, and come to class sessions where what they have learned can be distilled into discussions and experiments that allow them to put their learning into practice and test the limits of the knowledge they have accumulated.

It's Not Their Money

Two of every three graduating college seniors across the country in 2011 were in debt for their student loans. The average debt was $26,600 for those with loans (The Project on Student Debt, The Institute for College Access

& Success, 2012, p. 2). This figure is for student loans and does not include other types of debt, such as credit card obligations, mortgages, or loans from individuals, nor does it include the debts of students who failed to graduate but still had financial obligations accrued from their time in college. Furthermore, student debt would be much higher if so much of the cost of education were not covered by parents, some of whom also go into debt to pay for their children's educations. Many parents cut deeply into their own savings, so that their sons and daughters do not have to borrow funds to pay for college. Clearly, colleges need to find ways to reduce the costs of a college education so that our students do not end up deeply in debt.

One way that student debt could be reduced or eliminated would be to have the states or the federal government fully underwrite the costs, as occurs in many other nations. Tuition is free in many of the European Union (EU) countries, such as Denmark, Iceland, Norway, and Greece, for students from EU countries. Germany and France have tuition costs of under $1,500 per year (StudyinEurope.eu, 2013). However, for students who do not live at home, the cost of rentals and food in some European cities can sometimes make college unaffordable, in spite of the low tuition levels. Unfortunately, except in community colleges, government-underwritten low-cost college tuition is unlikely to be offered in the United States, as the present pullbacks in most states indicate, and as the federal government grapples with long-term needs for deficit reduction.

Another way that student debt could be reduced would be to have colleges cut their costs, so that the combination of tuition and fees they would need to charge would impose less financial burden on their enrollees. Back in the mid-1990s, several colleges did try to roll back their rates, but for the most part their efforts were not successful. The colleges that cut tuition prices did not gain large numbers of students and then found themselves needing to play catch-up with schools whose tuition had continued to grow, with the surplus assets being reinvested in newer and better campus amenities. In other words, for the schools that tried to do the right thing, some ended up worse off for their efforts.

Today, it is safe to assume that absent significant external pressure colleges will not cut their charges. That pressure is coming, though, and it is coming from multiple sources, including government exhortation, online programs, growing competition from the for-profit sector, and enrollment declines due to potential student inability to pay the costs of attending.

As bad as the debt problem is for our students who do attend college, an equally troubling issue is the fact that most of our four-year colleges and universities admit relatively few low-income students. Even students admitted to enhance racial diversity are generally not culled from disadvantaged groups, but rather from middle- and higher-income groups. One reason is that the pipeline to college, through family and high school teachers and advisors, does not work well for lower-income young people. Even talented low-income students rarely apply to selective schools. A second reason is that many independent colleges allow legacy admissions. These admissions, which privilege applicants whose families attended the college, normally benefit applicants from more economically well-off families. A third reason is that many colleges do not make strenuous efforts to recruit lower-income students. As the dean of the Michigan State University College of Education explained to the *New York Times*, "It's expensive. You have to go out and identify them, recruit them and get them to apply, and then it's really expensive once they enroll because they need more financial aid" (Pérez-Peña, 2013, p. A1).

For many colleges that profess to meet the needs for all or most of their students, the cost crunches they face are creating ethical dilemmas. In the past many of them did not screen for financial aid prior to offering admission, but now many more do so, although they are frequently hesitant to admit it except to colleagues.

Even for many applicants whose family incomes would have been enough to pay their college costs a decade ago, college is now unaffordable, without serious discounts and financial aid. The total costs have gotten too high for all but the most affluent applicants.

Consequently, college costs for students must, and will have to, be brought down. Colleges will have to find ways to be more efficient, or they will not survive. They cannot continue to thrive on the backs of their students' debts, because technology and the marketplace have now opened up new ways for students to gain college-level credentials at price points they can afford, or future debt levels they will be able to manage.

The trustees and other officials who set the costs for their college's tuition rates and fees do not do so in order to put students in debt. College and university trustees are normally selected from groups of business leaders, philanthropists, and ardent alumni. In a few states they are elected to serve on public college boards. In most states, the governors or legislatures appoint trustees to public boards. The boards of independent colleges are generally selected by the other board members. Many colleges have set aside one or more dedicated seats for student, alumni, or faculty representatives to serve as trustees.

Most of the trustees I have known are thoughtful and careful about allocating college funds and are particularly averse to raising tuition. If the student debts were their own, though, they might be even more averse to many of the decisions they make that serve to drive up the costs of education for people like Marianne. It is not their debt, though. It is not their money that is being spent. And it is not always being spent in the most appropriate ways to keep down the costs.

On the other hand, as several presidents of successfully growing and innovative nonprofit colleges reminded me, when surpluses are created at nonprofit colleges, the funds are used to benefit the students, not the stockholders. "Nonprofit universities are fundamentally different from for-profit ones," Danielle Ripich, president of the University of New England, told me. "We put any extra dollars we have left into enhancing student learning or providing better facilities." She added that higher education is a very expensive enterprise that needs to become more financially accountable, especially in terms of alleviating the continual rise of student debt.

"Motive matters," Paul LeBlanc, president of what may be the most innovative nonprofit college in the nation, Southern New Hampshire University, said. He added,

> We don't have shareholders. That makes a difference at the margins. We don't need to make the surpluses that for-profit companies may be pushed to deliver. We can live with lower or no surpluses. And when we have them, we invest them in improving the quality of our programs and services.

There is little doubt that there are different drivers of for-profit and nonprofit colleges. The trustees who sit on nonprofit boards are not doing it for the money. Often they are expected to donate considerable financial gifts for the privilege of sitting on those boards, particularly for private nonprofit colleges. The returns they enjoy are psychic enrichments, not monetary ones. Their rewards are derived from the satisfaction they experience from helping to make a difference in the life of their institutions.

Just the same, as one president of a large higher education corporation who had also been a nonprofit college president, told me,

> There is a palpable difference in the demands of the boards, in the sense of urgency, and in how sharp a pencil they use. In the public sector, my board expected an explanation of a problem. My present board says, "Tell us what is happening, what you are doing about it, and your time frame." And by time frame, they mean next week.

Presidents of profit-making companies can reap very rich rewards. Nonprofit college presidents compete for jobs in the same labor market, although most of them might not ever command the same salaries as presidents of high-tech companies. The median total compensation for public university presidents was more than $441,000 in fiscal year 2011–12, with four of them earning $1 million (Stripling & Newman, 2013). For presidents of independent colleges, the median pay in 2010 was almost $400,000, with 36 of them earning more than $1 million (Stripling, 2012).

Being a college president is a demanding job requiring long hours; few vacations; and skills in management, leadership, public relations, and fund-raising, just to name a few. The men and women who become college presidents frequently accept those jobs at lower salary levels than many of them could earn in industry.

Still, critics are raising questions as presidential salaries and perks continue to climb, while students at their colleges are deeply in debt and staff are being laid off. In a lead editorial in the Florida newspaper the *Sun Sentinal* citing six-figure base salaries, deferred compensation packages, housing and medical benefits, and a host of other perks given to public college presidents in Florida, one critic claimed that benefits were too much "to be supported by students struggling to obtain a college education" (Sun Sentinel Editorial Board, 2013, p. A16). The editorial listed several instances of salaries and benefits in the million-dollar range, stating, "In handing out our money, it appears too many boards of trustees approach the negotiating table with a blank check, rather than a posture of protecting the public purse" (Sun Sentinel Editorial Board, 2013, p. A16). Another critic, Claire Potter (2013), professor of history at The New School for Public Engagement, had this to say:

> It's time to investigate the various shenanigans by which wealthy universities retain their non-profit status; rely on vast amounts of temporary, student and non-union labor; maintain vast wage disparities between faculty; spend millions on athletic programs that are disconnected from the academic mission all the while charging high tuitions and running shell games that allow them to shovel millions of dollars towards their executives and stars.

Too many dollars are spent on salaries and benefits that are too high for nonprofit higher education institutions. Too much money on college campuses also is spent on buildings that are not fully utilized, or have been built as showplaces, rather than being more utilitarian. Too much money and time and decision making is given to intercollegiate athletic competition, especially football, when most of the educational institutions in other nations do not subsidize sports teams and stadiums with the tuition fees of their students.

Every time a few new midlevel managers are hired, the costs go up. Every time services that can be more efficiently offered by outside providers are kept in-house, the college pays extra for them. For every class that is not offered on Friday afternoons, because professors do not like to teach then, and students do not like to come to classes then, the waste accumulates, and the costs go up. Most of all, when decisions get postponed because of endless jurisdictional and governance disputes, the effort to provide a college education at a reasonable cost gets shoved aside.

A survey of board members of public and private nonprofit institutions indicated that the majority of trustees believed that their institution "costs what it should," while also agreeing that higher education was too expensive. Only 12% thought that their institution needed to do more to hold down costs (Association of Governing Boards of Universities and Colleges, 2012, p. 26). In other words, their tuition and fees were right, given the value their school provided. It was other colleges that needed to work to reduce their costs.

It is not too difficult to understand why this outcome occurred. Board members care about the colleges they serve. Board members often devote countless hours of volunteer time to their institution's meetings and issues. Many also contribute substantial gifts of funds to their college. They would not be so generous with their time or money if they did not think that the college with which they are affiliated was worth such an investment.

At the same time, they also recognize that they have approved the prior decisions that set tuition and fee rates. If you, as a trustee, find those rates appropriate, it is frequently because you feel satisfied with the positions you have previously taken. If you say that the costs are too high, you have to face the need to do something about it. And often, as a trustee, you would not know exactly what was required and what would work.

The trustees of most colleges want to hold tuition down and deliver programs at reasonable costs. They do not make or allow others to make bad decisions intentionally. Rather, many of the costs build up because they are relatively hidden in the new building budgets that trustees are assured will be paid for by donor dollars or over time through bonding or the one-at-a-time increases to provide additional staff to meet what seem like perfectly reasonable needs. And athletic budgets are partially buried all over the college budget, in every nook and cranny where some of those costs can be allocated.

What happens on boards of all kinds of nonprofit organizations is that it becomes too easy to go along, to not argue against every expenditure, to want to see the organization flourish, and to have its reputation grow because of its exceptional facilities or programs. People say yes to new or expanded projects because they do not see how the accumulated results of their decisions will make the institutions unaffordable to the people who will ultimately have to pay the bill, especially when those people are students who have not yet enrolled or, even more, amorphous taxpayers they do not know.

For those students and taxpayers, the latest budget addition has only minimum impact. It is the cumulative effect that is crippling. Together, the rising net costs of tuition, fees, and other costs, at both public and private nonprofit colleges, have gone beyond what average-income American families can afford. Public policies alone cannot, and should not, significantly affect the fee schedules of private institutions, but they should impact what public colleges do.

This does not mean that the problems of costs can be solved by having state governors start cutting their subsidies to state colleges. The reasons for the mismatch between what colleges cost and what students can pay are quite complex. There are numerous pressures on college boards to allocate resources as they do, in order to keep their institutions competitive in the marketplace. But unless they can reduce the distance between cost and ability to pay, most American colleges are about to lose their market share, and many will close and die.

The problems that higher education is facing are not the fault of inadequate boards or staffs. They are problems that come with a rapidly changing environment. The difficulty of adjusting to this rapid change is that neither the trustees nor the senior-level administrators are personally held to the fire. Time and again, with the best of intentions, they proceed down well-traveled pathways that no longer lead to the best outcomes, partly because they are not at personal risk, and partly because those are the only pathways they are really knowledgeable about and comfortable with. They know what used to work and find it easier to follow old ways than to make the much more difficult transition to new ways of providing educational content.

Marianne's school debt problem is in the process of being solved for future students. The market for higher education is warped right now. The institutions that provide college degrees have become too expensive for most students. Too many programs do not lead their graduates to the good jobs they relied upon getting when they enrolled in their schools.

When markets do not function well, change occurs. For a lot of people who are seeking a college education, the present offerings cost too much and return too little. A relatively free-market economy opens the door to new types of suppliers, offering new ways of getting what the demanders are seeking. The new suppliers include a mix of for-profit education companies, consortia of existing colleges, and bold new programs from risk-taking institutions. Most of the programs include online course offerings.

If Marianne were starting her college career just a few years from now, she might not go into debt. She could take classes from different schools, in different ways. Marianne might work during the day and take her classes at night or on the weekend. Some of her classes might be taken at the local industrial park, where a for-profit college rents space to offer its programs. Other classes might be taken online, through a different college's program.

The professor who does the online presentation would not be the same one whom Marianne questions about her work, either by phone or by computer. One teacher would do the instruction, another would assist with learning issues, and yet a third would analyze Marianne's performance and assess her accomplishments.

For her hands-on nursing classes, she might go to a laboratory or clinic, where clinic specialists would teach her and observe her. But she could also experience the same activities on her computer and have more time to think about what she is doing by going back and forth during the presentation, putting it on "pause" or "repeat" as needed.

Nearly one of every three college students are taking some of their classes online. Some faculty are teaching several hundred thousand students at a time, worldwide, and they are very committed to making more course offerings accessible to thousands of potential students, not only in the United States, but everywhere that access is available.

Some of these courses are offered free, and others have moved forward, developing a business model that will offer course credit for reasonable fees. Given the size of some of these classes, it is obvious that the link between teaching a class and grading the performance of its students has to be altered. Work on this is in process.

While consortia of large nonprofit colleges are moving forward on this concept, some companies that see a business opportunity are racing to develop low-cost course and program materials that will enable people to gain degrees without going into debt. They hope to capture much of the student market that has been going to traditional colleges.

How can for-profit schools offer lower-priced programs than nonprofit colleges do and still make a profit when our traditional nonprofit schools cannot even break even without public and donor dollars? The answer is that our traditional colleges have allocated a lot of their financial resources to programs and amenities that may enhance the on-campus experience for students but that are not essential for learning the material necessary to earn a college degree. Trustees of nonprofit colleges want the best for their students. They should feel this way, to be good trustees, but in making their judgments about how resources should be expended, they have focused on offering more, instead of charging less.

It is not their money. This is the bottom line for much decision making in nonprofit organizations, and it is particularly so for public institutions, where decisions are based not only on student and faculty needs, but on political positions as well. Our public colleges are subject to the vicissitudes of political favoritism, patronage, bargaining, and upheaval.

As Paul LeBlanc told me, "Private nonprofit colleges are more accountable than public ones. We have greater insulation from our sources of support."

Students Cannot Afford the Debt

According to an article in the *Cincinatti Enquirer,* an analysis of Federal Reserve Bank of New York data revealed that student loan debt has now reached $986 billion. The article points out that student debt levels have tripled since 2004, after adjusting for inflation. With such high debts, many former students are unable to save for their future needs, buy a home, or even own a car. As the article subtitle notes, "Loans gave them the college funds they needed to move forward, but now are holding them back" (Peale, 2013).

Students are graduating from undergraduate college degree programs owing an average of more than $26,600. Debt loads for students completing graduate and professional degrees are even higher. In addition, students forego many years of earnings in order to complete their graduate programs.

For medical students, becoming a licensed physician requires more than just eight years of undergraduate college and medical school. After they graduate and pass their medical licensing examinations, they must still complete graduate medical residencies, which can add from three to seven or more years of additional training, before they are allowed to be licensed to practice in their respective states.

Consider the case of 12 recent radiology residents. They had graduated from medical school and were working in residencies at St. Barnabas Hospital in New York. Radiology has long been one of the most highly compensated specialties in medical practice. Though one of the students said he was already $300,000 in debt, he and all his colleagues received sudden termination notices from the hospital, which said it was going to replace its residents with a company that reads radiological images remotely (Bernstein, 2013).

It is hard to blame the hospital. It was planning to save money. But it also upended the residents' lives, because most residency matches happen before students graduate from medical school, and the stranded residents will not be able to practice or pay off their student debts unless some other hospital finds a way to take them in.

Students at every level are experiencing the difficulties attendant to paying off their student loans. One significant problem underlying the debt that students accumulate is that far too many of them do not understand how debt grows, or that early payments of student loan debt go largely to interest, with little reduction of principal.

Neil Theobald, the president of Temple University, who is an expert in higher education finance, wants to change that for his Temple students. "Students need full information on costs and job prospects for their fields," he told me. "We need to give them the information they need to make good decisions." He says that many students do not understand that financial aid is a loan, or how to use credit cards. He is having Temple, which serves more than 37,000 students, provide special programs for its undergraduate students on financial understanding of debt. While the programs are being offered to students in groups of about 100 at a time, taking them is urged, but not required.

Temple is an urban university whose main campus sits in the heart of one of the poorest parts of the city and state. Peter Liacouras, the president of Temple from 1981 to 2000, pushed the university toward serving the needs of the poor and middle-class residents of the city, and many Temple professors have taken great pride in their sense of commitment to urban America.

Now Temple pamphlets trumpet the fact that Temple froze undergraduate tuition and fees for the 2012–13 school year, held tuition stable for most graduate programs, increased financial aid by 10.7%, and cut its operating budget by $113 million since 2010.

Theobald claims that another area that colleges need to work on is getting students through their undergraduate programs in four years. "Right now our four-year graduation rate is 48%," he said, noting that he wanted to see the graduation rate improve. In addition, Theobald said that there are three activities colleges should work on to help reduce the problem of student debt: containing costs; graduating their students within four years; and helping their students make smart decisions on debt, including not just college loans, but credit card debt as well.

At the same time that tuition and debts are increasing for college students, job requirements for earning a bachelor's degree are also increasing. Many employers are now raising the bar for entry-level jobs. According to a front-page *New York Times* article, in Atlanta some firms are now hiring only persons with bachelor's degrees even for entry-level jobs that pay only $10 per hour and require no college skills (Rampell, 2013). College graduates, the article noted, are seen as having demonstrated a sense of commitment, and being "career oriented" (Rampell, 2013, p. A3). It is part of the growing trend toward degree inflation, a phenomenon that occurs when the formal criteria for working in a profession are increased. This happened with pharmacists over the last decade. In the past, pharmacists needed only bachelor's degrees. Now the expectation is that pharmacists have doctoral degrees, so students pursuing this profession now must spend six or seven years studying for their degree, instead of four.

Physical therapy degrees are another example of degree requirement expansion. When I first became president of the University of New England in 1995, I found a flourishing physical therapy program, which required a baccalaureate degree. Its graduates had such good reputations that therapy centers were offering some of the students signing bonuses before they graduated. Not long after I arrived, the profession began requiring colleges offering the programs to make the master's degree the entry-level requirement for their graduates. Now the standard has expanded so that the preferred degree is a doctor of physical therapy degree, with the professional education program beginning at the postbaccalaureate level.

Advocates for the changes in pharmacy and physical therapy can rightfully argue that the expansion of training has been necessary to meet the expanded responsibilities and expectations of professionals in those two fields. They could be correct, but even so, the bottom line is that students in those fields must now pay tuition for two to three additional years of training—training that was not required in the past—and forego income for those periods as well.

Debt loads build up over those years, and the only way graduates can afford to pay back their loans is to earn more than their predecessors, in comparably valued salary packages. Most of the time, the compensation is not enough to fully reimburse them for the added debt they incur.

Degree inflation also occurs in other, less formal ways, such as when employers expect candidates they hire to possess more credentials than are actually required by the job. That is what the story about hiring practices at Atlanta firms indicated. As long as a surplus of credentialed persons is available to work in a field, employers can pick and choose whom they hire. That means that for employers who want to engage in seeking candidates who are overqualified for the positions, those candidates with more credentials have the hiring advantage.

Although there is a positive correlation between having a college degree and job and earnings success, many college programs knowingly enroll far more students than the marketplace can absorb in their particular field. They do this because they generally do not offer degrees in order to meet student needs or job needs, but to meet colleges' needs for given levels of enrollments necessary to sustain or grow the programs.

When an economy is strong and demand for employees is high, it can go relatively unremarked upon when some capable graduates do not find work in the field for which they trained. It is when the economy experiences increasing unemployment and severely tightened job markets that public attention begins to take note of the mismatch between postsecondary education career preparation and the opportunities available to graduates to find work in the careers for which they trained. It is then that, in addition to noting the mismatch, government and media begin to focus on the questions, What did the institution offering the degree promote as the job opportunities? and What prices did the students pay to get the training that was ultimately unable to provide them with the career they had been promised?

There are a great many problems facing higher education in America. Our world is changing very rapidly, but the traditions of shared governance in colleges generally forestall rapid change in favor of prolonged discussion and analysis. At a time when both the inputs and outputs of higher education are under attack, can American colleges rise to the challenges facing the sector?

Inputs, such as tuition costs and government support, are being tested. Students at many institutions may no longer be able to afford the costs of going to college, as the debt they owe for student loans becomes more than they may be able to pay back in a reasonable time frame, and the states whose budgets have supported many of the schools find that they can no longer afford to keep increasing higher education support. Outcomes, such as lack of degree completion and job placements, will be facing increased scrutiny from the public and governmental bodies.

Student debt levels have reached all-time highs, and as the information about debt, job paucity, and misleading educational recruiting efforts has become much more public, a shakeout has begun, in both for-profit and not-for-profit higher education institutions.

At the same time, the fiscal crisis that hit the federal government has also exposed the financial instability of many states. Among the largest expenses of state budgets are educational costs, including basic education and public higher education. States are asking more questions about the programs in higher education that they fund. The federal government is asking more questions and writing more regulations to protect students from predatory enrollment practices, especially those involving federal student loans.

As government scrutiny rises, it also demands more scrutiny from accreditation agencies. The federal government allows only accredited colleges to offer its federal student loans to students. Accrediting agencies examine colleges and their programs to ensure that they meet acceptable standards for institutions or programmatic areas; are fiscally sound; and have fair and appropriate policies for students and employees, among other requirements.

Alerted by constituent concerns and extensive media coverage of rampant problems in higher education, potential students have been exercising their displeasure by voting with their pocketbooks. Professions such as law, with large surpluses of graduates relative to available jobs, have seen declines.

In undergraduate programs, especially in the for-profit sector, some institutions have seen dramatic decreases in applications and enrollments.

In October 2012, the for-profit University of Phoenix announced that it was closing 115 of its more than 200 branches. At around the same time, the University of California System saw its state-supported budget slashed by $750 million. The cuts in the University of Phoenix branches were due to a drop in enrollments following a federal investigation into the high dropout and low graduation rates of the for-profit university's former students, as well as the high default rates of those students on their debts for their federal financial aid assistance (Lewin, 2012). The University of California sustained cuts in its state allocation due to the fiscal problems facing the state of California. Other states face similar problems. Higher education newspapers and online newsletters are replete with stories about the regular tugs of war going on among governors, legislatures, and representatives of state colleges about proposed cuts in budget allocations for the institutions.

Moody's, the bond-rating agency, has downgraded the credit ratings for many colleges over the last several years, going so far as to state, "The 2013 outlook for the entire US higher education sector is negative, including the market-leading, research-driven colleges and universities" (Moody's, 2013a). Because Moody's is a premier credit-rating agency, many colleges depend on its analysis of their creditworthiness when they float bonds to finance construction projects. The report found that all but the most elite universities face diminished student demand and increased price sensitivity (Moody's, 2013a).

National higher education associations agree that higher education is facing difficult times ahead. "Economic, demographic, marketplace and technological trends are converging to cause an unprecedented time of change for higher education," one organization spokesperson indicated in a conversation with a *New York Times* reporter (Martin, 2013).

Law schools across the country continued to see their applications and enrollments decline for the 2012–13 school year. As of January 31, 2013, law school applications were the lowest in 30 years. In 2004, there were 100,000 applications (Bronner, 2013). This number dropped to under 56,000 for the 2013–14 school year, a more than 44% decline (Ho, 2013).

This probably happened as the result of a confluence of several events. The economic downturn undoubtedly brought more scrutiny to the investment of three more years of high tuition. Then media stories reported that too many law school graduates could not get jobs, after going deeply into debt to pay for their legal education. It was also widely reported that there were nearly twice as many graduates each year as there were openings to absorb them (Bronner, 2013). A study by the American Bar Association showed that only 55% of students who graduated from law school in 2011 had a job nine months later that required passage of the bar exam.

The awareness of these problems and issues apparently affected the willingness of potential students and their families to commit to spending scarce dollars, or borrowing them, to finance their law school education. Law school is expensive. As one law professor pointed out, in a *New York Times* front-page story, going to law school in New York City can cost about $80,000 a year, when you include the cost of food and lodging (Bronner, 2013).

The legal profession has been shaken by the recognition of the gap between the promise of a legal education and the reality of getting a position as an attorney. The American Bar Association has set up the Task Force on the Future of Legal Education to explore solutions to the problem. The task force is considering some major changes, including reducing the curriculum needing to be covered from three years to two years of study, allowing college juniors to go directly into law school, and changing accreditation requirements.

Higher education, as we have known it since 1945, is not sustainable. Many colleges may not survive, and others may drastically reduce their services as they struggle to find ways to survive the changes that are assaulting them on all sides. Those institutions that flourish or grow will do so because they find new and better ways to remain viable.

For-profits, nonprofits, independents, and public institutions of higher education are all facing a new reality. The deep recession that began in 2008, with the collapse of the subprime housing mortgage market, exposed the fragile economic underpinnings of budgets built on future debt obligations, debts that many states and local communities cannot fund now, or may not be able to adequately pay down in the near future. This has undermined states' abilities to fund higher education at previous levels. As a result, many formerly low-cost public colleges have raised their tuition and other costs so high that many students can no longer afford to pay them. In addition, the costs of private colleges have risen much faster than the rates of inflation, potentially pricing many students out of the market. Even for those students who will enroll, regardless of the prices that their colleges are charging, it is unlikely that most of them will be able to earn salaries high enough to pay off their student loans when they graduate.

For our society as a whole, the problem is one in which the cost of higher education has been spiraling upward faster than the cost of inflation, with no sign of abatement. Higher education is human resource intensive, which makes it hard to capture the economies of scale that benefit other types of businesses. The nature of teaching has made it difficult to benefit from technological advances until now. Although the advent of online teaching has opened the door to potential enormous savings, classes will still be expensive because not all students can learn online, not all subjects lend themselves to off-site teaching, and the grading of work and up-front costs of successful online classes are still barriers to cost containment.

Moreover, although every college that can do so is entering the online market, the largest and wealthiest colleges have established a beachhead in offering large online courses and programs that are likely to expand that segment's share of the market. And no matter how desirable a degree from a well-known college may be, for-profit companies will undoubtedly grow their share of educational enrollment dollars, as investors give those companies more funds with which to promote and hone their offerings.

As state budgets tighten, and the availability of federal dollars for education is reduced, colleges will need to find ways to tighten their belts. This will be very difficult because, like the federal government, colleges have multiple constituencies wanting to be satisfied and have become accustomed to using financial resources to meet both constituents' desires and competition in the marketplace.

Colleges are not villains, of course. They are charging higher fees because their costs keep rising. American colleges find themselves buffeted by changes going on all around them. To not adapt to the changes is to lose ground in the marketplace, but the costs of change are often significant drivers of the need for budget increases.

For most colleges, competition from peers is a powerful stimulant for spending money in order to keep up with the colleges that are aggressively seeking the same groups of students. Whether it is fancier residence halls, faster Wi-Fi hookups, more successful athletic teams, or more famous professors, American colleges are obsessed with staying competitive and gaining ground.

They are experiencing more threats to their well-being than they are accustomed to, and it is hard for them to deal with, especially when most collegiate institutions make changes at a glacial pace, given their reverence for shared governance. Most decisions have to go through various committee approvals before they can be acted upon. This makes colleges responsive and generally improves the quality of decision making, by subjecting it to numerous levels of review, but slows down the ability to adapt to change.

Change is coming rapidly now, though, and few colleges are adequately prepared. Colleges face competitive threats not just from their historic peer institutions, but from lower-ranked schools spending the money to climb up; fast rising foreign universities drawing away top international students; other college and consortia online programs competing for their tuition dollars; and the swarm of for-profits like the University of Phoenix, emerging, it often seems, at warp speed.

Most American colleges would lose money if they did not receive public funds or donor gifts. It costs more to educate the average student than the colleges can reasonably, or even unreasonably, charge. Colleges manage to admit so many students who pay less than they cost, by getting money from other sources. For public colleges, state government (and sometimes local government) has historically provided much of the difference. For them, and for private nonprofit colleges, donations and grants allow the budgets to be balanced.

Yet there is a group of higher education institutions that does not get state dollars, or donations, or government or foundation grants (for the most part) that has not only been flourishing but growing phenomenally. These are the large, often publicly traded, for-profit college companies, such as the University of Phoenix. They are growing because they provide profits, or the promise of profits, to investors; because they have found ways to offer more convenient, easier to access ways to reach consumers of their college programs; and because many of them have lowered the barriers to entry for less-well-prepared or college-ready applicants.

The University of Phoenix is not the only or best answer to our American college costs problems, but it has been able to do what nonprofit colleges have not been able to accomplish: Balance the institutional budget and even turn a profit. If they can do it, why can't nonprofit colleges do it too? And with the for-profits in trouble for having such low graduation rates, what can or will they do to change? Obviously, there is something that the two kinds of institutions can learn from each other.

Our global society is changing rapidly, especially when it comes to how people communicate and receive information. One single class can be offered to several hundred thousand students at a time. Students can learn asynchronously, meaning that they can receive a class lecture at a different time than it was offered, and respond at a different time. All colleges will need to be able to offer online classes, but that alone will not adequately either balance a higher education budget, ensure appropriate student learning, or position a college to effectively compete in the marketplace. For that, our colleges will need to change. Those that cannot accommodate the necessary changes will not survive.

One significant harbinger of change is the acceptance of online instruction by students across the nation. Technology has opened a pathway for both profit-making and nonprofit institutions to reach potential students in different ways. Students no longer have to physically attend classes and, instead, can take their classes online. In 2012, the number of students enrolling in at least one online course was 6.7 million. That means that nearly one of every three persons taking college-level courses took at least one of them online (Allen & Seaman, 2013, p. 4).

The following sections examine what the different types of colleges can do about their problems, as well as issues about and potential answers for how to reduce costs to institutions and students in the face of the changing state and federal dollars available. Problems that confront traditional colleges are assessed, including competition from for-profits and other nonprofits, as well as the rapid growth and concerns surrounding online educational programs.

Competition in Higher Education

Although competition is growing in the field of higher education, it has not decreased student debt loads yet. In fact, across all sectors of higher education—public, independent, and for-profit—debt-related scandals are being exposed. Profit-making colleges are receiving most of their tuition funds through federal student loans, but high attrition rates are leaving students deeply in debt, with no degrees to show for their financial problems.

At nonprofit colleges, debt loads for students who are graduating are at an all-time high, and potential students are increasingly learning that the degrees in fields they had planned to enter and incur debt for are no longer able to guarantee the kinds of jobs and salaries that might justify accruing that debt. To attract and hold students, colleges must find ways to lower the overall cost and, hence, the overall debt.

Nonprofit higher education is experiencing rapid and radical change for which its cultural and financial models are unprepared. Terrence MacTaggart, former chancellor of the University of Maine System, and before that the State Colleges of Minnesota System, says that the three biggest trends confronting higher education are the business models of proprietary colleges, the contested areas between profit and excellence, and the opportunities that technology is providing for e-learning.

MacTaggart sees opportunities for blended offerings, combining campus-based programs with online programs, such as colleges like Southern New Hampshire University are now doing. He sees pressure for change, on both for-profits and nonprofits, coming from accrediting agencies and federal regulations. He told me, "There is a need for regulation. The pressure in the market is for mass, generic, adequate programs. The market will not automatically create quality options among proprietaries."

MacTaggart predicts we can expect to see some nonprofit colleges begin to imitate some of the innovations of the for-profit companies, with subtle changes in their own business models. In addition, he notes that there is still what he terms *lingering political support* in most states for their own public colleges.

Although observers would agree that the market has not yet produced outstanding for-profit colleges, the for-profit corporations that own colleges and college course delivery systems will improve them because it will be profitable to do so. They will pay close attention to any innovations that public and independent colleges will adopt, and some frankly state that they will use any of them that make both educational and financial sense.

In the same way, the world of nonprofit colleges needs to take seriously the lessons it can take from the profit-making side. The cultural model of shared governance and slowed decision-making processes of most nonprofit colleges has a rich and respected tradition, one that is worthy of maintaining in a traditional world. But the world of higher education is changing very rapidly, with stories about new types of online programs or new threats to finances or student career options released almost every few days, it sometimes seems.

The competitive environment of educational options, the rising and increasingly unaffordable cost of college tuition and fees, and the decline in the financial condition of states and markets signal a difficult time ahead for many of our colleges, especially the smaller, more tuition-dependent ones.

What will small, traditional, campus-based colleges do when the for-profit colleges and the big consortiums of large, richly endowed colleges attract away their students? Who are the people who will continue to go into debt to pay a second-rate college's high fees for what they may think is a third-rate education that is unlikely to get them a good job in the career for which they studied?

Interestingly, a survey of college and university presidents in mid-2013 found that although 62% of the presidents were excited about the future of their own institution, only 20% said they were excited about the future of higher education (Gallup, 2013). Clearly, something is amiss.

What is happening is that most higher education leaders recognize that the future is not going to be kind to many colleges, but most believe that their own colleges and universities will defy the odds, continue to flourish, and in fact be stronger and more successful. Most of the leaders I interviewed certainly subscribed to this set of beliefs. All of them saw some problems looming ahead, but each professed that his or her own institution was doing the right things to survive. Some were right, I am sure, and others were like ostriches, burying their head in the sand and ignoring the reality ahead.

In interview after interview with leaders of both nonprofit and for-profit higher education institutions and agencies, they expressed concern for the survival of smaller and less prestigious colleges, those that many referred to as "third or fourth tier."

Some schools will continue to thrive, perhaps, and many will stay above water. But unless there is fairly rapid change in the halls of academia, a lot of colleges are going to shrink, and some are going to die. As one higher education leader told me, there are only going to be 50 or so Harvard- and Swarthmore-level private colleges, ones that have the deep endowments and quality reputations to be able to either manage the changes or manage to survive without changing.

The colleges with very large endowments, such as Harvard, are able to spend their investment income in ways that other less well-endowed colleges strive to emulate. This leads to the so-called arms race of spending that is so detrimental to higher education. Recommendations for government policies to ameliorate some of the problems that result from very large endowments are discussed in chapter 7.

Let us imagine the options of a small independent college, Jane Doe College, facing a tough future. Beset on all sides by forces of change over which it has little control, it lacks deep pockets and is eating up its endowment. It lacks the funds to invest in major changes and cannot attract enough students who will pay its high costs because of the school's modest social cache.

For the last several decades, it has kept afloat partly because the market for college was expanding, and partly because it used a number of mechanisms to keep pace with its competitors, which were, for the most part, other schools with similar profiles. Most of Jane Doe's students had average grades, and many were the first persons in their families to go to college. Jane Doe College awarded large scholarships to many of those applicants, letting them and their parents know that even if Harvard was not admitting them, Jane Doe recognized that these students were worthy of support. Few of those families knew that most of the applicants to this college are offered these scholarships, and that they really are not scholarships but discounts offered to entice applicants to enroll.

Jane Doe College has built new facilities to keep up with the colleges down the road. It has done this with the help of loans and bonds, whose payback schedules assume that the residence quarters will be fully occupied in the future, and that there will be relatively full classrooms.

Jane Doe has never considered Harvard as competition, because the profiles of the students who enroll in the two institutions almost never overlap. Now, Jane Doe is facing a falling pool of applicants, as its net tuition price continues to rise faster than inflation, amid an economy still not out of recession and a lackluster job market for potential graduates. The local community college is increasingly becoming the first choice for many students, who take their first two years at the community college and then, if they make it, transfer to Jane Doe or another college in the area.

Another reason that the college's applicant pool is shrinking is that more of the college-going students in its region are being wooed away by for-profit companies, and free or low-cost online programs sponsored by big-name colleges. Jane Doe College does not have wealthy donors. Its program is decent but undistinguished. It needs a leader who can turn the college around, point it in a new direction, and set it on a path to success. But it is unlikely to be able to afford to hire such a leader, or keep one.

Even more stable colleges need to balance their budgets in a variety of ways. One important source of balance is provided by offering a mix of low-cost and high-cost courses. Introductory humanities courses such as history can be offered to a large number of students at a time by a relatively low-paid professor or even less well-compensated part-time adjunct professor.

Many of the courses that students take in their freshman and sophomore years are considered lower-level courses. Those are foundational courses that introduce subject matter, or cover parts of a field for which few or no prerequisite courses are expected. Many of these courses are taught by adjuncts and graduate students.

Such lower-cost offerings help provide the necessary fiscal balance for both higher-cost laboratory classes and upper-level courses. Laboratory classes are generally restricted to small numbers of students working in a laboratory at a given time. They are expensive to offer because of the larger number of faculty needed to support a given number of students, as well as the higher costs of facilities and equipment. For example, one professor with several teaching assistants may be able to teach a history class of 120 students, but in a chemistry laboratory only 16 students may be able to be in the class, therefore requiring seven or more teachers, for the same 120 enrollees.

Upper-level courses offer advanced, intensive study, presuming that students in those courses have already had significant exposure to the field. Senior professors, earning the highest salaries, usually teach these classes. And because many college students never complete more than two years, upper-level classes are frequently much smaller than lower-level ones. It is not unusual in academia to have senior seminars with 10–12 students in them.

When for-profit colleges and nonprofit competitors start offering introductory and other lower-level courses online with star professors doing the teaching at prices below what the traditional colleges need to charge, who will be attending the history class in the traditional college lecture hall? Who will be in the residence hall when they can take a class with some other institution while sitting in bed? Who will be eating in the school cafeteria when they don't need to be on campus? Just how will a college survive when its bread-and-butter courses become underenrolled because of economic competition from lower-priced, perhaps higher-quality content providers?

Elite colleges will continue to proffer what they have always really offered: an education based on small classes with really good professors; a rich, socially stimulating cocurricular life on a manicured campus; and a network of lifetime contacts in the business and professional world.

These colleges will perform a function similar to the role preparatory schools play at the pre-collegiate level. They will focus on attracting the best and the brightest of the propertied class, with a small percentage of diversity admissions added to the mix. These are the schools we all wish we had gone to, or desire to see our children and grandchildren attend.

Amid the potential gloom and doom of a scenario of some cherished institutions falling on hard times or collapsing must be framed the possibility that higher education, like the fabled phoenix, can be resurrected from its own ashes. Applied to higher education, the transformative power of exciting and regenerating new entrepreneurial ideas could open the doors of opportunity for learning much wider than they have ever opened before.

First and foremost among the competitors seeking to supplement or replace traditional higher education modes are the for-profit colleges that are expanding so rapidly across the nation. Some are small proprietary schools, serving a largely local constituency with a focused program, or limited degree offerings. Others, like the University of Phoenix, Kaplan, and the Education Management Corporation, are billion-dollar enterprises, with multiple sites and thousands of employees. They may offer their educational programs in conventional college-type settings; at sites in business parks; or virtually, through online courses. Jointly, large corporate college programs now enroll almost 10% of all higher education students nationally.

Competition to the traditional classroom-based nonprofit college offering is coming in other formats as well. One major online set of programs that is now being offered by and with nonprofit colleges, and that also will compete with those colleges, is massive open online courses (MOOCs). These are the courses that can have 50,000 or more students. MOOCs have the potential to significantly change the way classes are offered, thereby dramatically impacting higher education in ways we may not even be aware of yet.

Coursera is a company offering a platform for delivering these open courses online, especially in computer science, mathematics, and economics. The company, founded by two professors of computer science at Stanford University, is working with a group of as many as 62 participating universities to develop ways to allow students taking Coursera's classes to earn credit for them. At the same time, the universities would be able to charge students for certificate or degree processing, thereby having a way to generate revenue from the otherwise free coursework. In addition to Coursera, there are other academically based or partnered consortiums of universities that are involved in the delivery of open online courses, such as Udacity and edX.

Most of the MOOCs are being offered by professors at a few of the richest and most prestigious of U.S. universities. For the most part, the institutions in the consortiums are large elite schools with international reputations. The professors presenting the courses frequently are expected to be among the top people in the discipline.

The lectures are multimedia, with uplinks to videos, news clips, footnotes and data sources, connections to related topics, networks of potential colleagues, and more. Many of the presenters are among the best at holding audiences. For our media savvy generation of students, who now expect to be entertained in class, taking a MOOC will raise the bar in terms of student demands for spectacle and showmanship.

What will happen to the average state or independent American college when the classes it used to fill with its own first- and second-year students are being offered online, at lower costs and more convenience, not only by profit-making colleges but by very prestigious nonprofit universities as well? Will these smaller or less well-known colleges, which together educate the bulk of our students across the nation, be able to find new models of survival? Will they change in ways they have not yet planned, or even imagined, to cope with the new reality? Or will they just disappear, because the economic underpinning for keeping them going has seeped away?

According to Moody's, the institutional credit-rating service, the growing use of MOOCs in higher education, in one format or another, indicates a "fundamental shift in strategy by industry leaders to embrace technological changes that have threatened to destabilize the residential college and university's business model over the long run" (Kiley, 2013).

All is not well in MOOC land, however. There is growing competition among colleges between using MOOC platforms or those of Coursera and others. Some colleges are experimenting with both. Worse news for these programs, though, is that many faculties are resisting the use of these massive open online programs in their institutions. At some colleges, faculty have argued that administrative decisions to join online consortia were made in violation of faculty governance standards requiring faculty involvement in academic decisions. Other faculty groups have argued that the online courses do not offer the same quality learning experiences as traditional classroom-taught classes do. Because of faculty concerns about the rise of highly compensated superstar professors, the potential loss of academic positions, and the fracturing of the joint governance culture of higher education, the disagreements are not likely to be smoothed over, or to go away quickly, in the nonprofit sector.

For-Profit Colleges

For-profit colleges represent the biggest threat to traditional colleges. Many of them have deep pockets, they have investors willing to bet on them, they are innovative, and they are agile. Most of all, their command structures allow them to make quick decisions; step into opportunities rapidly; and jettison problem programs or projects that nonprofit, and especially public, colleges could often take years to disentangle.

While most American colleges would lose money without their fund-raising and grants, for-profit colleges largely have found a way both to live on tuition and to make a profit from it. Of course, for-profit colleges do not have to offer expensive but socially important programs, nor provide the moral and social extracurricular support to their students that we customarily expect our public and independent colleges to provide.

For-profit colleges do not make a profit by charging more than nonprofit colleges do. In fact, they receive less revenue per student, on average, than their nonprofit colleagues. They received just over $11,000 per student in 2008–9, compared with $19,000 in public universities and $38,000 in private nonprofit colleges (Bennett, Lucchesi, & Vedder, 2010, p. 21).

For-profit colleges turn a profit on a fraction of the per-student receipts that nonprofits receive, not because they charge more but because they spend less. They spend less in spite of, or perhaps because of, the fact that more than 85% of their revenue comes from tuition, while publics get only 17% and privates 36% of tuition toward their total revenues (Bennett et al., 2010, p. 21).

American for-profit higher education college companies are experiencing extraordinary growth. The University of Phoenix, the largest of the for-profit college corporations, has had stunning success. The university, part of the Apollo Group, had an enrollment of nearly 600,000 students in 2010. Just 10 years earlier, its enrollment was 100,000 (University of Phoenix, pp. 1–2, n.d.). Although the University of Phoenix closed a number of campuses in early 2013, the bulk of its operations is still ongoing.

For-profit colleges have made a lot of mistakes that they will need to overcome. They have misled prospective students about realistic job opportunities in fields in which the colleges offer degrees, and they have graduated far too few students.

They are likely to improve, though. They have a powerful incentive to do so: the profit incentive. They are in higher education for the long haul. They see a huge opportunity to make money. To do so, they are willing to learn from traditional colleges. The real question is, Will traditional colleges work to improve, so that they too will remain competitive, and if so, can and will they do it in time?

Discussions with leaders in for-profit education indicate high expectations of continued growth and expansion. Leaders suggest that every technological advance accepted for nonprofit colleges will be used by profit-making colleges as well. This topic is discussed further in chapter 4.

Massive Open Online Courses

MOOCs are here to stay. They may or may not solve all of the problems of higher education across the globe, but the technology to deliver courses to tens or even hundreds of thousands of pupils at a time is here, and its power cannot be denied.

There are professors who are going to want to offer MOOCs, and students who will want to take them. Whether they can find delivery platforms or business models that will enable them to be economically feasible is still a question that is being explored.

Although huge numbers of people have signed up for some MOOCs, the evidence is that most of those who enroll never even start a single assignment, and that very few complete the courses (Lewin, 2013).

"The best thing about the MOOCs is that they have validated online education," the president of Southern New Hampshire University told me. "There is virtue seen in them now that the elite universities have committed to them."

The president of a large nonprofit university, who did not want his name mentioned in connection with his response, told me,

> In the right setting, these can be fabulous. For adult learners, and as a supplement for undergraduates, they can be useful. I question the rush to MOOCs. They are not realistic for most students, with their 90% dropout rates. And if they are high quality, the costs are not substantially less than in-class courses. My biggest worry is that some providers could cheapen the quality of what is offered.

He added that the percentage of 18-year-olds who can manage an online course is minimal, in his opinion. "The market is adults, and people who already have degrees, but want to extend their learning."

Ever since the development of the electronic computer, college faculty have been seeking ways to increasingly connect with each other, and then with wider audiences. Once they were connected through the Internet, scholars began to reach out to help each other by sharing ideas and advice. Many began to post their syllabi online, so that they could illustrate to colleagues how they were approaching the teaching of their disciplines and learn from each other.

For several decades, some courses have been offered online, but generally, most of the courses presented by faculty were visually unappealing, sometimes offering little more than talking heads and blackboard notes. Some for-profit providers partnered with faculty, especially at smaller colleges eager for the extra enrollment dollars that came with these shared revenue programs. The for-profit providers in the 1990s provided the delivery platforms and also frequently owned the rights to the content, regardless of whether they or the faculty developed the material.

These companies were unable to offer academic credit for the coursework and thus needed academic institutions to partner with them. They provided the delivery system, and the schools offered the credit for their courses. This initially usually required at least some on-campus face time between students enrolled in the courses and the faculty from the credit-offering college. The face time could occur on weekends, or during a summer vacation week.

Accrediting agencies began to crack down on these types of offerings, generally demanding more traditional faculty involvement or control over the content of the courses being offered.

Given the inherent proclivity of faculty to share what they know, it was only a question of time before some professors began to put not just syllabi but whole course lectures online, for colleagues or interested persons anywhere to share. Next, some professors began to put all of their lectures for a given course online, making them freely available to all. They opened them up to unlimited enrollment, eliminating traditional course caps. Not only did they put the lectures online, but they provided forums and notes.

Then, in 2008, a number of major universities set up the OpenCourse-Ware Consortium, which now includes more than 250 universities and educational organizations. The consortium is committed to providing free coursework across the globe.

This desire to provide open access and share information and opportunities has undergirded much of the development of the web and its subsequent evolutions. Freeware and shareware came along, for example, concurrent with and in response to proprietary software applications that were developed for PDAs (personal data assistants).

MOOCs originally started as part of this type of movement, albeit MOOCs are specifically focused on providing expanded educational opportunities. These open online courses use streaming video, forums, quizzes, and other interactive techniques not only to simulate live classroom experience, but to extend well beyond its reach. Streaming video allows professors to offer materials with uplinks to audio, video, and all types of resources virtually, relatively simultaneously, and asynchronously. A person taking the class can participate anywhere; tune in anytime; set up his or her own shared networks with other users; and, most of all, learn at his or her own pace and demand.

Advocates for MOOCs point out that developing the class modules will help the instructors build collections of well-developed presentations they make, which can be used for other lectures and opportunities. Of course, many instructors have been doing just that with PowerPoint presentations for some time now.

According to a MOOC wikispaces guide, benefits of offering MOOCs include the opportunity for the presenter to learn new things as well "thanks to the unknown knowledge that pops up as the course participants start to exchange notes on the course's study," and the ability to make connections "across disciplines and corporate/institutional walls" ("Benefits and Challenges of a MOOC," 2013). Challenges of using MOOCs include the fact that participation requires digital literacy, time and effort, and "self-regulation" and can feel "chaotic as participants create their own content" ("Benefits and Challenges of a MOOC," 2013).

There are two other substantive problems. One involves developing secure ways to test people who take these massive courses. Given the rapid advances in technology, it is likely that methods of providing fingertip or eye scans, or other similar biometric methods, will be developed as MOOCs are being refined. The second problem, providing course credit or certification, is already in the process of being solved, as colleges and businesses offering MOOCs and other online educational coursework break barriers to establish new models of offering and measuring learning.

As of early 2013, only 2.6% of colleges reported having MOOCs, with another 9.4% in the planning stages. Most institutions say they are undecided about using MOOCs, and a third have no plans to use them. Most of the nonprofit institutions that are considering the use of MOOCs are research universities, perhaps because they are the only ones with deep enough pockets to finance their ventures (Allen & Seaman, 2013, pp. 3, 8).

During a webinar hosted by the American Council on Education (ACE) in May 2013, more than 300 academics from across the country were able to log in to a discussion about MOOCs by faculty who are using them either to teach with or to supplement their own classes. The webinar dealt with issues questioning how students benefit from MOOCs, how colleges are integrating them into their curricula, and how the quality of MOOC learning experiences can best be assessed.

One of the four panelists was Daphne Koller, cofounder of Coursera, Inc., and professor of computer science at Stanford University. She talked about how valuable the open online courses have been for poor people in remote parts of our world as well as those with health-related issues, such as a student with autism who greatly valued his course offering. She stated that more than 3.6 million students have now signed on for MOOCs, involving 374 courses, and pointed out that the certificates of completion of courses, even without credits, can help people access job opportunities. She also noted that online courses can enable the kind of mastery learning that historically required personal tutoring.

Elizabeth Allan, an associate professor of biology at the University of Southern Oklahoma and an ACE CREDIT faculty reviewer, talked about the multiple values of MOOCs, giving the example of an older, returning student who hoped to go to medical school, using a MOOC to strengthen his ability to do well in a face-to-face science class the following semester. Two community college representatives, Barbara Illowsky and Michelle Pilati, gave examples of the use of MOOCs in their colleges. Illowsky argued that if 100,000 persons took a MOOC, even with a 94% dropout or failure rate, that would still mean 6,000 people would complete the course successfully. "That is more students than I could teach in a lifetime in regular classes."

MOOCs certainly present a previously undreamed of opportunity to offer access to education to people wherever in the world they may live. At the same time, there are cautions in the air. One of the speakers at the webinar said that many community college faculty in California were avoiding collaborating with MOOCs because they feared the state would substitute MOOCs for faculty, as a way to deal with the need for more access to community college courses. In addition, a Gallup poll released in May 2013 indicated that only a minuscule 3% of college presidents strongly agreed that MOOCs could improve student learning, and only 2% strongly agreed that MOOCs will help to solve the financial challenges facing colleges (Gallup, 2013).

Interestingly, when academic conferences discuss MOOCs, they do so in terms of the promise they offer, or ways to overcome the obstacles to using these open online courses most effectively, but they rarely discuss them as vehicles for competing with for-profit colleges, whose growth represents such a looming challenge for nonprofit higher education. Undoubtedly, this is because the for-profits are still not seen as quality rivals, in any sense. Instead, they are seen as purveyors of inferior programs to nontraditional students, many of whom are considered not college ready. The dismissal of the for-profit sector could be considered somewhat warranted in the past, but it is a huge mistake for the higher education establishment to close its eyes to the potential of growing quality levels along with competitiveness developing in some of the for-profit arena.

The biggest problem for MOOCs is finding a way to monetize them. Even though MOOCs can enable one professor to reach thousands of students, the technology and platforms are not free, nor is the professor's time. Most MOOCs are free right now, and many colleges and experts are trying to find ways to recover costs or make a profit while using them.

Coursera, Udacity, and edX

Several companies and consortia are in the process of developing ways to enable massive online courses and monetize them at the same time. Coursera founders Andrew Ng and Daphne Koller are both computer science professors at Stanford University.

Presently, all of Coursera's courses are offered at no charge, but some changes are on the way. Coursera has received about $16 million in venture capital for the company to expand. It is developing a business model, because without a way to fund the investment in its work, Coursera cannot survive.

During the ACE webinar, Koller (2013) stated that the 94% dropout rate from MOOCs is not really a failure rate and is misleading. She said that many people log in with no real intention of actually completing the courses. Of those who indicate seriousness by being what she termed *signature students*, she claimed there was a more than 90% successful completion rate.

To fund its programs and growth, Coursera intends to own the platform on which it provides its classes. Charging students for providing credit for taking the classes may be a feasible way for Coursera to underwrite the costs of the programs. Nonetheless, some of its for-profit potential competitors do not think the present business model will be able to fully fund the programs.

Coursera has offered several hundred courses in the humanities, science, and engineering over the last few years. Currently, it provides a platform for about eight courses, centering on computer science with some math, economics, and linguistics. In February 2013, ACE endorsed five of its course offerings. ACE has received funds from the Bill & Melinda Gates Foundation to explore how such courses might help students complete college (Kolowich, 2013).

ACE is not an accrediting agency, however, so it can endorse and recommend that its member colleges accept Coursera offerings for credit, but that does not ensure that they will do so. In fact, some faculty groups have already gone on notice that they are resistant to acceptance of such credits.

Udacity, MITx (developed by the Massachusetts Institute of Technology), and edX, the newer version of MITx, are differently structured but similar ventures looking for ways to turn open online courses into business models that can offer creditable coursework for reasonable costs while providing profit centers for the institutions that host them.

Udacity is a private company, founded by another Stanford professor, Sebastian Thrun, who famously had 160,000 students everywhere on the globe enroll in his free online class in artificial intelligence in 2012. The experience was life-changing for the professor, who said that he could not return to teaching at Stanford again, where he typically lectured to only 20 students in a class (Hsu, 2012). ACE has been exploring recommending Udacity courses, in addition to those from Coursera.

There has been continued conflict over the use of such courses and their potential entry into the marketplace is sure to create upheaval in traditional college enrollments. Interestingly, Sebastian Thrun himself has decided to have Udacity now concentrate on offering corporate training. An experiment in offering college courses at San Jose State University in 2013 was not successful. Thrun said that his online education medium was not a good fit for the disadvantaged students targeted by the pilot (Straumsheim, 2013).

StraighterLine

The president of a major accrediting association directed me to look at StraighterLine, and what that company is offering in the marketplace, to see how intertwined all of the online companies and traditional colleges are, and how they are overlapping and integrating, in cyberspace offerings. Straighter-Line provides higher education courses online. Its courses already have been recommended by ACE for college credit, even though StraighterLine itself is not accredited. What the company has done is partner with colleges that are accredited and that accept StraighterLine courses for academic credit. The StraighterLine offerings are courses that provide general education credits. They are low cost and, therefore, quite competitive. Prospective students can sign up with StraighterLine for just $99 a month plus $49 for each course, or they can subscribe for an entire freshman year of college for $1,299.

Regarding college credit transfer, the company's website notes, "A StraighterLine Advisor can build you a personalized degree plan that lists all of the courses you can take that will transfer" (StraighterLine, 2013b). Furthermore, the site notes on its business courses page that these "affordable online business courses are your inside track to starting a career in business and finance without burying yourself under a mountain of debt" (StraighterLine, 2013a).

StraighterLine's 50 or so course offerings include English Composition, College Algebra, General Calculus, General Chemistry, Accounting I and II, Spanish I and II, and American Government. All the courses listed appear to be first- and second-year courses, rather than advanced ones.

The most interesting thing about StraighterLine is the mix of colleges with which it partners. Some are for-profit companies, some are independent colleges, and quite a few are public colleges. The for-profit partners include companies larger than StraighterLine, which by midyear 2012 had grown to 22 employees ("Higher-Ed Startup StraighterLine," 2012). For example, StraighterLine's website lists among its partner institutions, which accept its courses for credit, the University of Phoenix, Kaplan University, and Ashford University. It also lists Liberty University Online, a private Christian university, as a partner. Liberty University, through its online programs, is one of the fastest growing colleges in America. It has 12,500 residential students and more than 80,000 studying through Liberty University Online, according to its website (www.liberty.edu/online). Liberty itself is now a major competitor to traditional, for-profit, and Coursera-type higher education providers. Some of the state colleges that accept StraighterLine credits are Albany State College, Thomas Edison State College, SUNY Empire State College, and Northern Virginia Community College.

Other Models

As the possibilities for online learning abound, we are likely to see many other potential models emerge. Many will be blended versions of technologies already on deck. Others will be even more paradigm shifting than MOOCs, for example. Whatever types of models are developed, they will have to demonstrate that learning occurs through their usage. Moreover, in a marketplace that will be filled with new ideas and products, those that want to succeed in capturing large numbers of customers or users will have to find ways to demonstrate their superiority over other claimants for student tuition dollars.

Some providers are already at work building assessment tools and programs, honing their transfer of knowledge methods with metrics that yield continuous quality improvements and allow them to showcase their successes. These providers will be the leaders of the pack. Some of these vanguard colleges and companies are explored in chapter 6.

Reasons for the Problems

Higher education is facing a perfect storm as a number of events, trends, and innovations with negative implications for nonprofit education converge somewhat simultaneously. Costs continue to rise faster than inflation. Tuition and fees for colleges have risen beyond affordability for many potential students. Government funding sources are deeply in debt. New ways of offering classes are upending traditional teaching methods, and for-profit colleges are luring away hundreds of thousands of students.

It could be bad karma, or it could be that the new forces that are descending on the old reliable colleges are upending the way the higher education business is done. Some theorists, such as Clayton M. Christensen, think higher education is in for vast changes, in much the same way that industry has experienced changes in the way products are manufactured and delivered, and in the companies that have profited from or lost business due to those changes.

In *Disrupting Class: How Disruptive Innovation Will Change the Way the World Learns,* Christensen, Horn, and Johnson (2008) examined major changes in business markets that occur when new entrants to a marketplace create innovations that disrupt the existing market and replace the existing production or service models. In their early stages, these new entrants use their new technologies or delivery methods to lower costs but often also provide lower-quality services. Established firms often ignore the incursions of these new entrants, because the price point at which they sell is too low, or the volume involved is too small to offer large enough profits (pp. 46–47).

Over time, some of these new companies develop stronger products and become disruptive innovators in the marketplace. One example Christensen, Horn, and Johnson (2008) give is the Japanese automakers, whose originally inferior products later became leading sellers in the American auto market (p. 58). Another, highly relevant example he gives is Apple. Apple's original microcomputers were not competitive with the huge computer systems that major computer firms of the time were manufacturing and servicing. As Apple increased its earnings, it invested its profits in upgrading its product, and now it is one of the most successful companies internationally (pp. 48–50).

Christensen, Horn, and Johnson (2008) see education, both basic and college level, as rife with disruptive innovations. Both technological changes and process changes are creating new methods of offering instruction. In a book on K–12 education, he and his coauthors note that everything in the K–12 system "is designed to treat all students the same" (p. 133).

But new online courses, offered stand-alone or blended with in-class support, have reached the level of development where they can respond to perceived as well as expressed needs from learners for more explanation or information. The technology is still in its early stages, with enormous promise for allowing adaptive strategies to ensure that deep learning can take place.

In a more recent book, Christensen and Eyring (2011) posit that increased pressure by accreditors and regulators to document learning achievements will redound to the benefit of online companies, which will have the tools to both assess and refine their offerings. They argue that online instruction technology has enabled online courses to get "demonstrably better, now equaling or exceeding the cognitive outcomes of classroom instruction. At the same time, the economic downturn that has forced cost cutting at traditional universities has given the financial edge to the for-profit educators, many of which have strong balance sheets and access to capital markets" (p. 212).

Even as competitors abound, nonprofit colleges find themselves unable to lower their costs, or even hold them steady. In the world of business, if a rival company sets up a store near you, you offer sales, you cut your prices, or you provide noticeably better products or services.

So, in a logical world, you might expect American nonprofit colleges to compete more effectively, by either lowering their prices or improving the quality of their classes. Instead, they concentrate most of their efforts on improving the same thing they have been improving for the last 60–70 years: the facilities and amenities on their campuses. For perhaps 20% of the students, that really does matter, but for the vast number of prospective students, most of whom are nontraditional, college facilities are the least of the things for which they are willing to go into debt.

Traditional colleges have ignored the for-profits for too long, because the for-profits served a segment of the market that selective colleges did not want: older students, lower-income students, and less academically able students. Much like the businesses Christensen, Horn, and Johnson (2008) cited that ignored rising competitors who initially served the less desirable market segments, before they grew strong enough to capture majorities of their markets, nonprofit colleges are making the same mistake. They have assumed that the for-profits offer an inferior product, one they need not worry about.

But as long as our traditional colleges postpone the inevitable reforms that they will need to undertake for most of them to remain viable, their competitors will grow and strengthen. And as long as the conditions under which their classes are offered remain inflexible, and the costs keep rising, prospective applicants will compare and frequently select other options.

Given the competition and other problems facing public and independent colleges, it is reasonable to wonder why the cost of college is still increasing, even in the face of all the public attention to, and criticism of, the tuition policies of colleges and college systems. It is rising because as states cut their support of public colleges and private colleges continue to compete for students by providing more and fancier amenities than the colleges down the road, none of them really know how to cut their costs. They all want and need more money, both to be competitive and to make improvements they feel will add to the quality of their offerings.

Lack of money is the biggest reason for the problems of the nonprofit colleges, Judith Eaton, president of the Council for Higher Education Accreditation (CHEA), an association of 3,000 degree-granting colleges and universities, told me. CHEA is the national umbrella organization that recognizes 60 institutional and programmatic accrediting organizations.

According to Eaton, "The current business model is not working. State subsidies are declining. Colleges are more dependent on federal aid and grants, which subject them to more control." She adds that "the idea of college is changing. More courses are online, and going to college is more episodic" for many students, who stop in and out, between jobs, or when financing is available. Eaton, like several other accrediting agency leaders, sees small, private colleges as those at greatest risk. She notes with concern, "We can expect less support for counseling, student activities, and other student needs," due to the financial crunch that colleges are experiencing.

The economic recession of 2008 brought higher education tuition and funding issues into sharp relief. Parents lost savings and jobs. States found their budgets unable to be balanced. Prospective students began to realize that the jobs for which they were investing in college educations might not be available to them even if they were able to graduate from their college programs.

At the same time, most colleges across the spectrum—from profit to nonprofit, public to private, small to large, and religious to secular—were experiencing financial problems. The gamut of problems included decreases in prospective student applications as well as in donations from supporters who were experiencing their own financial problems. Many colleges also experienced large drops in their investment portfolio values, along with drops in credit ratings. For public colleges across the nation, there was an increasing threat, and the reality, in many cases, of drastic cuts to state allocations.

In fact, analysis has shown that the major reason for tuition increases and budget problems at public universities is that states have been cutting back on their support of their colleges. According to a recent report by the Center on Budget and Policy Priorities, states were spending 28% less per student on higher education nationwide in the 2013 fiscal year than they did in 2008, when the recession hit (Oliff, Palacios, Johnson, & Leachman, 2013). When state support dollars are adjusted for inflation, all but two states are now spending less per student on higher education than they did prior to the recession. Eleven states have cut funding by more than one third per student, and two states have cut their higher education allocation per student in half (Oliff et al., 2013).

There is little doubt that these cuts would have eventually been made, even without a recession, because so many state budgets had serious debt issues of their own building up for a long time. Over the last two decades, as basic education, health care, and prison budgets all grew, states responded by cutting the percentage of state colleges' costs that they had previously provided. What the recession did, by putting so much overt pressure on public budgets, was just speed up the process.

States have been cutting back on their share of their publicly supported state colleges and universities for some time. According to a study by Demos, "While state spending on higher education increased by $10.5 billion in absolute terms from 1990 to 2010, in relative terms, state funding for higher education declined." It adds that real funding per public full-time equivalent student dropped by 26.1% from 1990–91 to 2009–10 (Quinterno, 2012, p. 2).

Furthermore, the prognosis for state funding in the near future is grim for most state colleges. An analysis in *The Kiplinger Letter: Forecasts for Management Decisionmaking* (Kiplinger Washington Editors, 2013) argues that states "have a rough budget road ahead, perhaps for much of the decade for some" (p. 1). The article noted that two thirds of the states have unbalanced budgets, to the tune of about a $25 billion shortfall (Kiplinger Washington Editors, 2013).

In the face of declining state support, state colleges have charged students more, in order to make their college budgets work. Some of these increases are obvious, in higher tuition prices. Other increases have been assessed through higher costs for room and board, and all kinds of fees, including laboratory, parking, athletic events, and general fees.

Although the costs of attending four-year colleges have more than doubled over the two-decade period from 1990 to 2010, median household income rose only 2.1%. There are a lot of reasons for the steep escalation in college costs, which are discussed in chapter 3. Whatever the reasons, though, the response has been not to cut costs, but to increase charges, putting the burden of paying for the problem on the backs of students.

As a result of the dramatic increase in the cost of a college education, college-enrolled students have come up with the necessary funds by borrowing them, thereby creating significant debt loads that in many cases will limit their future options. For example, the average medical school student graduating in 2012 had incurred a debt of greater than $166,750 (American Medical Association, 2013). For those who wait until after their residency to start paying it off, the debt escalates considerably, due to interest obligations. Many students who enter medical school dreaming of becoming family practitioners or of being physicians in underserved communities find out upon graduation that their debt status often precludes their opting for lower-compensated medical positions, pushing them into higher-paying specialties.

For both public and private nonprofit colleges, the inability of future students to afford to pay what is being asked of them, coupled with cutbacks in public support, raises the specter of underenrolled classes and potential budget crises. If we add to this the growing competition that these traditional colleges will face from aggressive for-profit colleges, more competition from colleges in other countries, and the MOOCs that the wealthiest and most prestigious schools will be hosting, what will be left for these traditional colleges to build their budgets on? Who will be sitting in their classes, or even taking their classes online, and will there be enough students enrolling to pay for building maintenance, faculty and staff salaries, and other financial obligations?

Community colleges will survive. As one business leader said, "Their price point is right." Community colleges are doing a lot of things right. They cost much less than four-year schools, and their tuition is lower than that for most for-profits. Community colleges have been growing and stretching, and educating poor students, students who are the first in their families to attend college, returning adult students, and students who need a fair amount of remedial work. In fact, 44% of community college students are first-generation college attendees, and more than half are over age 22 (American Association of Community Colleges, 2012, p. 8). In the 2010–11 school year, more than 8 million degree-seeking students attended two-year colleges (Koebler, 2012).

Community colleges will be sustained because they deliver a lot more bang for the buck than senior colleges. The smallest or weakest ones might have to merge or close, but in general community colleges are the institutions that best meet the needs of their local communities, for specialized job training or other programs. For-profits are not required to offer programs that the local public sector needs, but community colleges can be mandated to do just that.

Students enroll in community colleges for a variety of reasons. Some come to gain an associate's degree, or to earn enough credits to transfer to a four-year college and earn a bachelor's degree; many want to receive a certificate oriented to a particular job in industry; and others just want to take a few courses to develop some expertise in a career area. In fact, about 15% of community college students already have a bachelor's degree but return in order to gain credits for, or licensure in, a new career.

For four-year schools, however, the prognosis is gloomy. According to a report by Moody's (2013a) bond-rating service, the outlook for the future of the entire U.S. higher education sector is negative. Moody's analyst Eva Bogaty said that most universities will have to lower their cost structures to achieve long-term financial sustainability and fund future initiatives. She also pointed out that the report states, "Strong governance and management will be needed by most universities as they navigate through this period of intensified change and challenge."

As American colleges face dismal prospects for the next five years or so, more is being asked of them than ever before. State governments are raising the bar for their expectations of job readiness preparation of graduates, and the ability of academic institutions within a state to offer programs that help attract new cutting-edge businesses to the state. The federal government wants evidence that students are graduating, getting jobs, and being able to earn enough in the marketplace to pay off the federal student loans that helped to finance their college education.

As a nation, for several generations now, we have looked to higher education to play a transformative role in our society. Earlier in our nation's history, basic public education was seen as the glue that cemented people from diverse backgrounds into one union, by socializing children through a common education. Public schools were also the medium through which social mobility was provided, by giving children of the poor and middle class the same exposure to knowledge and ideas that only the rich and powerful had enjoyed in many other parts of the world.

Today, completion of a high school education is just the embarkation point for entry into the higher education programs that enable most Americans to attain at least a middle-class lifestyle. Numerous recent studies have demonstrated the enormous average annual and lifetime income differentials between college graduates and individuals with just high school diplomas (Longley, 2013)

Colleges are under more scrutiny to see how well they are succeeding in accomplishing their own missions of producing educated citizens, as well as the extent to which they meet governmental expectations. Colleges also need to be able to respond to rapid change, in an era when the social modes of communication are changing long before most people get acquainted with whatever the newest methods are.

It is difficult for anyone to keep up with all the technological changes that are confronting us. However, when it comes to higher education, it is especially difficult to respond to such changes because of the culture of higher education, where input from constituent communities such as faculty and students is a routine expectation, and the value of discussion and analysis, sometimes to the point of oblivion, is seen as consistent with the model of teaching and learning that underpins our concept of informed and thoughtful decision making in our educational institutions.

Some form of shared decision making is almost ubiquitous at our top colleges and universities. Accrediting agency teams often note with displeasure the signs of managerial monarchial standards of operation, and for good reason. The best professors frequently will not stay at such colleges, and the most sought-after students often will not attend them or will transfer from them except at military and some religiously based institutions.

Yet, colleges are faced with such pressing problems right now that the inability to respond rapidly to both threats and opportunities can consign an institution quickly to a less competitive status, if not an outright financial or other emergency, especially given the overwhelming amount of competition coming from sources that were either nonexistent or unable to offer effective challenges in the past.

The people who govern our nonprofit colleges are aware that our institutions are faced with growing fiscal problems. The senior staff and the boards of trustees are educated and successful people, for the most part. Most of them are businesspeople. Few would be likely to make the kinds of decisions for their businesses that they routinely approve for the colleges they oversee. Successful businesses do not usually spend more than they earn, and the investments they make are expected to lead to increased business.

When successful firms see threats to their markets, they make the kinds of changes necessary to hold or grow their market share, or they alter the business they are in, so that the firms can continue to survive. Not only do they make big changes, but they often make them very quickly, to capitalize on trends they see emerging.

In the nonprofit world, decisions are made very differently, and for a lot of reasons. First and foremost is that most nonprofit organizations, including colleges, have been established to support a cause or mission. This mission serves as the foundation of the organization. It drives its activities and the ways that it measures and values its performance.

In a well-functioning organization, goals and objectives are planned to help it carry out its mission. In the case of a nonprofit, the goal is not to increase market share or profits, but to cure cancer, or improve services to children, or provide a high-quality liberal arts college. Some nonprofits have a goal of changing the world, or changing some aspect of it.

Businesses have goals too, but for most businesses, those goals all relate to present or future profits. If the businesses are public corporations, they are responsible to their shareholders. Public corporations are businesses that sell stock that is traded on an open market. While a public corporation is managed by a board, it is owned by its shareholders.

For many nonprofit college leaders, it often feels like everyone owns the colleges. States oversee their licenses and activities, even when they are not publicly funded. Boards of trustees, administrators, faculty, students, alumni, the local community, and donors all have input into what college leaders feel they can and cannot do. All collegiate decisions also must be made with an eye on future constituencies, particularly the potential students that the colleges wish to recruit. For colleges, the future is always more important than the past, no matter how glorious or important it has been.

Nonprofit colleges are especially dependent on charitable donors, to help them bridge the gap among what students pay in tuition and fees, what government provides for them, and the costs of their enterprises. Most nonprofit colleges in the United States are not subject to income tax, and their donors can deduct the value of gifts they give them from their taxable income. In addition to tax benefits, donors may give to build a legacy, to create or sustain a certain type of program such as a cancer research center, or to enable poor students from their home town to have scholarships to attend the college. Few colleges in America could continue to provide their present level of programs and services without this type of donated support.

The Role of Accreditation

To qualify for federal financial aid eligibility for its students, a college must be accredited. If a for-profit or a nonprofit college is not accredited by a federally recognized accreditation agency, its students will not qualify for federal aid, and many would then not be able to afford to enroll in the college.

Accreditation assures potential students that a group of academic professionals has reviewed what the college presents and that the institution has passed an inspection process. The process is intended to document that a college is providing an appropriate education to its students, complies with public laws, and meets expected educational standards. Without our system of accreditation, students would have no way of knowing whether a college is legitimate.

In the United States, college accrediting is not done by the government, as it is in most other nations. Neither the federal government nor state governments accredit colleges, although states do require that colleges be licensed to grant academic degrees within their boundaries. Accreditation is done by accrediting agencies that the secretary of the U.S. Department of Education (2013) "determines to be reliable authorities as to the quality of education or training provided by the institutions of higher education and the higher education programs they accredit."

Accreditation agencies are voluntary nonprofit organizations composed of member institutions that set the standards for the institutions or program fields they evaluate. The agencies use peer review processes. Members of other colleges conduct the evaluations.

There are two basic types of accreditation organizations: institutional and specialized. Institutional accreditation is done through regional accrediting bodies that evaluate entire institutions rather than specific programs, although they look into the range of programs and can examine how well any particular program is structured and offered.

There are six regional accrediting organizations in the nation. Each accredits colleges largely within its own distinct geographic area, such as the New England states. The regional accrediting associations were developed in order to help colleges assess the preparation of high school students applying to their institutions. They have played a key role in enabling students to transfer credits from one accredited college to another, by ensuring that the standards for credit attainment are reasonably similar across accredited institutions.

Institutional accrediting bodies examine the mission of a college they are evaluating, and the extent to which it is achieved. They look at governance, to be sure that the separate responsibilities of board and staff are respected, that board members set policy, and that staff members work on implementing policies.

A specialized accrediting body evaluates particular units, schools, or programs within an organization. Specialized accreditation, also called program accreditation, is often associated with national professional associations, such as those for engineering, or with specific disciplines, such as business, teacher education, psychology, or social work. Some professions require their licensed practitioners to have graduated from accredited programs.

Many for-profit colleges seek accreditation through national accrediting organizations that evaluate schools offering their specialized programs, such as trade schools, or institutions offering programs such as theology, art, music, or cooking.

Accrediting agencies normally refer to institutions that offer only undergraduate programs as colleges and those that offer graduate programs as universities. They also designate government-funded colleges as public and those that are independent of government as private.

In the rest of the book, I use the term *colleges* to indicate all levels of accredited higher education institutions that confer earned academic degrees except where the name of a particular institution or set of institutions is involved, such as Duke University. To further simplify terminology and eliminate possible confusion between nonprofit and for-profit private colleges, I use the term *independent* for all private nonprofit colleges.

References

Allen, I. E., & Seaman, J. (2013, January). *Changing course: Ten years of tracking online education in the United States: Executive summary.* Babson Park, MA: Babson Survey Research Group and Quahog Research Group, LLC.

American Association of Community Colleges. (2012, April). *Reclaiming the American dream: A report from the 21st-Century Commission on the Future of Community Colleges.* Washington, DC: Author. Available from http://www.aacc.nche .edu/21stCenturyReport

American Medical Association. (2013). *Background: Student debt statistics.* Retrieved from http://www.ama-assn.org//ama/pub/about-ama/our-people/member-groups-sections/medical-student-section/advocacy-policy/medical-student-debt/background.page

Association of Governing Boards of Universities and Colleges. (2012). *The 2012 AGB survey of higher education governance, college prices, costs, and outcomes: Who's minding the gap between higher education and the public?* Washington, DC: Author.

Benefits and challenges of a MOOC. (2013, December 3). *MoocGuide.* Retrieved from http://moocguide.wikispaces.com/2.+Benefits+and+challenges+of+a+MOOC

Bennett, D. L., Lucchesi, A. R., & Vedder, R. K. (2010, July). *For-profit higher education: Growth, innovation and regulation.* Washington, DC: Center for College Affordability and Productivity.

Bernstein, N. (2013, March 28). Dream jobs disappearing for radiology trainees. *New York Times,* pp. A21, A22.

Bronner, E. (2013, January 30). Law school's applications fall as costs rise and jobs are cut. *New York Times,* pp. A1, A14.

Buddin, R. (2012, August 28). *The impact of charter schools on public and private school enrollments.* Policy Analysis No. 707. Retrieved from http://www.cato.org/publications/policy-analysis/impact-charter-schools-public-private-school-enrollments

Carnavale, A. P., & Strohl, J. (2013, July). *Separate and unequal: How higher education reinforces the intergenerational reproduction of White racial privilege.* Executive Summary. Georgetown Public Policy Institute Center on Education and the Workforce. Retrieved from http://www9.georgetown.edu/grad/gppi/hpi/cew/pdfs/Separate&Unequal.ES.pdf

Christensen, C. M., & Eyring, H. J. (2011). *The innovative university: Changing the DNA of higher education from the inside out.* San Francisco, CA: Jossey-Bass.

Christensen, C. M., Horn, M. B., & Johnson, C. W. (2008). *Disrupting class: How disruptive innovation will change the way the world learns.* New York, NY: McGraw-Hill.

Finn, C. E. Jr. (2013, May 16). Why private schools are dying out. *The Atlantic.* Retrieved from http://www.theatlantic.com/national/archive/2013/05/why-private-schools-are-dying-out/275938/

Frey, W. H. (2011, February 7). A demographic tipping point among America's three-year-olds. *Brookings.* Retrieved from http://www.brookings.edu/research/opinions/2011/02/07-population-frey

Fry, R. (2013a). *Hispanic high school graduates pass Whites in rate of college enrollment: High school drop-out rate at record low. I. Overview.* Retrieved from http://www.pewhispanic.org/2013/05/09/hispanic-high-school-graduates-pass-whites-in-rate-of-college-enrollment/

Fry, R. (2013b, May 9). *Hispanic high school graduates pass Whites in rate of college enrollment. II. Immediate entry into college.* Retrieved from http://www.pewhispanic.org/2013/05/09/ii-immediate-entry-into-college/

Gallup (2013, May 2). Gallup's college and university presidents' panel—inaugural survey findings. *Presidents bullish on their institution's future, but not on massive open online courses and higher education generally.* Executive Summary. Retrieved from http://www.mtsac.edu/president/board-reports/Gallup_Presidents_Panel _Report.pdf

Harden, N. (2012, December 11). The end of the university as we know it. *The American Interest.* Retrieved from http://www.the-american-interest.com/articles/ 2012/12/11/the-end-of-the-university-as-we-know-it/

Higher-ed startup StraighterLine moving out of ETC. (2012, July 17). *Bmore.* Retrieved from http://www.bmoremedia.com/devnews/straighterline-expansion-071712.aspx

Ho, C. (2013, June 2). Law school applications continue to slide. *Washington Post.* Retrieved from http://articles.washingtonpost.com/2013-06-02/business/ 39697850_1_american-bar-association-accredited-law-school-legal-job -market

Hoover, E. (2013, June 18). Demographic change doesn't mean the sky's falling. *The Chronicle of Higher Education.* Retrieved from http://chronicle.com/blogs/ headcount/demographic-change-doesnt-mean-the-skys-falling/35223

Hsu, J. (2012, January 25). Professor leaving Stanford for online education startup: Thrun's surprise announcement says he's taking his college courses to different level. *NBC News.* Retrieved from nbcnews.com/id/46138856/ns/technology_and_ science-innovation/t/professor-leaving-stanford-online-education-startup/# .UdrEh1PrHJw

Jamrisko, M., & Kolet, I. (2012, August 15). Cost of college degree in U.S. soars 12 fold: Chart of the day. *Bloomberg News.* Retrieved from http://www.bloomberg .com/news/2012-08-15/cost-of-college-degree-in-u-s-soars-12-fold-chart-of-the -day.html

Kahlenberg, R. D. (2004). *Left behind: Unequal opportunity in higher education.* New York, NY: The Century Foundation.

Kiley, K. (2013, January 17). Nowhere to turn. *Inside Higher Ed.* Retrieved from http:// www.insidehighered.com/news/2013/01/17/moodys-report-calls-question -all-traditional-university-revenue-sources

Kiplinger Washington Editors. (2013, April 12). The Kiplinger letter: Forecasts for management decisionmaking. *Kiplinger, 90*(15), 1.

Koebler, J. (2012, April 21). Report: Community college attendance up, but gradu-ation rates remain low: Community colleges place a greater emphasis on student achievement. *U.S.News & World Report.* Retrieved from http://www.usnews. com/education/best-colleges/articles/2012/04/21/report-community-college-attendance-up-but-graduation-rates-remain-low

Koller, D. (2013, May 28). *MOOCs and the completion agenda: ACE webinar.* Retrieved from http://www.acenet.edu/events/Pages/MOOCs-and-the-Completion-Agenda. aspx

Kolowich, S. (2013, February 7). American Council on Education recommends 5 MOOCs for credit. *The Chronicle of Higher Education.* Retrieved from http:// chronicle.com/article/American-Council-on-Education/137155/

Lewin, T. (2012, October 17). University of Phoenix to shutter 115 locations. *New York Times*. Retrieved from http://www.nytimes.com/2012/10/18/education/university-of-phoenix-to-close-115-locations.html?_r=0

Lewin, T. (2013, April 30). Colleges adapt online courses to ease burden. *New York Times*, p. A1.

Liberty University. (2014). *Liberty University online*. Retrieved from http://www.liberty.edu/online/

Longley, R. (2013, August 17). *Lifetime earnings soar with education: Masters degree worth $2.5 million income over a lifetime*. Retrieved from http://usgovinfo.about.com/od/moneymatters/a/edandearnings.htm

Marcus, J. (2013, April 14). Why some small colleges are in big trouble. *Boston Globe Magazine*. Retrieved from http://www.bostonglobe.com/magazine/2013/04/13/are-small-private-colleges-trouble/ndlYSWVGFAUjYVVWkqnjfK/story.html

Martin, A. (2013, January 10). Downturn still squeezes colleges and universities. *New York Times*. Retrieved from http://www.nytimes.com/2013/01/11/business/colleges-expect-lower-enrollment.html

Moody's. (2013a, January 16). *Announcement: 2013 outlook for entire US Higher Education sector changed to negative*. Retrieved from http://www.moodys.com/research/Moodys-2013-outlook-for-entire-US-Higher-Education-sector-changed--PR_263866

Moody's. (2013b, June 27). *Announcement: New state adjusted pension liabilities show wide range of obligations; effect of new discount rates highlighted*. Retrieved from http://www.moodys.com/research/Moodys-New-state-adjusted-pension-liabilities-show-wide-range-of--PR_276663

National Catholic Educational Association. (2013, May 25). *United States Catholic Elementary and Secondary Schools 2012–2013: The annual statistical report on schools, enrollment, and staffing*. Retrieved from http://www.ncea.org/data-information/catholic-school-data

Oliff, P., Palacios, V., Johnson, I., & Leachman, M. (2013, March 19). *Recent deep state higher education cuts may harm students and the economy for years to come*. Washington, DC: Center on Budget and Policy Priorities.

Peale, C. (2013, May 19). Student debt weighs on economy, local students: Loans gave them the college funds they needed to move forward, but now are holding them back. *Cincinnati Enquirer*. Retrieved from http://news.cincinnati.com/article/20130519/NEWS0102/305190006

Penn University Archives & Records Center. (2013). *Tuition and mandated fees, room and board, and other educational costs at Penn since 1900: 1950–1959*. Retrieved from http://www.archives.upenn.edu/histy/features/tuition/1950.html

Pérez-Peña, R. (2013, May 31). Limited success as colleges seek to attract poor. *New York Times*, p. A1.

Potter, C. (2013, June 18). Go into academia, win valuable prizes. *The Chronicle of Higher Education* Retrieved from http://chronicle.com/blognetwork/tenuredradical/2013/06/go-into-academia-win-valuable-prizes/

The Project on Student Debt, The Institute for College Access & Success. (2012, October). *Student debt and the class of 2011*. Retrieved from http://projectonstudentdebt.org/files/pub/classof2011.pdf

Quinterno, J. (2012, March). The great cost shift: How higher education cuts undermine the future middle class. *Demos*, p. 2.

Rampell, K. (2013, February 20). It takes a B.A. to find a job as a file clerk. *New York Times*, pp. A1, A3.

StraighterLine. (2013a, March 25). *Business*. Retrieved from http://www.straighterline .com/online-college-courses/business/

StraighterLine. (2013b, March 25). *How does college credit transfer work?* Retrieved from http://www.straighterline.com/how-it-works/credit-transfer/

Straumsheim, C. (2013, December 18). Scaling back in San Jose. *Inside Higher Ed.* Retrieved from http://www.insidehighered.com/news/2013/12/18/san-jose-state-u-resurrects-scaled-back-online-course-experiment-mooc-provider

Stripling, J. (2012, December 9). Pay and perks creep up for private-college presidents: Some of the highest paid get cash to cover taxes, too. *The Chronicle of Higher Education*. Retrieved from http://chronicle.com/article/PayPerks-Creep -Up-for/136187/

Stripling, J., & Newman, J. (2013, May 12). 4 Public-college presidents pass $1-million mark in pay. *The Chronicle of Higher Education*. Retrieved from http://chronicle.com/article/4-Public-College-Chiefs-Pass/139189/

StudyinEurope.eu. (2013). *Compare tuition fees schemes in Europe*. Retrieved from http://www.studyineurope.eu/tuition-fees

Sun Sentinel Editorial Board. (2013, May 19). Rein in outsized perks given Florida's college presidents. *Sun Sentinel*, p. A16.

University of Phonix. (n.d.). *Fact sheet: An overview of University of Phoenix activities*. Retrieved from http://www.apollo.edu/content/dam/apolloedu/pdf/Apollo-Group-UOPX-Fact-Sheet.pdf

U.S. Census Bureau, U.S. Department of Commerce. (2012, December 12). *U.S. Census Bureau projections show a slower growing, older, more diverse nation a half century from now*. Retrieved from http://www.census.gov/newsroom/releases/ archives/population/cb12-243.html

U.S. Census Bureau, U.S. Department of Commerce. (2013). *The 2012 statistical abstract, the national data book*. Money income of households—Median income by race and Hispanic origin, in current and constant (2009) dollars: 1980 to 2009. Table 691. Retrieved from http://www.census.gov/compendia/statab/cats/ income_expenditures_poverty_wealth/household_income.html

U.S. Department of Education, National Center for Education Statistics. (2012). *The condition of education 2012* (NCES 2012-045). Table A-49-1, p. 287. Washington, DC: Author.

U.S. Department of Education. (2013). *Database of accredited postsecondary institutions and programs*. Retrieved from http://ope.ed.gov/accreditation/

Walsh, M. W. (2013, June 28). Ratings service finds pension shortfall. *New York Times*, p. B1.

2 Nonprofit Colleges
Strengths and Weaknesses

O ur states and our federal government put a lot of resources into higher education because it is seen as a merit good. A merit good is something that we want people to have because we think it will benefit them, as well as our society as a whole.

For instance, we want children to be inoculated against dangerous diseases to protect their health, but inoculating a child also helps to protect other people's children from becoming infected. Similarly, higher education is seen as a merit good because we want ample numbers of citizens in our communities to possess the skills that such education provides for them as well as for the community at large, so that we all may benefit by having adequate access to ample numbers of trained schoolteachers, physicians, electrical engineers, and agricultural specialists available to provide vital services for us.

It is because higher education is seen as a merit good that communities are willing to pay taxes to support it, individuals are willing to give donations to its providers, and millions of students receive subsidies for their education. State governments give significant subsidy dollars to their public colleges. The federal government provides aid in the form of grants and loans to students. The students can use the aid at any accredited college in the nation, be it public, independent, or for profit.

Some states also provide direct student aid but may specify in which colleges, programs, or geographic regions that aid can be used. Some states provide scholarships for students studying in needed fields such as medicine or have in-state undergraduate tuition rate compacts with bordering states. Some states offer scholarship stipends to students whose grades are above a designated cutoff. Some limit the use of such scholarships to colleges in their own state.

Nonprofit colleges do not have owners or shareholders. They are governed by boards of trustees, who are appointed by the college or by governmental bodies. They do not seek profits, and if they have surpluses, they are expected to use those funds to benefit their present and future students and communities by awarding scholarships to their students, hiring more or better qualified faculty and staff, improving their facilities, or making other enhancements.

If a college is designated as a 501C-3 nonprofit organization by the Internal Revenue Service, it is able to receive donations for which its qualifying donors are eligible to claim federal tax deductions.

What Our Public and Independent Colleges Do Well

In its rankings of universities internationally, the British magazine *THE (Times Higher Education)* ranked 7 American universities in its top 10 selections for 2011–12. Among the top 20, 14 were from the United States, 4 were from the United Kingdom, and there was 1 each from Canada and Switzerland ("World University Rankings 2011–2012," 2012).

American nonprofit colleges are strong institutions for the most part. Most are regionally accredited and provide good training or teaching for the students in their programs. Even though there are many criticisms about whether American colleges are adequately preparing students for the world of work, or to meet the needs of the nation for scientists and engineers, the fact is that many foreign colleges, in all parts of the globe, are trying to emulate the American model of higher education.

There are two major advantages that some European and British Commonwealth colleges have over American ones. One advantage is in the time it takes to achieve a college degree. In Germany, for example, it takes three years to earn an undergraduate degree. In many other countries, students can also earn a "pass" degree in three years or an honors degree in four years, although there have been slow but consistent efforts to move to three-year degrees across Europe.

In 1999, educational leaders from 29 European countries met and adopted the Bologna Accord, which sought to standardize college offerings across national boundaries. The Accord is not a set of laws with which nations must comply, but rather a set of agreements toward which there has been movement, although compliance has been uneven. The Accord advocates a three-year bachelor's degree, a two-year master's degree, and a three-year doctoral degree.

The other advantage is in cost. For the most part, colleges in other developed nations cost less to attend than American colleges do. The major reason is that most other developed countries subsidize the cost of higher education at much higher levels than is the case in the United States. A second reason is that housing is not provided for most students, nor is it luxurious, where provided. A third reason is that many amenities such as athletic stadiums, upscale residence halls, fitness centers, and student unions with climbing walls and multiple pools and ever fancier cafeterias, which are routinely built at American campuses, are not part of the college offerings in most other countries.

Meet Societal Needs

Public colleges exist for the benefit of the public, of course. But what that means is that the states that fund them can require them to offer programs deemed necessary for the well-being of the citizens of the state. The state, through its agencies or its funding mechanisms, can also direct its colleges not to offer programs.

This latter effort has mainly been used by higher education system offices to try to compel their colleges to avoid unnecessary program duplication, especially in areas of high cost or low demand. Where undertaken, these efforts rarely fully succeed in cutting back extant programs. They are more likely to be somewhat effective in curtailing new offerings brought before system administrators or boards, especially if the new programs entail additional degree approvals, or specialized accreditation.

Many duplicative programs, even new ones, get established under the radar, because it is so easy to pick a name or a specific slant for a new program, and thereby assert that it is new and different from others being offered.

And many duplicative programs can and should be offered because there is adequate demand for them from students, and from eventual employers. Think of nursing programs, for example. Our colleges are unable to meet the demands in their own states and regions for more nursing graduates, because the pipeline is constricted outside of their control. There are not enough hospital sites willing to absorb more nursing students, for the training that is necessary to meet accreditation and licensing requirements, to allow most colleges to expand and more fully meet the need for nurses.

Independent colleges and for-profit colleges do not have to offer a program if it is too expensive, or does not draw enough students to be cost-efficient, or for any other reason they wish. Public colleges, on the other hand, can be pushed to meet the needs or desires of public officials, because although many states are providing a lower level of financial support for their state schools than they used to do, the amount of money they do provide is still significant enough that publicly funded institutions cannot afford to lose that support.

Agriculture programs are still largely provided by state colleges, particularly the land-grant colleges. Agricultural studies may or may not be cost-efficient, but for many states, these historically have been extremely important programs to offer.

In every state a land-grant college, and sometimes more than one state college, also support county extension services. The extension services offer information to farmers and other citizens in their service areas on agricultural and related issues. In states with large agriculture-based economies, many residents see these services as crucial. And you do not have to be a farmer to get information. Any resident can call to learn more about insects or growing conditions in their areas.

Most, though not all, states also offer important graduate programs through their state colleges, such as programs in medicine, dentistry, pharmacy, and law. States require licensure for practitioners of these programs and frequently ensure that at least some of their schools offer these degrees if the private sector does not. Many of the top medical centers in the nation are at major public research universities, where the university-owned hospital, the medical school, and other university health degree programs jointly enable medical excellence.

Manage the Curriculum

An appropriate college degree consists of more than just a collection of courses strung together willy-nilly. Undergraduate degrees are awarded in subject areas or fields such as mathematics, sociology, chemistry, or mechanical engineering. A small number of schools offer just one generic degree, such as liberal arts.

Nearly one of every three of the 1.7 million bachelor's degrees in 2010–11 was awarded in just two fields: business-related programs (21%) and social sciences and history (10%) (National Center for Education Statistics, 2013).

Regardless of the degree awarded to a student by an accredited college, the expectation is that the collection of courses taken to fulfill the requirements for the particular degree makes good sense and will help enrich the student's ability to understand and work in the field in which the degree is offered.

Regional accrediting associations require all four-year colleges to ensure that a minimum number of general education credits be completed by every student graduating from their college (e.g., the minimum requirement of the Southern Association of Schools and Colleges is 30 credits). These credits, frequently referred to as the core curriculum of an institution, include offerings in the humanities, social sciences, and hard sciences.

At most colleges, students are offered a menu from which they must select a given number of courses or credits from each menu part to meet the necessary minimum number of general education credits. In addition, students must complete a number of courses in their major, the area of study in which they seek their degree.

Who puts these course requirements into place? They are not specified in any external official documents or laws, nor are they completely agreed upon in their multiple manifestations. Rather, there is a broad, cultural consensus as to the types of studies that can legitimately be seen as general or liberal education. In most colleges, faculty across the academic disciplines, together with their deans, agree upon the core foundation options for their students.

Faculty within the departments or divisions that offer majors are the ones who choose the requirements for those majors. The members of the faculty in a particular department generally try to offer courses that replicate the predominant fields within that academic discipline. In political science, for example, a department would probably want its graduates to have taken coursework at least in American politics, international politics, political theory, political philosophy, and social science statistics or research methodology. Students can exceed the minimum requirements in each area, or they can fill out their remaining class time with electives that appeal to them.

Because faculty determine the offerings, we can be comfortable in knowing that those closest to understanding a particular field of study are shaping the program that students will receive. They do not shape the program to make money, or to create quick degrees. They design the program out of respect for, and commitment to, the field to which they have devoted their careers. Their disciplinary journals frequently provide guidelines, offered by respected leaders in the field, for the key areas of study to include within the particular discipline.

If this sounds too ideal to be true, that is because it is the ideal. It is also the case that most faculty members fight over curriculum design because they care so much about it. Trying to change a curriculum can evoke deep and protracted battles within departments. But just because people care about their field does not mean they will make good decisions about it.

Some faculty fail to keep up with the emerging arenas in their field of study. In addition, less productive faculty may feel threatened by changes. Many disagreements occur as a result of honest differences of opinion about the correct way to view or teach particular issues. Human nature often leads faculty to seek to replicate their own views and areas of interest in the new faculty whom their departments are seeking to hire.

Worst of all, course offerings within departments often get slanted to benefit senior professors with clout, who may opt to largely offer boutique courses attuned to their pet theories or writing projects, rather than base offerings on what students need in order to complete their programs, or have the broadest possible exposure to the field that a faculty of a given size can present.

Although far from perfect, the system of faculty design of curriculum is still one of the great strengths of the American system of higher education.

The challenge for faculty is to continue to control curriculum development, while finding ways to make more rapid and timely changes, and constraining personal distortions in curricular offerings.

Ensure Social Well-Being and Good Citizenship

Most nonprofit residential colleges have historically seen promoting the well-being of their students as part of their mission. From the beginnings of our first colleges in the United States, developing citizenship was a crucial part of the obligation of good colleges.

The mission statement of Yale College (Yale University, 2013), the undergraduate part of Yale University, states:

> The mission of Yale College is to seek exceptionally promising students of all backgrounds from across the nation and around the world and to educate them, through mental discipline and social experience, to develop their intellectual, moral, civic, and creative capacities to the fullest. The aim of this education is the cultivation of citizens with a rich awareness of our heritage to lead and serve in every sphere of human activity.

Most colleges have longer mission statements, but few so clearly and efficiently summarize the prevailing ethos of a college's fundamental commitments.

Of course, at one time, citizenship was understood to refer to America, and the effort was to provide socialization to its cultural norms. Today, that goal has been greatly attenuated, or greatly expanded, depending on one's point of view. It is no secret that teaching respect for our country's culture or history is not a major goal of faculty or institutions today. Some see citizenship more in terms of global expectations. Others see it as irrelevant to a college education. And some faculty see their obligations in terms of challenging received orthodoxy.

However, most colleges and their constituencies do want to provide learning that is more than just career focused, and that strives to develop a sense of social responsibility in the students they graduate. Committees that design mission statements for colleges, and for professional programs, agonize over finding just the right focus to develop what they consider the principles that must undergird the knowledge and understanding that their graduates should possess.

In addition to the commitment to social responsibility, colleges must focus on other forms of social well-being for their students. This focus is even more paramount now than it was in the past. For example, colleges need to be able to demonstrate that they seek and support diverse populations, including students whose educational needs, such as special testing accommodations, may diverge significantly from the norm.

Many colleges, especially elite independent colleges, have highly developed cocurricular programs. These include the establishment of numerous clubs and activities, along with large staffs devoted to ensuring that students are encouraged to "get involved."

Most colleges also offer wellness programs, providing mental health as well as physical health counseling, activities, and support. Student activities' staff work to engage students in campus efforts to create peer bonding, community outreach, school loyalty, and countless other efforts intended to promote happy, healthy students.

Although a residential for-profit college might be required by accrediting agencies to provide some of the student support systems in order to be accredited, citizenship and student emotional health programs are not fundamental drivers of what the constituencies and managers of for-profits see as the fundamental underpinnings of their educational enterprises.

Most of the for-profit colleges are focused on course delivery. Course delivery, not social responsibility, is their mantra, for the most part. They may offer a course in ethics, but the ethical development of the student is not their fundamental concern.

As the federal government increases its focus on dropout and job placement rates at many for-profit colleges, career outcomes will increasingly become a necessary focus for these colleges as well.

Provide Scholarships

Even though American colleges do a poor job of making college affordable, many colleges do provide a great deal of scholarship support for students whom they really want or need to attract. American colleges are expensive, and the major way they lower the real cost of attendance is to offer some of their students scholarships. These scholarships may underwrite part or all of the costs of tuition, and sometimes even some fees and residence charges.

Many scholarships are given based on need. These allow students from families with limited incomes to pursue their education at colleges they might otherwise not be able to afford. Nonprofit colleges spend a lot of time and effort seeking charitable donations for these need-based scholarships. Other scholarships are often offered to attract students with skills the college seeks to have in its student body, such as students with outstanding academic credentials, athletic skills, or leadership qualities.

A large number of scholarships are also offered to students as a way to lower the price enough to get them to enroll in the college. This is especially true for independent colleges. It is particularly important for them because the sticker price for entrance to most independent colleges is much higher than that for most public institutions.

Although public colleges are subsidized by their states (and occasionally by their local governments), the level of state support has been declining in most states over the last two decades. From 1990 to 2010, state funding per public full-time equivalent student dropped by 26.1%. Over the same period, the published prices for tuition and fees at public four-year universities rose by 112.5%, after adjusting for inflation (Quinterno, 2012). Furthermore, state and local appropriations have fallen every year over the past decade, dropping from 70.7% in 2000 to 57.1% in 2011 (Chakrabarti, Mabutas, & Zafar, 2012).

Nonetheless, state support still is substantial in terms of actual dollar amounts. State support allows publicly supported colleges to have much lower tuition rates than most independent colleges. State support to state higher education institutions amounted to an average of $5,906 per full-time equivalent student in 2012, down from $7,667 in 2007, in constant dollars. The total public support for public higher education across all the states was $78.4 billion (State Higher Education Executive Officers Association, 2013, pp. 24, 31).

For independent schools, the need for scholarships is obvious. The aforementioned more than $5,900 in support from the state means that public colleges can charge $5,900 less in tuition than independent colleges can, on average. Of course, the averages can conceal considerable differences in funding levels. Some states are much more generous to their public colleges than others are. And there can be significant differences in charges between elite independent colleges and less well-known independents.

The funds to underwrite scholarships come from two sources. The first and primary source of scholarship dollars comes from grants and donations to the college specifically intended to reduce tuition costs. Many donors give gifts that they target for support of scholarships, and many endowment gifts stipulate that interest income accrued in the fund must be allocated to scholarships. In addition, foundation grants to colleges are often given to support student tuition needs.

Colleges with very large endowments may also choose to allocate other endowment-generated income to support the awarding of additional student scholarships. This gives schools such as Harvard and Haverford, with large endowments, a huge advantage in attracting top students who have their choice of schools.

The second source of scholarship funds results from internal decisions by colleges to allocate more dollars to scholarship funding than is available through gifts and endowment income. These dollars are shifted within the institutional budget, to create additional scholarships for the institution to offer.

The basic reason that this is done is to lower the actual cost of attendance to some students, in order to maintain or increase enrollment in the college. Some colleges do this to attract more competitive students, so that they can raise their academic profile or ranking; other schools want to ensure an adequately diverse pool of enrollees; and still others want to attract enough students to enable their school to remain financially viable.

Particularly for this last group of colleges, the awarding of scholarships is funded largely by using a share of the anticipated funds due from the expected new enrollees. Basically, these schools, some of which may be close to the financial edge, set a tuition sticker price high enough to allow them to redirect much of the money they receive from tuition back into scholarship awards. Those colleges that do this are engaging in the practice of lowering the actual price for some students at the expense of having to charge more for those students who end up paying the full price.

For the small independent college, competitive pricing of the final net tuition cost is a must, if the college is to survive. The actual price that a given student will be expected to pay cannot appear to cost more than it would at similarly situated schools with which the college competes for enrollment. This effort to use scholarship awards to attract students has led to what is often referred to as a discount war.

Discounting, which is more thoroughly explored in chapter 3, occurs when colleges intentionally use scholarships as a means of recruiting enough students to fill their classes and meet their total tuition dollar needs. It requires a complex blending of cost estimates, realistic tuition sticker prices, and enough of a surplus available to enable the lowering of costs to some cohort of students, whose total dollar yield will be in excess of the cost of admitting and educating them.

What Our Public and Independent Colleges Must Do Better

There are a number of actions that our public and independent nonprofit colleges need to take in order to hold down or lower tuition, manage institutional costs, and be academically and fiscally sound. A brief overview of necessary undertakings is explored here. A more in-depth analysis is provided in chapter 5.

Reduce Costs

Simply put, a college education costs too much money. According to the College Board, "About 60% of students who earned bachelor's degrees in 2011–12 from the public and private nonprofit institutions at which they began their studies graduated with debt. They borrowed an average of $26,500" (College Board Advocacy & Policy Center, 2012).

Tuition and fees are part of the problem. The average cost of tuition and fees at public colleges was $8,893 for state residents for the 2013–14 academic year. The average published price for independent four-year colleges was $30,094 for the 2013–14 academic year (College Board Advocacy & Policy Center, 2013).

People hear those numbers and focus on them, but those charges are only part of the story—there are a lot of other charges that must be paid. Foremost among them are room and board. Room and board costs for the same 2013–14 school year were $9,498 for public colleges and $10,823 for independent colleges. For students who attend public colleges and choose to live on campus, room and board often costs more than their tuition and accounts for more than half of their total costs (College Board Advocacy & Policy Center, 2013).

These costs translate to about $160,000 over four years for an education at an independent college, and a good deal more if a student exceeds four years to graduate, as most now do. For students at public colleges the average sticker price with room and board amounted to $17,860 per year, or more than $71,000 over four years. And for too many students, the reality is that they will pay tuition, fees, and some expenses for more than just four years. Where will the resources come from to support these kinds of average costs?

Of course, prices differ greatly by institution and by state and many students do not pay the full listed price. According to a study done by the College Board Advocacy & Policy Center (2012), about two of three full-time undergraduates at public four-year institutions received an estimated average of $5,750 in grant aid from all sources and federal tax benefits to help them pay their tuition and fees, lowering their net annual tuition and fee costs to under $3,000.

Although financial aid may cover some to most of the cost of tuition for some students, very few get anything other than loans to pay for their fees and room and board. Just a small number of students get free or reduced room costs, by serving as resident advisors. There is one group of students who do get free room and board, though, and for the most part, they are football, basketball, or ice hockey players, at schools fielding highly competitive Division One teams in the National Collegiate Athletic Association.

When I first arrived as an administrator at the University of Minnesota Duluth, a few weeks before classes began, I noticed a group of solidly built young men sitting around some dining hall tables with huge displays of food in front of each one. I had never seen anything quite like it before. Each student had lined up glasses of milk and juice, four to a side, and several in the middle, surrounding their food plates like three sides of a large square.

These were the incoming and returning ice hockey players. They were having training workouts, and because of the number of calories they were apparently burning in their practice sessions, they had to consume huge portions of food to maintain their energy levels. It was an amazing sight, and only these athletes were part of it.

These big eaters all had free room and board. Some of the football players had similar levels of support. Free room and board is a very special kind of perk. It is part of a scholarship package that is usually offered to athletes in sports that fans buy tickets for.

Scholarships for academic merit will ordinarily not defray college fees, including room and board, but athletic prowess and the recommendations of the appropriate coaches will. It is fair to ask: Where are the academic standards and the academic integrity that drive these disproportionate awards? Surely, you would think, if athletes get such awards, other types of meritorious students should get them too. But most of them don't.

Of course, students do not have to choose to live on campus, although many colleges are located in communities far from their students' homes. Still, students can commute from home, or find lower-cost off-campus housing if it is available and if they are allowed to live off campus. Many colleges require first- and second-year students to live in campus housing. Some require juniors to do so as well.

There are several reasons that many four-year colleges require students who come from outside the local area to live on campus for at least their first year or two. First, there is the belief that it helps students to become better adjusted to college life, and to form friendships with other students. Second, having an adequate number of students on campus in the evenings is crucial to developing clubs and cocurricular activities. Commuters are unlikely to be on campus enough at night to ensure a good turnout for many campus activities. Finally, requiring certain classes of students, such as freshmen and sophomores, to live on campus ensures that the residence halls can be filled, and that enough students will purchase meal plans to support the catering services. These are frequently necessary requirements for small colleges.

One of my sons attended Columbia University. We were actually thrilled to pay the university room and board fees for the dismal facilities he occupied at the time, because the alternative, renting an apartment in Manhattan, was unthinkably expensive for a young student.

Blog sites contain numerous stories of students who live in RVs, yurts, or other lower-cost housing options. At the University of New England, groups of four or five students often would jointly rent a beach home off season, when the rentals were cheap, making the expense reasonable and affordable for each student. Over time, this option has become somewhat less viable, as more of the coastal homes have been bought, demolished, and rebuilt as mansions. People building mansions don't need the income from winter rentals to help pay off their second homes.

Some colleges, especially the higher-priced independent schools, wrap most of their fees into the tuition cost, so that they do not have the appearance of nickel-and-diming their students. Public colleges, however, find themselves needing those extra nickels and dimes, especially as state funding levels have failed to keep pace with costs, and so many are imposing every kind of fee that is not specifically denied to them under state regulations.

For example, in Florida, which has the 11th lowest tuition level among the states for its four-year colleges, fees are higher than in some other states. To prevent its state colleges and universities from continually increasing fees, Florida's K–20 Education Code places caps on how high some fees can be, how much they can be increased from year to year, and in some cases the processes that must be followed to determine what the fees will be. There are nine pages of requirements and limits on fees that may be charged. One statute mandates that "the sum of the activity and service, health, and athletic fees a student is required to pay to register for a course shall not exceed 40 percent of the tuition established in law or in the General Appropriations Act" (K–20 Education Code, 2012, § 1009-24[e]).

One state is trying to do something potentially groundbreaking: Reduce the immediate cost of college for its students attending state colleges. The Oregon legislature approved a plan in July 2013 that could allow students to attend state colleges without paying tuition or taking out loans. Instead, they would reimburse the state by paying it a small percentage of their earnings until the debt is fully paid. Under the bill, Oregon's Higher Education Coordinating Commission is charged with designing a pilot program that will have to meet legislature approval. The state would have to provide the start-up funds, and it has been estimated that each student who uses the program would have to pay back about 3% of his or her earnings over a period of about 20 years (Pérez-Peña, 2013). Although this is a potential creative way of helping students to afford to go to college, it does not do anything about the high costs imposed by the institutions.

Graduate Students in a Timely Fashion

Even if colleges delivered everything that they promised or that was expected of them, it still would not justify their escalating costs. Students go into debt to enroll in higher education institutions because they believe that four years later they will be able to get a good job in the career for which they studied, or be accepted into a graduate program that will appropriately train them for their aspired profession.

Although many for-profit colleges have been in trouble with their accreditors or the U.S. Department of Education for not graduating most of their matriculants, they are not the only colleges with poor graduation rates. For most American public and independent colleges, graduation rates are dismal, though less so than is the case for the for-profits. Of those who do graduate, far too few do so within the anticipated four years for a bachelor's degree. For public colleges, the overall four-year graduation rate is only 31%, and for independent colleges the rate is 52% (de Vise, 2012).

Because most students do not graduate within four years, federal tracking on degree attainment is largely done by examining completion rates over six-year intervals.

In fact, only 58% of students who started as full-time students at a four-year college in the fall of 2004 were able to attain a bachelor's degree at that college six years later. Students at independent colleges were the most likely to graduate within six years. An average of 65% did so, compared with just 56% at public colleges, and only 28% at for-profit institutions (U.S. Department of Education, National Center for Education Statistics, 2012).

Therefore, our typical imagined four-year pathway to a bachelor's degree seriously underestimates the length of time it takes the average student to complete his or her degree programs. This means that the cost charts we use to predict college expenses frequently woefully underestimate the true cost of degree attainment. When we multiply the annual costs by six years instead of four, the costs can be really frightening.

There are several reasons why students take more than four years to graduate. Some may fail a course, or not take enough course credits per semester. They may also attend part-time, or start off full-time but need to change to part-time. They may drop out because of family obligations, work needs, or illness.

There are some problems with the way the measurements are done by the U.S. Department of Education. The measurements are based on reports known as IPEDS (Integrated Postsecondary Education Data System), which colleges must file annually, through the National Center for Education Statistics. The main weakness of the findings is that they consider only students who are first-time, full-time enrollees to a college, and who graduate from the same college, in the database. The reason is that tools are not yet available to track the progress of students who change colleges, drop out for a while, or drop back in after a prolonged absence from the college market. None of these students are counted in the estimates of time to graduate. This is completely unrealistic because about a third of all students do change schools (Hossler et al., 2012). Many transfer from community or junior colleges to four-year colleges, but some transfer in reverse, from four-year to two-year, perhaps to save money. Most transfers involve students moving from two-year to four-year programs. In fact, 45% of all four-year degrees are earned by students who were previously enrolled in a two-year institution (National Student Clearinghouse Research Center, 2012).

Students transfer in order to go to a school with a stronger program in their major, to be closer to home, because their significant other has changed colleges, or just because they do not like the school where they have been enrolled. Whatever the reason for changes in institutions or status, the federal statistics on the length of time to graduate clearly illustrate how long the process of getting a degree is for much of each year's student cohorts. Students who transfer typically have to take additional courses at their new college in order to meet different requirements, or because they have changed programs, and some of the work they have previously done will not count toward a degree in the new program.

"Higher education is no longer monolithic," Richard Winn, senior vice president of the Accrediting Commission for Schools, Western Association of Schools and Colleges (ACS WASC), told me. "Only about 19% of the students are traditional 18- to 24-year-olds. The others are married, part-time, returning, or older. An average student today picks up credits from several colleges. When they transfer, they lose nearly a quarter of their credits. Students need to be offered seamless transfer policies."

Because the federal statistics do not capture information about many students in the college pipelines, six higher education associations have gotten together to sponsor a new and more comprehensive tracking system for measuring student advancement and completion of their college studies. These associations are the American Association of Community Colleges, the American Association of State Colleges and Universities, the American Council on Education, the Association of American Universities, the Association of Public and Land-grant Universities, and the National Association of Independent Colleges and Universities (Mangan, 2013). They represent public and private two- and four-year colleges and are urging their association members to participate in this new tracking system.

Of course, if we tracked data on length of time to graduate for all students, not just first time, full-time enrollees, the results could look better for those colleges that graduate their transfer students within two years. However, the overall results could look far worse than the numbers that are presently causing the concern about length of time to graduate.

The federal government would like to make schools responsible for collecting such data, but it is still too difficult, although new data collection tools could make it more feasible. Basically, students would have to be tracked as individuals, with electronic educational records, much like the new electronic medical records that will follow us all. Are we all prepared for such a further intrusion on our privacy?

Focus More on Students Than Faculty

Our public and independent colleges profess to be all about educating their students, but in fact, most colleges are primarily concerned with maintenance and enhancement of their institution, including the building of reputations and endowments, to ensure healthy institutional futures.

Moreover, schools with the most positive reputations have yet another consideration that looms much larger than the welfare of their students. That consideration is the quest for the best faculty, generally meaning those faculty who are well published, who are recognized as authorities in their fields, who bring in grants, and whose affiliation with a college helps to raise the status of the institution in the eyes of its academic peers.

College presidents often joke that faculty are the real "owners" of their colleges. They mean this in the same way that people refer to civil service employees in government jobs. The politically appointed directors come and go with elections, but the regular staff outlasts all the political changes. Similarly, college deans and presidents come and go, but most of the tenured faculty remain at the college.

Faculty know that although their students pass through their programs in four, five, or six years and their senior administrators come and go, most faculty will stay at the school for their entire career. But even if that is true, the top tier of faculty do have options. Other aspiring programs at other colleges may solicit strong faculty. Colleges need to keep their top people satisfied. That is why New York University (NYU) has given loans for summer homes and other extravagant perks to its top faculty.

Great research faculty are crucial to the quality of an institution's research reputation. Having a great teaching faculty is key to a college being perceived as having a quality learning environment.

The curriculum for each major a college offers is presumably designed to provide its students with the best possible knowledge and training in that particular field. However, there is little doubt that the offerings conform to the strengths and desires of the particular faculty in a department, and that both the sets of offerings and the times of offerings are generally more contingent on faculty preferences than students needs, although pressure will be brought to bear if things get too much out of balance.

Even though the very best research faculty may be recruited by other colleges or research centers, or for leadership roles outside of academia, the culture of tenure ensures that midlevel, mediocre faculty can stay in their jobs at their colleges as long as they wish. Even poorly performing faculty can be hard to part with, because the standards for removing someone from tenure are set so high in terms of what levels of performance can be used to enable their removal. In essence, barring criminal behavior, within the academic realm tenure provides most faculty with a lifetime job.

By contrast, the average term of service for a college president is just seven years (American Council on Education, 2012). This means that college presidents and deans (who also experience regular turnover) know that their faculty will outlast them. There are few things that college presidents fear more than a faculty vote of "no confidence," which frequently leads to a president having to step down from his or her office and more often than not find another position somewhere else.

Donors are another important consideration. A 2011 survey of 1,622 college and university presidents found that presidents increasingly spend their time on fund-raising, budgets, community relations, and strategic planning. More than two thirds of presidents of private bachelor's, master's, and doctoral institutions reported that they spent most of their time on fund-raising (American Council on Education, 2012, pp. xi, 34.)

There is no getting around the fact that you cannot offer a great education without great faculty. The best public and independent colleges have been serving faculty needs before student needs, but the direction of that relationship is about to be reversed. This reversal will take place as a result of the changes the for-profit colleges and the for-profit enterprises owned by consortia of nonprofit colleges (such as Coursera and Udacity) are making. They are changing the model of course offerings from a design where students are under one professor's tutelage in a classroom to one where they can pick and choose their favorite provider and method of delivery (i.e., in their home, office, or residence hall).

Great faculty who can master the presentation of online material will still be in the catbird seat, so to speak, but they will wield their power over the dollars they can command from the content-providing organization's overseers, rather than through the governance of their institutions. They may only incidentally be offering their classes on a campus, with any students sitting in the same room with them.

Stop Overbuilding Facilities

Most facilities on most college campuses are not well utilized. At small private colleges, many or most of the buildings are closed for the summer. In fact, because the average length of the two semesters offered is about 30 weeks, many of the facilities may be unoccupied or closed for more than 40% of the year.

Some colleges run summer programs, but these are usually small programs. Colleges in areas that attract summer tourists may offer adult noncredit classes or rent rooms in their residence halls to alumni and others who wish to visit in the area, as several colleges in the upper Midwest do, but these are rarely real moneymakers. Rather, they help in a minimal way to defray building maintenance costs.

A number of colleges host business conferences, or camping programs, or even summer school offerings for their own students. And some, especially universities with numerous graduate programs, may have some classes taking place all year long. But whatever the model used in the summer, few places are full, though the more programs they offer, the more of their auxiliary facilities, such as libraries and dining halls, they need to keep open.

Think about it. It may make sense for schools in warm areas to close or reduce activities for the long summer break. Northern areas, such as New England, are places where people like to vacation in the summer. In such summer tourist areas, it could make a lot more sense to have classes run all summer, and close for part of the winter, saving on heating and snow removal bills, and attracting students and staff who might like to vacation in ski resorts and then vacation in hotter climates during their long winter breaks.

Summers are not the only downtime for colleges. Every weekend will find most colleges substantially empty of students and staff, unless there is a big football game taking place. Additionally, classes at most schools that are not in urban areas also aren't running in the evenings; too few traditional-age students are willing to attend evening classes.

On the other hand, courses such as those that are required to retain teacher certification are the types of evening classes that some older students are willing to attend for graduate credit, although even on colleges that offer these programs, there are still very few students on campus at night.

Saturday and Sunday classes also are rarely offered. Weekend classes are generally attended only by older students taking part-time so-called "executive" programs. These programs that cater to working adults also do not generate many enrollees, but they may provide extra income for schools providing such offerings. They may provide an opportunity for a returning student to complete a degree program. Schools often see offerings such as executive MBAs as cash generators. They can offer a desired degree to students they might not admit to their regular programs while taking in high tuition dollars without having to expend college funds on the auxiliary support programs they provide to their traditional students.

The norm for holding classes for college course offerings, in colleges around the nation, has been a three-hour-per-week class scheduled one hour per day on Mondays, Wednesdays, and Fridays, or four hour-and-a-half sessions on Tuesdays and Thursdays. Senior professors at many schools historically demanded the two-day-per-week, Tuesday/Thursday schedule as much as possible, often claiming the need for adequate research time. In recent years equity concerns have led many departments to eliminate this practice and rotate schedule opportunities

Friday afternoons are another dead time because few professors are willing to host classes, and few students are willing to attend. It is not unusual for senior academic leaders at colleges everywhere to discover that occasionally some professors with three-day afternoon schedules simply do not meet with their students on Friday afternoons. Often, no one discovers it is happening because none of the students complain.

Both professors and students who do not want to artificially shorten their courses simply do not sign up for afternoon classes that meet on a Monday-Wednesday-Friday block. This well-known phenomenon leaves many classrooms more utilized during mornings than in the afternoons.

It is true that many businesses are closed evenings and weekends, too, although those that deal directly with the public, such as retail establishments, often have extended hours in the evening and on the weekends. There are also businesses that cater to seasonal tourism, but many either close for the off-season or reduce their staffing. However, few businesses that are seasonal have so many buildings or so much acreage sitting idle as colleges routinely do.

Once they are built, college buildings are not a free resource. Buildings must be cleaned, heated or cooled, repainted, regularly repaired, and otherwise maintained. As buildings age, the cost of their care increases. The costs of maintenance are frequently not faced as regular budgeted items, especially when large costs, such as for new heating units or roofs, are involved.

Deferred maintenance problems are a frequent reality for most colleges. In the crush of competing expenses confronting an administration and board at budget-making time, those costs that can be deferred generally get considered last, as an add-on, for future consideration. Sooner or later, though, these costs must be met.

The state of Louisiana is facing some of these costs right now. The price tag for dealing with the deferred maintenance issues on its public higher education colleges and universities has been projected as $1.7 billion. In a statement about the extent and seriousness of the problem, Louisiana Commissioner of Higher Education Jim Purcell claimed, "The cost of deferred maintenance on Louisiana's college campuses has reached the point where it's more than double the amount of money schools will have available to educate students next year" (Addo, 2013).

Some of the buildings have mold problems, others have leaky roofs, and some are still not adequately accessible to those with disabilities. Yet more than $100 million a year is still going toward new construction. Some Louisiana educators say that their schools face "major health and safety concerns as repair requests languish for years or even decades in the capital outlay pipeline" (Addo, 2013).

Tighten Managerial Control

In many ways, public and independent colleges are like the American government. James Madison argued in Federalist Paper No. 51 (1787) that because men are not angels it was important to build checks and balances into the design of government to guard against the concentration of too much power in one place. In our colleges, faculty are frequently fiercely protective of their "right" to control the curriculum, fearing exactly what Madison warned about, the concentration of power in the hands of a board or senior administrator. Faculty distrust the business model of college management for two reasons: First, they believe the creation and imparting of knowledge cannot be appropriately assigned a dollar value; and, second, they do not trust their leaders.

American governments, at all levels, have multiple constituencies. Local governments have voters, parents of schoolchildren, police, state officials, and businesses to deal with. Even on small issues, such as many involving real estate disagreements, there may be lots of different viewpoints and coalitions of concern. National governments have to consider all the branches of government; all the many players in their political space; and, of course, international concerns.

For college administrators, it is much the same. Faculties think their presidents have too much power, but most presidents know they have very little real authority. A war may be declared if a president bucks a faculty decision on the awarding (or not awarding) of tenure to someone. Boards fire presidents when new board chairs with different agendas take over. Although many newly hired college presidents fire their entire senior staffs when they assume office, they need to do it quickly, before their honeymoons end, and the perceptions of their power dwindle.

Presidents are beholden to boards, student leaders, faculty leaders, alumni, and powerful community interests. A vote of censure, or even the threat of one, by a faculty senate has cost many a president his or her job. For those in the public sector, the governor, key legislators, and system leaders can all sway support against presidential actions. Even in the independent sector, for a school whose athletic programs have strong booster organizations, a football coach may have far more real power than the president.

In all too many places this means that no one is totally in charge. Someone may nominally be in charge, in terms of day-to-day decisions, but no one may be in a safe position from which to administer major reforms, even where and when they are desperately needed.

For-profit institutions can exert tight managerial control. It is an advantage they have over nonprofits, but it is a mixed blessing, for if a college president in a for-profit school can rearrange the chairs on the deck of the institution, what will ensure that the integrity of the educational process, within any particular discipline, is respected and that academic standards are adhered to? Faculty may sometimes abuse their rights, but the bottom line is that of all the players involved in the process of educating college students, faculty are the ones who, at their best, are the guardians of academic standards.

We can have colleges without administrators, but we cannot have colleges without faculty. We can provide them in person, or virtually, but we must have them present the curriculum to students, even if, or where, we provide others to evaluate students' ultimate progress.

References

Addo, K. (2013, May 20). *Backlog of maintenance: Colleges, universities suffer $1.7 billion maintenance lag.* Retrieved from http://theadvocate.com/csp/mediapool/sites/Advocate/assets/templates/FullStoryPrint.csp?cid=5997316&preview=y

American Council on Education. (2012). *The American college president 2012.* Washington, DC: Author.

Chakrabarti, R., Mabutas, M., & Zafar, B. (2012). *Soaring tuitions: Are public funding cuts to blame?* New York, NY: The Federal Reserve Bank of New York.

College Board Advocacy & Policy Center. (2012). *Trends in higher education.* Figures 10A and 10B. Retrieved from http://trends.collegeboard.org/student-aid/figures-tables/loans

College Board Advocacy & Policy Center. (2013). *Average published undergraduate charges by sector, 2013–14.* Table 1A. Retrieved from http://trends.collegeboard.org/college-pricing/figures-tables/average-published-undergraduate-charges-sector-2013-14

de Vise, D. (2012, June 2). *Public universities pushing 'super-seniors' to the graduation stage.* Retrieved from http://articles.washingtonpost.com/2012-06-02/local/35461441_1_students-graduate-graduation-rate-public-universities

K–20 Education Code, Fl. Stat. §1009.24(e). (2012).

Hossler, D., Shapiro, D., Dundar, A., Ziskin, M., Chen, J., Zerquera, D., & Torres, V. (2012). *Transfer and mobility: A national view of pre-degree student movement in postsecondary institutions.* Signature Report. Herndon, VA: National Student Clearinghouse Research Center.

Madison, J. (1787, November 22). Federalist No. 15: The Same Subject Continued: The Union as a Safeguard Against Domestic Faction and Insurrection. *New York Daily Advertiser.* Retrieved from http://www.ourdocuments.gov/doc.php?flash=true&doc=10&page=transcript#no-51

Mangan, K. (2013, June 24). Higher-ed groups unveil alternative to federal student-success measures. *The Chronicle of Higher Education*. Retrieved from http://chronicle.com/article/Higher-Education-Groups-Unveil/139981/

National Center for Education Statistics. (2013). *The condition of education, undergraduate fields of study*. Figure 2. Retrieved from http://nces.ed.gov/programs/coe/indicator_cta.asp

National Student Clearinghouse Research Center. (2012). *Snapshot report*. Retrieved from studentclearinghouse.info/snapshot/docs/SnapshotReport6-Two-YearContributions.pdf

Pérez-Peña, R. (2013, July 4). Oregon looks at way to attend college now and repay state later. *New York Times,* pp. A13, A15.

Quinterno, J. (2012, March). The great cost shift: How higher education cuts undermine the future middle class. *Demos*, p. 2.

State Higher Education Executive Officers Association (SHEEO). (2013). *State Higher Education Executive State higher education finance FY* 2012. Boulder, CO: Author.

U.S. Department of Education, National Center for Education Statistics. (2012). *The Condition of Education 2012* (NCES 2012-045), Washington, DC: Author.

World university rankings 2011–2012. (2012). *THE (Times Higher Education)*. Retrieved from http://timeshighereducation.co.uk/world-university-rankings/2011-12/world-ranking

Yale University. (2013). *Mission statement of Yale College*. Retrieved from http://catalog.yale.edu/ycps/mission-statement/

3 Why College Costs Are So High

To see how the cost of going to college might be brought more in line with the ability to pay for it, it is necessary to explore the reasons why college educations are so costly and to think about which costs could be reduced without damaging educational programs.

Colleges are complex organizations. They are expected to provide quality educations to their students, yet educators, the government, and the public at large do not all agree on what the components of a quality education are, or how we might best measure its attainment. We entrust to the colleges and their accrediting agencies confidence in their capacities for doing the job right when we send them our sons and daughters.

Colleges try to find the right mix of classes and cocurricular activities for their students, and the right balance of teachers and researchers to offer their academic programs. They seek the best possible blend of student bodies, and the most appropriate and competitive sets of facilities that their particular institutions can develop.

Although they are not seeking profits, public and independent colleges must find a variety of ways to fund their institutions and meet their goals. Because they must provide at least one faculty member for every class and have adequate staff to recruit students, manage financial aid, oversee the library, arrange activities, provide security, raise funds, coach athletics, and perform myriad other essential and nonessential services, colleges need a lot of personnel. Hiring a big staff is costly.

The shared governance model of higher education also raises costs because decision making often takes a lot of time and effort in many facets of a college's programs. Senior college administrators generally lack the authority to unilaterally make many of the kinds of decisions that their counterparts in the for-profit sector can make.

Over the last several decades, there has been a lot of staff expansion in higher education institutions. Some of that increase has occurred because of efforts to enhance programs, but a lot of it has also been required to cope with regulatory requirements. Colleges have experienced increased regulatory and reporting requirements from a slew of governmental agencies, as well as accrediting agencies, athletic conferences, collegiate associations, and donor organizations, among others. These reporting requirements necessitate staff to monitor compliance, compile data, and perform analysis.

Mission creep also increases costs for institutions, and even more so for students. Mission creep involves the expanding ever upward of requirements for degrees in specialized fields, additional off-site college campuses, and the movement of colleges from two- to four-year status or college level to university level.

Offering tenure to faculty secures faculty positions but holds down flexibility in managing academic needs and costs and changing programs. Although there are clearly some benefits to tenure, the costs outweigh the benefits.

Tuition rates, discounting policies, and federal financial aid all affect the final costs that students will pay for their education. In fact, many of the policies that help to reduce the sticker costs to students today may actually help to increase the net costs in the long run.

Building more and fancier facilities than are needed places long-term burdens on college budgets. The overbuilding of residence halls and student unions and athletic facilities, in an era of growing online education, is going to lead to colleges having to pay off underutilized facilities that reduce their flexibility to move money into program areas in need of support.

Intercollegiate athletics is an area that needs significant rethinking. Most for-profit colleges do not offer intercollegiate athletics as part of their educational package, nor do most nonprofit colleges in most other nations. Athletic programs not only cost a lot of money, but also divert colleges from their proclaimed missions and standards. Many college teams in the United States have ardent supporters who strongly believe in the benefits the teams convey to their institutions, but the evidence to support those beliefs is meager, and the costs are very high.

Unfortunately, in nonprofit higher education, there are a lot of cost drivers. In addition to intercollegiate athletics, these include regulatory compliance, the inability under tenure rules to part with less productive faculty, and student recruitment costs. Competition in recruitment often leads to discounted prices and added new activities or facilities to attract more students. Buildings are easier to fund than academic programs. These additions or expansions, which often are planned as revenue enhancers, eventually begin to encumber higher costs as they build their own bureaucracies.

Economic Issues

Both independent and public colleges are facing hard times economically. As the cost of a college education has increased faster than earnings, the need to discount rising tuition sticker prices has bedeviled independent colleges. For many, the net tuition they receive is no longer keeping pace with increases in their costs.

Public colleges are straining too as states cut back on higher education allocations. Even when state budgets for higher education have increased due to growth in student numbers, the amount of state support per student has been declining in most states. Consequently, tuition and fee costs for students attending state colleges have risen dramatically over the last few years.

For the most part, higher education does not function like a normal market. Nonprofit colleges, for example, do not try to maximize income or sales. They behave more like private clubs. Their eyes are firmly fixed on reputational status and acknowledgments. They prize the ability to become more and more selective as to who—students and faculty alike—will be admitted to membership.

Innovations that bring grant dollars or academic awards are highly valued, but proposed innovations in the way learning is offered are looked at askance. Academics may be accused of leaning leftward in their politics, but in their willingness to take risks with fundamental redesigns of curriculums or methods of presentations, they are decidedly conservative.

"We need to skate to where the puck is going to be, not where it has been," a trustee of Florida Polytechnic University said at a board meeting, quoting ice hockey legend Wayne Gretzky. The trustee was telling us to design our new programs to meet future needs, rather than imitate academic programs already saturating the market.

Most colleges do not skate to where the puck is heading. They are not opposed to change per se but are agnostic about its applicability to their own institutions and needs. The operant philosophy seems to be, "Show me who else is doing it."

Fear of accreditation issues, board or political disapprovals, potential new costs, faculty recalcitrance, student resistance, and other innumerable possible objections stop many innovations before they get very far. Unlike the world of business, colleges do not feel the need to develop new models each year, as the auto and computer industries do.

Public and independent nonprofit colleges offer mixes of programs and courses, which sometimes vary widely in what it costs to provide them. For example, it costs a lot more to offer a class in animal husbandry than a class in English literature. The latter course requires only that the college provide a professor and a classroom. For the animal husbandry course, there must be a professor, some animals, facilities to house the animals, and staff to care for them, at a minimum. Similarly, most classes in dentistry require a lot more support than most classes in philosophy.

For-profit colleges do not have to offer expensive, money-losing programs or courses. Some public institutions have to offer them, and some independent colleges may feel obliged to offer them. These nonprofit colleges manage their support for their high-cost programs by balancing them with some less expensive, or more profitable, programs.

As commercial providers have entered the higher education market, they have made a beeline for the low-cost, revenue-enhancing programs, such as part-time MBAs. Zemsky, Wegner, and Massy (2005) note that colleges have only two sources from which to subsidize unprofitable programs: funds generated from other, profitable programs or funds from endowments, governmental appropriations, or gifts (p. 66).

Within a given college there will be multiple contenders for such funds. For starters, the programs generating profits or gifts expect to benefit from their own efforts. Programs experiencing increased demand will want funds to support their growth. Even programs doing poorly will have their advocates, claiming that more financial support from the central administration could help them reverse their slide.

As a vice chancellor at a public university and later as a president at an independent university, I was subjected to numerous requests for increased levels of financial support, as well as regular visits by faculty and staff with "wonderful new projects" for us to invest in. When I asked how we might pay for those programs, I frequently was told, "Oh, you will easily be able to raise money for this project. Lots of people will support it, and you are very good at fund-raising."

It was rare for requesters (other than faculty who regularly received large public research grants) to offer to raise the funds themselves. Faculty often have wonderful ideas for new programs and projects. They are brilliant and creative people, after all. College leaders cannot accept all of the grand proposals that are presented to them because their institutions never have enough of the monetary or time resources. Neither is ubiquitous.

Because the ideas college faculty and staff want to explore are often quite exciting, most of us affiliated with higher education institutions wish we could fund more than we do. Students, faculty, staff, senior administrators, and board members for the most part want to do as much as they can to allow their college to pursue excellence, build its reputation, enhance its programs, and construct bigger and better buildings.

Historically, in the imaginations of many, colleges have been venerated as citadels of learning, fonts of wisdom, creators of new knowledge, providers of social networks, developers of good citizenship, and arenas of athletic splendors. They have also represented, to many donors, physical repositories for cultural explorations and artifacts, which may be expected to last for generations, thus ensuring that time will not diminish or destroy one's legacy. In fact, some of the finest art museums in our nation are on college campuses.

The reality is that some colleges have lasted for several centuries or longer. However, with the nature of the potential delivery of education undergoing extraordinary change, it is hard to know just how likely most colleges are still to be standing another century from now.

We live in a world with finite resources. And although the last 70 years have been very good to higher education, the next 10 or 20 are unlikely to support the previous levels of growth. That is because for most colleges, be they public or independent, subsidies are necessary to keep them fiscally sound. Those subsidies can come from taxpayers, through government allocations, or from donors.

The fundamental reality for colleges is that the cost of providing a traditional college education exceeds the amount that can be charged for it. As the National Association of College and University Business Officers (NACUBO, 2002) has stated, "In essentially every instance, the cost of providing an undergraduate education exceeds the full 'sticker' price charged to students and their families in the form of tuition and related fees, by anywhere from a few hundred dollars to as much as $20,000 or more" (p. 10).

The 2002 NACUBO study, which dealt only with the costs of undergraduate education (graduate education is generally more expensive to deliver), indicated that at community colleges and four-year public colleges 85% of the budgets were used for instruction and student services. Independent colleges and universities allocate only about 70% of their costs to instruction and student services, because they use so much of their income on providing financial aid for so many of their students.

Human Resource Intensive

The most frequently noted fact about the high cost of higher education is that college tuition and fees have been growing faster than the rate of inflation. Sandy Baum (2012), the analyst of an important study on college costs, while documenting that the level of college cost growth has exceeded rates of inflation also has noted, "It is revenue shortages rather than expenditure growth that have driven the recent rapid rises in public college prices" (p. 7).

Some college costs can be controlled or reduced through eliminating waste and duplication. Some costs can be reduced through redesign of management systems, but some discrepancies between inflation rates and tuition/fee rates are likely to remain. That is because there are complex reasons why both public and independent colleges' prices have risen faster than the rate of inflation.

The most significant reason is that colleges are human resource dependent. Their product is a service, generally provided by reasonably well-compensated human beings. Classes are offered by professors who have generally spent many years of study in preparation for presenting their accumulated knowledge to their classroom tutees. Cocurricular activities, such as glee clubs and athletic programs, are presided over by trained and sometimes high-cost student service professionals.

Organizations that are human resource intensive cannot easily increase productivity over time the way that manufacturers of goods can. The economist William Baumol, with his colleague William G. Bowen, demonstrated this problem in an article in 1966 analyzing the economic problems facing performing arts organizations (Baumol & Bowen, 1966). Baumol later expanded the analyses to cover many other kinds of nonprofit and human resource–intensive institutions.

Baumol pointed out that persons working in areas such as the performing arts, which may not experience productivity gains similar to those captured in manufacturing areas, still compete in the overall job market. Therefore, their wages will rise along with those of workers whose jobs do experience gains that bring them higher pay.

The cost of a given level of computing power keeps getting reduced, while the cost of a musical performance keeps going up. After all, the same number of musicians is needed to play a piece for a string quartet now as in the past. Unlike the manufacturer, who can develop efficiencies that reduce the number of laborers needed to produce a given number of widgets, the musical group cannot do so. They cannot effectively perform the quartet piece with just a trio of players, nor play the piece twice as fast. However, their wages must go up anyway, to keep pace with the increasing wages of workers in more labor-productive areas. Similarly, a professor cannot effectively teach a class twice as fast without changing the nature of what is offered, or the time spent on an individual student's teaching and learning needs, although technology is altering the number of students that can be taught in a class, through distance education options.

Student services present similar problems. The basketball coach may be able to attract more paying fans to an event but cannot work with or offer playing opportunities to more students. The band director cannot manage more bands at one time. The director of financial aid may be able to employ software systems to replace some personnel, but most students still want to meet with live advisors.

The college medical school competes with the private sector for the physicians who train its students. Programs such as Nurse Anesthesia find it hard to keep faculty, who can earn far more at hospitals and clinics than as faculty. Law school faculty have to be compensated with an eye to what they could earn as partners in lucrative practices. And so it goes. Colleges have to pay their personnel commensurate with the wider marketplace, even though the institutions have a hard time increasing productivity.

The challenge for colleges is to find ways to keep the best of what they offer while changing the delivery mechanisms enough to lower tuition, stay afloat, and where possible turn a profit.

Little Managerial Control on Costs

It is no secret that our colleges are not cost efficient, at a time and in a society where efficiency is an expected concomitant of management success. Many academics eschew the use of the concept of efficiency for their colleges, believing it to be part of the sellout of higher education to the business-oriented board members who govern their institutions.

Yet higher education must engage in creating efficient teaching and learning institutions if our colleges are to remain competitive, let alone thrive. As a former dean of the Rutgers School of Business–Camden pointed out, "Higher education is so rife with inefficiencies that even modest reforms could yield outsize gains. The barriers are not structural, but human." He added that the "institutions are inward-looking, and self-satisfied" (Leontides, 2007, p. 18).

Obviously, management control of costs is essential if colleges are to be healthy. One way of exerting strong internal control is to make units within a college more responsible for their own assets and expenditures. The University of Pennsylvania uses a model of management control likened to the concept of "every tub on its own bottom."

The model basically delegates to units within the overall university the rights and responsibilities of managing their own costs. This decentralized model means that each unit brings in its own resources, such as tuition dollars or donor dollars, and exerts a degree of control over how it allocates its resources in terms of the number of people it hires and the salaries it pays them. Institutional parameters must be adhered to, and institutional costs are assessed. For example, units pay rent to the university for the space they occupy, and they are assessed costs for their shares of institution-wide expenses.

Other large colleges are adopting some aspects of this model. One president told me that his university needed to be more decentralized, by which he meant that its divisions had to take more responsibility for managing their incomes and expenses. "We need to budget at the school level to be more nimble," he said.

Cost control is difficult for public and independent colleges, for three reasons. The first reason is the fact that these colleges have multiple constituencies whose preferences come into play when changes in funding allocations are considered. The second reason of difficulty grows from the tradition in higher education of shared decision making. With multiple centers of power, it is often hard to make tough decisions because there are so many ways for opponents of given changes to go around their putative leaders. The final reason is the bureaucratic expansion that has occurred over the last two decades or so. One study of nearly 200 public and independent universities demonstrated that "the number of administrators for every 100 college students increased by 39 percent from 1993 to 2007, while the number of professors and researchers rose by 18 percent during that period" (Green, 2010).

Professors are very much aware of this disproportionate growth and frequently criticize their institutions for what they consider administrative bloat. Expansion of administration has taken place for several reasons. One type of expansion occurs when a college notices that another college with which it competes has added a new and specialized position. Copycat hiring may then creep in.

Other expansions occur because of mismatches between institutional needs and the lack of appropriate skills of people filling the jobs associated with those needs.

Although colleges will insist that every position at their institutions is necessary, every organization with more than a few employees, from the business world to government and higher education, has people whose job definitions no longer describe what they are actually able to do.

Some are hangers-on who have not kept up with advances in their fields of expertise. Others have powerful supporters who prevent them from being let go, even if they produce very little useful work. Still others work hard doing jobs that are essentially redundant because the institution has not clarified its task allocations.

One example of duplication is the tendency for many academic departments to insist on teaching their own versions of other programs' courses, sometimes creating needless redundancies. For example, the sociology, geology, nursing, and business departments at a college may each decide to offer its own statistics courses, with examples from its own field. There may be special reasons why duplication is desirable, but frequently it is not necessary.

By and large, the increase in administrative positions is due to two factors: the competitive necessity to offer enhanced amenities or hire more specialized staff in order to be competitive in the college selection market; and the need to hire enough personnel to meet the demands of government, accrediting agencies, athletic conferences, and others for data aggregation and reporting responsibilities. The need to compete for students is the greatest cost driver for most colleges, both nonprofit and for-profit. For the for-profit sector, recruitment is the sine qua non. Without students, there is no source of funding.

For independent colleges, the top 50 or so elite institutions with large endowments and stellar reputations, the intention of recruitment is not for dollars; it is for the best and brightest students, the largest proportions of applications relative to the number of students admitted, and the highest percentages of acceptance rates of students who finally enroll.

For these schools, status rankings are more important than the financial yield from a given year's enrolled class. They will almost always make their budgeted tuition dollar expectations because they each have waiting lists of prospects eager to replace any admitted person who does not end up as an enrolled student at the college.

Some public colleges, such as community colleges that are in high-demand areas and are cash strapped, may also not feel that high-cost recruiting efforts are warranted. Some community colleges, such as those in states where funding cuts or lack of increases is coupled with increasing numbers of applicants due to the lack of jobs in the regional economy, may find the need to cap enrollments in some programs. And sometimes, as is happening in California, students may not be able to enroll in required classes in a timely way because budget problems prevent the college from offering enough class sessions.

Other community and state colleges invest dollars and efforts in recruitment because they need to draw enough students to justify their existence as separate institutions. For some small four-year public colleges in the University of Maine System with enrollments under 1,000 total students, fear of proposed closures or mergers has driven one to seek Canadian students over the border, and another to recruit students from the Caribbean.

In addition to needing to demonstrate viability, public colleges, just like many other government entities, often seek to enhance their footprints by growing their importance, their size, and consequently their budgets.

Public entities also often try to spend all the dollars allocated to them so that future allocations will not be reduced or surpluses recaptured by the funding sources. For some colleges, as for some public entities, there is a desire to expand their budget needs to match the available dollars that college leaders believe they can receive.

For all but a small number of independent colleges, recruitment is job number one. Private nonprofit colleges do not have dedicated state dollars to undergird their budgets and most do not have the annual donor dollars or multi-billion-dollar endowments of a Harvard or Princeton.

Although Harvard University had more than $32 billion in its endowment in fiscal year 2011, many colleges do not have such substantial financial cushions ("Harvard Endowment Rises," 2011). Numerous independent colleges with small endowments exist close to the margin necessary for keeping the doors open. Some colleges are regularly visited by accrediting agencies worried about ongoing budget deficits, papered over with bank loans, long-term debt obligations, or drawing down of endowments to potentially unsustainable levels.

I have participated in accreditation visits at quite a few colleges with small endowments and seen how close to the bone some of their finances are. For some of these schools, the difference between 50 students, more or less, in a new semester can be the difference between opening for business once more and shuttering the gates.

That puts enormous pressure on these college leaders to bring in students. They have to have enough students enrolling and enough students paying a high enough percentage of the sticker price to support the scholarships or discounts offered and accepted, as well as the academic and student programs of the college. It is not always easy to find enough students to attend, or to find the formula that will make the budget work.

Administrative Bloat

Once upon a time, small and medium colleges had mostly faculty on their staffs, along with a small number of administrators. There were presidents, deans, a few secretaries or assistants, and then there was the rest of the staff, most of whom were engaged in student services such as admissions, dormitory management, food services, student activities, and athletics.

Lots of institutions had just one dean. The move to additional deans often followed the move to expand the mission of a largely liberal arts institution to offer degrees in professional fields or graduate areas, a move often undertaken to enhance the bottom line of budget-stressed colleges.

When my former institution, the University of New England, merged with Westbrook College in 1996, Westbrook had a very lean administration: a president; one academic dean; and a handful of other mid- to senior-level positions in student services, development, and the library.

A lot of administrative expansion over the last 50 years has occurred as a result of federal and state government mandates, as well as reporting requirements from accrediting agencies, athletic organizations, and many other imposed conditions of operation. Colleges can assign this work to anyone they wish, including persons who already work for them, but no matter how it is assigned, it is extra work and generally needs the hiring of extra hands to take on the jobs.

In addition to such mandate-forced increases to staff, colleges have hired more administrators as they have sought to upgrade their status or take on new responsibilities. For example, if a college decides to sharpen its research focus, suddenly there will be an expectation of a research office with a freshly appointed new director or even a vice president of research. There will be a budget for supporting promising faculty projects, and programs set in place to assist in the process. Along with the new director, there will soon be an associate director, an assistant for each director, telephones, computers, offices, calling cards and stationery, and an often inadequately planned-for budget expansion.

One major area of expansion across nonprofit higher education has been in development. As public institutions have seen their state shares of their expenditures shrink, they increasingly have had to focus the time and efforts of senior management on raising external funds. Many public college presidents did little fund-raising in the past, but now it is expected by their boards and constituencies.

Most independent college leaders always had alumni giving as a major focus, but today, with the costs of running institutions of higher education outpacing the rate of inflation, college leaders are more pressed than ever to raise large sums of money. Donna Shalala, president of the University of Miami, told me that she entertained prospective donors an average of four nights a week, with a goal of raising over a billion dollars for the institution. It takes a lot of staff work to help a president organize, participate in, and follow up on such events.

Then again, there is probably a lot more staff expansion in higher education than might be absolutely necessary. As is the case in government, once you establish an office or program, it will seek to sustain and frequently enhance its footprint. In fact, according to a *Forbes* article by Daniel L. Bennett (2009) of the Center for College Affordability & Productivity, between 1997 and 2007 the administrative and support staffs at colleges expanded by 4.7% annually, double the rate of enrollment growth.

Documenting this increase requires a certain amount of "iffiness" at best because different colleges have different ways of deciding which positions are administrative and which seemingly administrative posts are called "faculty." In some colleges, librarians are counted as faculty. In others, academic staff positions below the rank of dean (assistant dean, associate dean, director, etc.) are often counted as faculty, especially when the persons filling the positions still teach one or more courses a year or still hold faculty status.

And counting faculty numbers is made difficult because of the growing use of adjuncts. To make reasonable comparisons, even among programs in the same university, for example, it is generally necessary to count by full-time equivalents (FTEs) rather than individual faculty members. After all is said and done, however, it remains obvious in most nonprofit institutions that the number of staff positions, whether called administrative or not, has grown even when the FTE size of the faculty has not.

There used to be basically four levels of academic employees at most colleges: faculty members, department chairs, deans, and presidents (who usually had risen from faculty ranks at their own or other colleges). Now there is a glut of positions between the president and the faculty.

Some of these staff increases have arisen because a college needed a sinecure for a longtime employee who was being removed from a key position and wanted to maintain face. Some positions get added in order to retain a valued employee who wants a more important title or set of responsibilities. If there are no appropriate open positions to accommodate the person, a new one is added.

The academic vice president of a college recently told me about his opportunity to hire a brilliant researcher from a distinguished university, who could add some real gloss to his program. However, the researcher wanted a sweetener. He wanted the position only if he could have his own institute. In this particular case he was not hired because of financial concerns, but such requests are often met when the institution wants and can afford the applicant.

A lot of senior staff positions are added this way. Opportunity knocks, and college officers rush to open the doors, even if they have not thought through how they will pay for the new opportunity. At several institutions where I worked, I saw cancer researchers, poets, and assorted big names, many of whom really were outstanding, hired on what seemed like the spur of the moment, to capture the glow of a new star.

In general, instead of responding willy-nilly to the latest "I'll come if you offer me a program with my name on it," college leaders need to plan in advance for the kinds of special centers they want at their institutions. If a college has a good reason for wanting to grow in a field and hire a star in that field, the availability of such an opportunity should be widely circulated, so that many strong candidates will apply and the institution can select the one with the best fit for the task.

Still other new positions have developed to address the numerous regulatory issues colleges now deal with. These issues include tracking the disposal of science laboratory wastes through appropriate Environmental Protection Agency (EPA) procedures and ensuring protection of privacy of patients, for programs that provide clinical services to the public, under the Health Insurance Portability and Accountability Act of 1996 (HIPAA). Many health-oriented colleges have had to spend hundreds of thousands of dollars in consulting and software fees to meet compliance requirements.

As institutions have expanded their nonfaculty staff, they have paid for them in two ways. One way, of course, has been to increase tuition. The other way has been to cut the relative costs of faculty. This has been done by replacing tenure-track faculty with temporary faculty and, worse, replacing full-time faculty with part-time adjuncts.

Whatever the reasons for expansions, colleges should have mostly full-time faculty. To pay for them, they need to strip back their midlevel administrative positions, by carefully assessing their needs for the positions and ranking the importance and value of individual positions to the colleges' missions. Painful as it might be to cut administrative support, the fact is that classes can be taught without a lot of administrators, but they cannot be taught without adequate faculty.

Mission Creep, Branch Campuses, and Degree Inflation

Mission creep is the gradual expansion or escalation of an original objective. In a study titled "Mission Differentiation vs. Mission Creep," David Longanecker (2008) states that expanding the mission of a college is often referred to as mission creep in public policy circles. Mission creep is flagrant in higher education.

Three major types of mission expansion have been taking place in higher education, especially over the last several decades: the upward migration of the level of degree offerings, the multiplying of branch campuses, and the inflation of degree requirements. I discuss each of these next.

Upward Migration of College Levels

Many community colleges really want to be four-year colleges and too many four-year colleges really want to be universities. There has been considerable expansion at each of these levels.

A study by the American Association of State Colleges and Universities (AASCU) points out that over the last 20 years or so, the number of community colleges offering baccalaureate degree programs has steadily increased, threatening "to upset the existing balance between the two- and four-year sectors in the American higher education system" (Russell, 2010, p. 1). AASCU represents public four-year colleges and universities, which have legitimate concerns about where community colleges are heading, but also have competitive concerns because students matriculating at community colleges for their baccalaureate degrees are frequently students who might otherwise have enrolled at the four-year institutions. However, all but a handful of the community colleges offering four-year degrees only provide them in a limited number of fields, such as nursing, applied technology, and teacher education.

Although most community colleges do not offer four-year degrees, the trend is definitely upward in many states. In Florida, for example, 22 of the state's 28 community colleges are now designated as part of the Florida College System and have been approved to offer at least one four-year degree. One of the largest of those colleges, Miami Dade College, has more than 161,000 students, spread over 8 campuses and 21 outreach centers. It currently offers two types of baccalaureate degrees, one in science and one in applied science. Each degree includes several program options, such as education, nursing, and public safety management.

Critics worry that as community colleges move toward four-year status they will increasingly lose their historic focus on open access and developmental education, especially as more community colleges make the transition. In 2004, there were 21 community colleges in 11 states that were able to offer some baccalaureate degrees. By 2010, there were 54 colleges in 18 states doing so (Russell, 2010, p. 2).

Community colleges are not the only colleges seeking upward mobility in degree-offering status. The really big movements are the jumps from college status to university status. More and more public and independent colleges are making this move.

Public and independent colleges seek to transition to university status for a variety of reasons. For many, enhanced stature in the eyes of the public and the students they are seeking to recruit is the major reason. Another reason is the possibility of increased odds for successfully competing for foundation or research grants. For public institutions, yet a third reason is the hope of better funding from their legislatures, with enhanced status.

With university status come other potential benefits for nonprofit colleges as well. One is the ability to attract stronger faculty. Another is the opportunity to offer some graduate degrees that might be revenue enhancing, although this is true for only a narrow range of programs.

Colleges cannot just rename themselves into universities. If they are public institutions, their state departments of education, their state governing boards, their legislatures and governors, or all of them must approve the changes. If they are independent colleges, in most states, the state education department must still sign off.

In all cases, the regional college accrediting agency must approve the status change for the colleges. This often means demonstrating the ability of the institution to offer graduate-level programs and degrees. Regional accrediting agencies require colleges undergoing what they term *substantive change* to file a request to go through a process for approval before they can offer higher degrees than those for which they have already been approved.

Most colleges seeking to gain university status have already been offering at least one or more graduating degrees, for which they had previously gained approval. The name change usually is sought after the college is actually offering some university-level programs.

Moving from the community college level to a four-year college level or from college level to university status may bring additional enrollments and the attendant tuition dollars. However, the upward trajectories also subject these institutions to expected enhancements to go along with their new status. Ultimately, what is often done to increase revenue instead increases costs.

Branch Campus Expansions

Another way to expand a college's mission is to open branch campuses. Frequently, public community colleges and four-year colleges that serve large cities or large geographic areas will open additional campuses and centers in order to better serve their constituencies.

Colleges like to do this because the branch campuses can bring in revenue and generally the cost is less per student than at the main campus. One reason the cost is less is that many of the senior executive positions are filled only at the main campus. Another reason is that the additional campuses often serve only commuter students, who require fewer amenities and services.

As branch campuses grow, they need campus managers and other refinements. On the whole, though, they do tend to be less expensive to operate than the main campuses.

Program and Degree Inflation

Not only does higher education indulge in mission extension; it has runaway credential inflation as well. Credential inflation occurs when professions for which academic degrees are awarded up the ante for entry to the profession.

Since the mid-1990s, a number of fields have inflated their requirements for degrees, for licensure, or for accreditation of college programs. Occupational therapy, which used to be an undergraduate program, now requires what is referred to as an "entry-level master's degree" or else a doctoral degree. Physical therapy, which also was an undergraduate program, briefly made a transition to master's-level degrees, before moving on to the doctor of physical therapy, the preferred degree now. Pharmacy degrees went through a similar change, from four-year degrees to master's degrees to doctor of pharmacy requirements.

Many law schools changed the name of the degree they offered from a bachelor of laws (LLB) to a juris doctor (JD), although no new requirements were added. Perhaps the degree was renamed to make it more clear that it is a postbaccalaureate degree, so as to be competitive in the titling of one's profession with all those other new doctoral degrees. There are even a few JDs now demanding to be addressed as "Doctor," friends have informed me. And how does one explain that an advanced law degree is titled a master of laws?

Professional degree inflation reflects the tendencies of members of a profession to increase the requirements for licensure or credentialing for those who come up behind them. It can be a way to restrict entry without violating regulations against restraint of trade.

Degree inflation also occurs in professions such as physical therapy and pharmacy because of the vastly expanded health- and medical-related information expected of qualified professionals in these fields today. The arguments about the needs for more advanced training have legitimacy, but what do those offering the arguments then say about all the present practitioners who have been grandfathered in, without the advanced degrees, many of whom are superb at their jobs?

In the case of pharmacy, not only have the credentials required increased, but so have the number of pharmacy schools offering the degree. As one higher education leader remarked to me about this phenomenon as we talked about degree inflation and the oversupply of professional schools, "Ten years ago there were 78 pharmacy schools. Now there are 124. Where will the graduates of all of those schools be able to find jobs?"

Tenure

Basically, tenure is a contract between a college and a faculty member. It guarantees a faculty member that he or she will be let go only for "just cause." In practice, this conveys a lifetime contract for most faculty members once they have been granted tenure. Furthermore, tenure allows them to work for as long as they wish because under the law today you cannot discriminate based on age. The American Association of University Professors (2013) states: "After the expiration of a probationary period, teachers or investigators should have permanent or continuous tenure, and their service should be terminated only for adequate cause, except in the case of retirement for age, or under extraordinary circumstances because of financial exigencies" (p.4).

Some unionized colleges, particularly public community colleges, have union contracts that stipulate automatic tenure except for those few faculty members who have been denied repeat contracts during their first two or three "trial" years. Most American colleges do not offer automatic tenure. They have established processes by which the right to receive tenure status, or the denial of tenure, are agreed upon. The norms for granting tenure generally require a faculty candidate to teach for five or six years as an assistant professor before standing for tenure and promotion. During that period, and for the tenure review, evaluations may be undertaken of the person's teaching skills, research and publication success, and service commitments to the program or the college. Obviously, the more selective the school is, the more selective the tenure process.

When almost all of a college's faculty have tenure, the college has little flexibility to make new hires, even if it wishes to start new programs. Because so many members of the college's staff have lifetime jobs, responsiveness to market opportunities is almost impossible because personnel shifts cannot be made.

One way that some colleges have dealt with the problem of having too many members of their academic staff tenured has been the imposition of board caps on the percentage of the faculty who may be tenured going forward. Although this can help, it penalizes newer faculty hires, at the expense of long-term faculty.

The most frequent way that colleges deal with the problem is not by capping tenure awards, but rather by preventing the opportunity for large numbers of faculty to even be considered for tenure. This is done either by recapturing positions that were previously held by tenured persons who have retired or left or by not approving positions needed to accommodate growth.

What happens is that when a replacement full-time position is needed, approval is withheld while the department needing to fill the position is permitted to fill it with temporary, non-tenure-track, or part-time adjunct professors. In fact, although we tend to conflate non-tenure-track faculty with for-profit schools, tenured and tenure-track faculty now account for less than 30% of the faculty at nonprofit colleges. At public community colleges, only 17.5% of the faculty is tenured or on tenure track, and almost 70% of the faculty is part-time (Kezar & Maxey, 2013).

Until relatively recently, faculty fought for and expected to win the right to have the positions in their departments filled with tenure and tenure-track faculty. When I was the vice chancellor of academic affairs at the University of Minnesota Duluth, from 1991 to 1995, we had to take a sudden, large budget cut. I learned about the cut the week I arrived on the job. The state had just cut back the budget of the University of Minnesota, and the system officers were having campuses and schools add additional give-back money to the pot to create a fund for innovation, even as the cuts were being taken.

Our campus had a tenured and unionized faculty. We could not let any tenured faculty go, and we could only lay off untenured faculty in reverse seniority order. With the advice of administrators who knew the programs, we looked at the departments that had people in not yet tenured positions, and especially those departments with declining enrollments.

One of the positions we decided to defund was in the foreign languages department. The department had nine professors teaching French, Spanish, and German. Members of the department, and much of the faculty as a whole, argued against our taking the one position there. The university faculty argued that being on a tenure track was a commitment with the expectation of tenure if the standards of the institution or its programs were met, even before a tenure status was actually awarded, and that the only ways someone should be removed from the tenure track was for cause or because they failed to meet the tenure standard. The department members also argued that they needed to teach all of the necessary courses for each of the three languages, and for this, they had to have at least nine professors. They made this argument even though their enrollment numbers at the time did not justify more than six or possibly seven positions.

I understood the desire of the faculty to offer everything that they thought was important. They had a harder time understanding why economics should interfere with their program. In fact, when someone tried to introduce me to the foreign languages department chair, perhaps in an effort to be a peacemaker, the effort backfired when the chair refused to shake my hand. "To me, you are just a faceless administrator," he said.

Four years later, when I was leaving the university I told the story to a group of faculty, explaining that I understood and had respected his anger at me. After all, a person who has devoted his life to studying a subject ought to care intensely about it. The man who had made the remark came up to me at the end of the event. He said that he was sorry he had said that and wished I would not keep talking about it. "You misunderstand why I tell the story," I said. "It is not out of anger. It is because the one thing I want to ensure in my life is that I will never be 'faceless.' "

While I am a not a fan of tenure, I am a fan of having good faculty. Today, adjuncts constitute most of the staff at many for-profit colleges. Those colleges are justly criticized for their use of adjunct faculty. However, nonprofit colleges across America are almost as guilty of abusive use of part-time people as the for-profit schools are.

Public and independent colleges use far too many part-time faculty, who often teach a majority of the classes. The institutional teaching budgets are balanced at the expense of these part-time faculty, who may have to teach at several colleges at a time to splice together enough work to earn a meager living.

When you are employed as a short-term faculty member, you may work hard to earn a more permanent berth, but you frequently lack the commitment to mission that semipermanent people have. After all, you generally are not considered to be a regular faculty member nor expected to take part in most faculty and department decisions.

Adjunct faculty can have a strong and appropriate role to play in higher education, especially when they offer specialized expertise and hands-on experience for technical, upper–level, and professional programs. For example, in an aeronautical engineering program, an adjunct from a corporate flight design company can expose students to practical applications not otherwise accessible. Likewise, a surgical cardiologist who comes into a medical classroom to give a lecture imparts invaluable information. On the whole, though, students suffer immensely from having too many classes offered by adjunct professors who are not available after class except maybe for an hour once a week, or who may not care much about the students or their programs as a result of their own teaching and grading time being split between too many campuses and colleges.

These adjunct faculty are often hired just days before classes begin, and sometimes even after classes have started. They have little time to prepare for their classes, and frequently have few opportunities to learn or understand the goals of the programs in which they are teaching. As an important article in the magazine *Trusteeship* puts it, in many colleges these faculty are not able "to provide the quality of education that meets institutions' goals for student learning and graduation" (Kezar & Maxey, 2013, p. 15).

Of course, the costs of a college education at most institutions would be much higher if all of the adjuncts were converted to FTE employees, with the benefit packages that it would entail. However, that neither justifies the use of part-timers nor guarantees its long-term success. The use—or really the misuse—of part-time people is wrong for the institutions that use them, wrong for the students, wrong for the part-time faculty, and wrong for our nation.

Right now, colleges hire these adjunct professors because they are cheap, and because they are easily replaceable. The current market for adjuncts is strong because the demand for full-time faculty is low and the supply of persons qualified to fill full-time positions is high. In the long run, however, this may cease to be the case.

Both nonprofit and for-profit colleges have benefited from the oversupply of potential faculty. This oversupply resulted from professors in doctoral programs encouraging their preferred students to pursue careers in higher education, even as it became obvious that in both the humanities and the social sciences far more graduate students were being trained for academic careers than the marketplace could absorb.

Now, as more media attention is focused on costs, debt loads, and career opportunities of given colleges and degree programs, talented young people may start to more realistically calculate both the true costs of their potential doctoral training (including foregone job income) and the actual opportunities for gaining decent academic jobs and salaries after graduation.

In a market economy, as jobs in a sector dry up, people normally shift their career intentions to other, more marketable career options. Although there is always a certain amount of imbalance due to up-and-down market shifts, the pipelines for professorships, especially in the liberal arts and sciences, has not adequately reflected the shifts we would expect to see.

How can we explain why some of the best and brightest young people in America continue to invest in doctoral degrees, which they expect to bring them professorships, when evidence indicates how few of them will succeed? It can only be for one of two reasons. The first is that they have unrealistic hopes and expectations and believe that they will be the exceptions who get hired for tenure-track positions by top-tier colleges. The second reason is that their doctoral studies professors lead them on, disingenuously, by allowing too many students into their programs in order to maintain their own faculty numbers and perquisites.

Markets do catch up eventually, though, and the oversaturated market for academically oriented PhDs will slow down. When it does, the oversupply of trained educators is likely to diminish enough to force educational institutions to make enough full-time hires to properly deliver their academic programs, and to use adjuncts more appropriately as outside experts who deliver special content and real-world experience to their classes.

Tuition, Discounting Wars, and Federal Student Aid

For many colleges, finding the right mix of enrolled students, scholarship offerings, and net yield from tuition payments is an ongoing battle. Colleges whose incomes are highly tuition dependent must be able to attract enough students each year at a high enough average tuition payment to cover their costs. Many do not know if they will be successful until the day newly enrolled students actually show up for classes, as last-minute registrations and withdrawals are completed.

Tuition Rates

For many colleges, sustaining enrollment levels has become an annual battle. Finding the right price point is the first priority and tuition pricing can be perverse. Although the purchasers of higher education services have some price sensitivity, the presence of scholarship, discounts, grants, tax support, and government loans all distort market transactions. Furthermore, students purchasing the same sets of courses at the same institution may be paying very different prices for the classes and amenities they are offered. And as Robert Zemsky has pointed out, a college selected by an applicant may choose not to sell its product to that potential enrollee. And if the student needs financial aid, "the selling institution may spend considerable amounts of its own funds to educate the customer" (Zemsky et al., 2005, p. 36).

The average college faces four issues in deciding how to set its tuition and fee rates (the fourth issue is discussed in the next section). The first issue is to figure out how much income the college will need for the following year. For many small independent colleges, without state dollars to subsidize those costs for the students, the money to meet the income needs will have to come substantially from student tuition payments.

Once the college determines how much it needs, it faces its second issue, which is the need to estimate how many students it is likely to be able to enroll. That figure is usually based on the prior year enrollments mixed with possible expectations of shortfalls or increases. Most of the students who will enroll in the following year are already at the college. Next year, those who return will be sophomores, juniors, and seniors. They will not all return, but most small colleges work hard to try to bring back as many as possible and to get as firm a handle on their prospects as they can. Although some colleges enjoy a spurt of transfers in, especially from community colleges, in the junior year, many traditional residential independent schools see only a small number of new enrollees transferring in.

The third issue for the college is to set a tentative tuition rate. This will be largely determined by the current year's rate because one of the hardest things to do in higher education is to increase tuition by more than what students and parents perceive to be an average rate of tuition cost increases in the region.

Just as there are different price ranges for different makes of automobiles, there are different tuition price ranges for different types of colleges, ranging from most selective down to less selective ones, but also determined by the type of programs being offered, the amenities on campus, the desirability of the geographic area, and other factors. A college needs to assess its price point, which is the ticket price that someone who receives no discount might reasonably be willing to pay.

Jane Doe College can use a consultant to help find its price point, or it can compare its costs with its competitors'. The college can find out who its competitors are by purchasing data from the organizations that administer the SATs or the ACTs, the standardized college testing organizations. These data enable a college to do two things. First, the data provide the recruitment office with the names, addresses, and e-mail addresses of high school seniors and others across the nation who have taken the tests. Many of the students have given permission to have their test scores given to "eligible users." Colleges can then purchase names from selected geographic areas or with SAT or ACT scores above a certain level. Second, colleges are able to access information that enables them to find out which other colleges their applicants apply to. Of course, the colleges do not get information for individual applicants indicating the other colleges they are interested in, but previous year cohort group printouts show which colleges have overlapping applicants with Jane Doe College. Many of them are likely to price their tuition rates in the same range.

Discounting

The fourth issue that a college faces in deciding how to set its tuition and fee rates is finding a way to provide different discount amounts to different applicants while ensuring that the mix of net prices somehow yields enough dollars to meet the financial needs of the institution. It does not always work out.

Discounting involves lowering the actual cost of enrollment through the device of scholarships, an important part of the process of putting together a plan for recruiting the next year's class. Planning for the amount of aid to be offered is a complex task.

Jane Doe College must consider what price most of its applicants are actually willing to pay. Again, knowledge of the net cost offered at other colleges is essential. There is no fixed net cost, of course. There is only an average net cost, which is arrived at based on the budget needs. The net cost is what students pay after they receive scholarships, grants-in-aid, and other forms of support, including student work opportunities.

This scholarship and other forms of support, by whatever labels they are referred to, are really discounts much more than awards. They allow the college to offer a discount off the sticker price, in order to be able to compete on the net price necessary to attract students who are being offered scholarship/ discounts at other colleges. Many independent colleges would probably close if they eliminated the process of discounting, unless their peer institutions did the same thing.

While the discounts may be used to help a college attain the mix of talents and strengths it seeks, these discounts serve the primary function of helping to deliver enough students to the campus to keep the college doors open and the budget in the black. The size of discounts offered by a particular college are allocated based on the needs of the school. For example, if the college wants or needs more students enrolled in its science programs, it may offer larger discounts to strong science applicants. If the college wants to attract more students from a particular geographic area, it may provide deeper discounts for that purpose.

Most colleges do offer at least some scholarships based on need, enabling some students whose families cannot afford the cost of the institution to benefit by having part or all of the cost of attendance covered by the scholarship.

Other scholarships are awarded to students the college wants because they are gifted athletes or musicians or scholars. But they are awarded even more liberally by many colleges simply to make sure that they attract enough students.

About a dozen years ago, enrollment consultants began advising tuition-dependent colleges to offer scholarships to high school seniors even before the prospects applied to the college. The idea was to jump the gun on competitors by sending a letter informing prospects that given their grade point average and SAT scores the college was offering them a $5,000 or $10,000 scholarship if they maintained their grades, graduated from high school, and enrolled in the college.

Colleges refine the process by juggling the amounts offered based on grades, scores, diversity, major likely to be selected, and other criteria that fit the college profile and needs. Offering a mix of aid packages is a gamble and a very risky one for colleges with small endowments.

Sometimes, too many students who have been offered large discounts show up at registration, and too many of those counted on to carry more of the financial burden end up going elsewhere. If the college recruiting office guesses wrong about how many students will enroll at given aid levels, the college can face substantial financial pressures.

Even for highly selective schools, estimating the yield, which is the total number of students who will actually show up on the first day of school, can be difficult. Law schools and medical schools, which may have class size limits set in their accreditation approvals, occasionally end up with more potential student acceptances than they are able to actually admit. When that happens, a college may offer some students generous scholarships in return for their willingness to have their admission deferred for one year.

To find the right price point, or position the college to be branded in a way related to sticker price, an institution may decide to increase, lower, or hold tuition levels flat. Each strategy has potential problems for a college.

When a college tries to raise tuition by more than the rate of inflation, it risks serious blowbacks. Students, parents, and faculty may all speak out or even hold demonstrations against the college administration and board. Institutional leaders need to be prepared to present strong defenses for their position. Even when they do, it may not quell the questions or allay the anger some people will feel.

There are about a dozen or so colleges in the nation that have not historically charged tuition. Most have rigorous admissions standards. Few cover costs other than tuition, and many require doing some work on the campus. When the Cooper Union for the Advancement of Science, which had been tuition free for more than 100 years, announced in early 2013 that it would need to start charging tuition to undergraduate students, many students staged walkouts, faculty promoted noncompliance with administrative directives, and the occupying of a college building took place, along with other displays of resentment.

Cooper Union had conducted a two-year study of tuition options because its operating deficit had risen to $12 million a year. The college had considered a number of ways to shrink the deficit, including reducing the number of students it admitted and selling property, but none made enough of an impact on the budget losses (Kaminer, 2013, pp. A1, A19). So even given compelling reasons for raising tuition (or, in the case of Cooper Union, reducing the scholarship support), tuition increases will often be antagonistically received.

During my years at the University of New England, we raised tuition between 5% and 6% most years, even though the rates exceeded inflation. We did it for several reasons. One was that we desperately needed the additional revenue it would yield us. Another was that we thought our price point was a little too low but had to raise it in small increments over a period of years. In addition, we were determined to use part of the income to allow us to hire strong faculty and pay them higher wages. And last but not least, we wanted to be able to give back much of the rest of the added income to strong student applicants in the form of additional student aid.

Fortunately, the quality and reputation of the college was growing at the same time that tuition was increasing. Today, the formula for determining tuition levels must obviously be quite different.

It is not easy, in a book about the importance of lowering tuition costs for students, to admit one's own culpability. The fact is, as a president, and in my previous other administrative positions, I was guilty of every sin I argue against. "It takes one to know one," as they say. Having committed the mistakes makes it easier to understand why they happen, the problems and pressures that build up on college presidents, and the potential remedies for those problems.

In past years, some colleges have tried to reduce their tuition. Usually this has been done by reducing the discount level. This has meant lowering the sticker price and eliminating many or most scholarships. In effect, the discount is eliminated, and prospects can compare the low sticker price with the apparent sticker price of other colleges that they are considering.

Most of the colleges that tried this approach in the 1990s did so because they were facing increased competition in their regions and were losing ground in enrollment numbers. They hoped that the lower tuition sticker price and the integrity of the process would benefit them. For the most part, they were not as successful as they had hoped to be and did not attract the additional students they had anticipated.

These schools, and others that held tuition levels flat while other colleges increased their costs, faced another difficult problem. Once they wanted to get back in the game and match their competitors' rates, to get back to those levels, they had to impose much greater than average tuition increases, which their students were loathe to accept.

Another issue that colleges face is determining whether to offer larger one-year scholarships or smaller multiyear ones. For students who receive scholarships, whether from the colleges, their states, or other sources, such aid is sometimes front-loaded. This means that a scholarship is awarded for first-year support. Sometimes students and their families do not realize that many awards are for only one year. Colleges do give multiyear awards, of course, but first-year awards are prevalent across higher education.

The colleges or organizations that give one-year awards do so for several reasons. One thousand dollars of scholarship support for four years costs $4,000. This can fund one $1,000 award for one student for four years or four students for one year each. Organizations like awarding more rather than fewer scholarships, and colleges like being able to have more awards to offer to new students. They hope that the new students will stay on for the next year, with less aid. All too frequently they do not.

Organizations and external donors are free to give any kind of support they wish, and we should all be exceedingly grateful to the generous people who help fund college educations. But colleges themselves should not front-load their own scholarship awards. To do so is to dangle a come-on in front of a susceptible applicant while often not stressing enough the finite period for which the offer is eligible. Even when students do understand the limited term for which a front-loaded award is made, they may imagine that after the first year the college will find other sources of scholarship aid for them. Sometimes it does happen, but often it does not.

Many college leaders bemoan the problems caused by the competition in discounts. In a survey of private college business officers, almost half said that the current discount rate was unsustainable. In fact, "many institutions with softer demand increased the use of institutional grant dollars to raise their enrollment, while other colleges with stronger demand tried to scale back on their discount rate" (NACUBO, 2013, p. 9).

Federal Financial Aid

Federal financial aid is offered to students through the Office of Federal Student Aid of the U.S. Department of Education, which awards about $150 billion a year in grants, work-study funds, and low-interest loans to more than 14 million students. Although federal financial aid is available to students, not institutions, students must access this aid through the colleges at which they enroll. Those colleges can offer students federal aid only if the colleges are accredited by accrediting agencies acceptable to the Department of Education.

Students at almost all nonprofit colleges are eligible for federal financial aid. The rare exceptions are mostly new colleges that are preparing for and awaiting accreditation or existing colleges that have lost accreditation. There are a few colleges, such as Hillsdale College and Grove City College, that have chosen to forgo all public support, including student financial aid, rather than comply with federal standards or mandates.

Some for-profit colleges have long had eligibility to offer federal aid, but for newer for-profit colleges, it is a door that has opened into a room full of opportunities. Even though the average tuition at for-profit colleges is lower than it is at most private nonprofit colleges, it is still more than most of their students are able to pay. Because of federal grants and loans, low-income and working adult students can borrow the dollars for tuition at the for-profit institutions.

Federal financial aid is the magic potion that has smoothed the path for for-profit colleges to grow and flourish. There is a bitter pill in the potion, however, for these schools. The pill is the 90/10 rule. The rule requires that for-profit colleges get 10% or more of their revenue from sources other than Title IV federal student aid. If a school exceeds this amount, it becomes ineligible for its students to receive federal student aid.

When Corinthian Colleges, Inc. schools got too close to that margin, Corinthian raised its tuition an average of 12% across its colleges. Corinthian is not the only college-education corporation keeping its eye on the 90/10 rule. Education Management Corporation has tried to increase its foreign student enrollment, and Kaplan University, University of Phoenix, and Career Education Corporation have all developed strategies to attract non–Title IV dollars, in order to stay compliant with the rule (Blumenstyk, 2011).

The federal government spent over $35.5 billion on Pell Grants in 2012. For that kind of expense, the government has the right to ask tough questions. The first set of questions concerns the nearly one fourth of Pell Grant dollars going to for-profit colleges, even though they enrolled only about 12% of all college students.

There are other issues that are being raised about federal financial aid. Some deal with the maximum amount of an annual grant for an individual student, which was $5,550 for the academic year 2012–13. In recent years, some critics have argued that the amount is too large whereas advocates have argued that it is too small.

A more important argument involves the question of whether increasing the maximum awards for Pell Grants actually helps students pay for their college education by decreasing the net cost for students, or simply allows colleges to increase tuition and fees. Do the loans partially camouflage the reality of increases in college costs if students are given more money in their grants with which to pay for the increases?

Certainly, tuition has been increasing by more than the rate of inflation. But that is more likely because of the enormous expenditures that colleges have made to enhance facilities and services than because of rising grants. Tuition levels for future years are usually set by colleges well before congressional actions on grants take place. This is necessary because colleges need to start recruiting each class at least a year before the class will start and must list tuition and other costs in order to compete for interested applicants.

Whether federal financial aid helps lower the costs students pay for their college education or mainly allows colleges to raise their rates, without the availability of federal student aid, including both the grants and the loans, most could not afford to go to college, and most colleges would be forced to find ways to reduce their costs, get additional state or local aid, or close their doors.

Pell Grants are a major source of support for college students, most of whom depend on the grants to help them pay for college. No matter how anyone feels about supporting Pell Grants, though, in the years ahead they are unlikely to be able to rise as fast as tuition has been rising. As Pell Grants flatten out and state aid wanes, how will the slack be taken up between what colleges need to charge and what students can afford to pay?

Expansion of Facilities

For the last 50 years or so, colleges have been on building sprees. New colleges have sprouted like weeds across the country, and many older colleges have expanded and remodeled their campuses. Part of the growth has reflected the twin trends of population growth and an increasing desire and need for a college education throughout the nation. But an equally important driver of the building growth has been competition among colleges; those with new facilities can trumpet their edge.

Moreover, what responsible officials would not want the best for their colleges, just as decent, responsible parents want the best for their children? Good trustees approve funding new facilities because they care about the college on whose board they serve and want to see it keep pace with or exceed the level of facilities on the campuses of its peer institutions. They want to do the best they can for their college and believe that fine new buildings testify to that commitment.

Although being the best college always has been construed to relate more to programmatic excellence than to the quality of facilities, newer and better buildings have been an important way to signal improved stature at a college. Colleges seem to believe that given otherwise similar types of college options students will select from among those with the finest facilities.

To build up their physical campuses, colleges have gone into considerable debt, especially in recent years, as competition for students has gotten more intense. Although interest rates on much of that debt are at historically low levels, many college budgets will have large debt repayment loads to carry for years to come.

Some critics have termed the love affair that academic institutions have with continually putting up newer and more expensive buildings as an *edifice complex*. Institutions are also frequently accused of building Taj Mahal–type facilities. In fact, colleges that can afford it have often hired internationally renowned architects to design their new campus facilities, be they laboratories or classrooms or residence halls. For example, in 1994, Frank Gehry designed a museum for the University of Minnesota. In 2012, Santiago Calatrava, the architect for the new World Trade Center, designed the first building for the new Florida Polytechnic University, which did not yet have any students. Although the building is poetically beautiful and will no doubt be iconic, it is an extremely expensive facility for a brand-new public institution.

According to an article in the *New York Times*, the binge to build "inordinately lavish" academic buildings "to attract students—has left colleges and universities saddled with large amounts of debt. Often, students are stuck picking up the bill" (Martin, 2012, p. A1). In fact, students almost always have to pay for the new facilities at independent colleges. Although a donor may have his or her name on the building, it is a rare donor who pays more than a fraction of the cost of that facility. Naming rights imply, but rarely require, donating the full amount necessary to construct John Doe Hall. Instead, a donor who is asked to pledge support is often shown a printed list of naming opportunities structured to fully fund building the facility. Some donors choose to name an auditorium, some a wing, and some the building itself.

Although donors contribute to public college facilities as well, the bills for such projects are largely paid by taxpayers. Frequently student fees also may be raised to help fund specific projects. In addition, tuition may increase to pay for ongoing maintenance of new facilities.

At small private colleges without large endowments, donor gifts can help fund some facility expansion. However, most of the time considerable debt financing is involved, and thus future tuition increases are part of the projections on which bonds or other forms of lending are approved.

Debt incurred for building new residence halls and sports facilities and classrooms has spiraled in recent years, affecting every sector of higher education. A *New York Times* article on debt buildups due to an academic "spending binge" on new buildings referenced a study by Bain & Company and Sterling Partners, private equity firms, showing that colleges have become overleveraged. "Much of the liquidity crisis facing higher education comes from having succumbed to the 'Law of More.' Many institutions have operated on the assumption that the more they build, spend, diversify and expand, the more they will persist and prosper. But instead, the opposite has happened" (Martin, 2012, p. B4).

Donor Preferences

When most colleges build new facilities, they rarely dip into their endowments. Instead, if they are independent colleges, they authorize a fund-raising campaign, to acquire as much of the capital needed as possible in the form of donations. If they are public colleges, they seek state support and raise funds for as much of the balance as they can.

Donors support college building fund drives for a variety of reasons. They may want to see their alma mater thrive. They may also be grateful for the education they received at the college and want to give back. Furthermore, they may be convinced that the facility is badly needed. Finally, they see college facilities as relatively stable and long lasting, places they can point to throughout their lives with pride.

But naming opportunities do figure into college funding plans. Any good capital campaign consultant will ask the college trustees and senior staff to develop a list of naming opportunities early in, during the so-called silent phase of a campaign, when prospective donors are grilled about how much they think their friends and contacts might give to the campaign while they and the leads they generate are being considered as prime targets for asks.

Naming opportunities refer to the buildings, wings of buildings, rooms within buildings, and other options for putting a donor's name (or the name he or she wishes to honor) on a plaque or across a wall. The donor for whom the building as a whole will be named is usually among the first people asked to consider a major donation.

Most donors of multi-million-dollar gifts expect to be recognized in some special way. Buildings offer a very visible way to say "thank you." That is one reason why it is generally easier to receive gifts for buildings than for programs, or even scholarships, named centers, or collegiate units. Few donors want to give money for a plaque thanking them for supporting heating and air-conditioning costs, for instance.

Long-Term Financing

Another reason campuses get overbuilt is that financing favors facilities. It is easier to get a $20 million loan with a 30-year payoff if you are going to use the loan to build a new building than it is if you are going to use it to pay additional faculty salaries or to lower student tuition costs. Long-term mortgage financing is part of our culture. Long-term operating financing is not. In addition, buildings can be used as security against the debt.

Residence halls are among the easiest buildings to borrow for because future student housing fees can be pledged against the debt. For the lenders, making the funds available is generally contingent on the assumption that the college can demonstrate that it will be able to fill the rooms in the residence hall for all of the years that the debt will be held.

Many colleges seek to borrow their funds through public bonds packaged by state bond-offering agencies in order to lower the premiums they must pay on their debt. Most bonds floated through state agencies are tax free and thus enjoy lower interest rates. The state agencies must assess the creditworthiness of each project they include in a state-approved bond offering, of course. For public colleges, the state's sovereign credit obviates the need for other collateral as long as state officials or voters approve the proposed projects.

For private colleges, in recent years, borrowing has not always been easy, but it has been achievable because banks and other lenders assumed that most colleges would last for generations. They were clearly among the more stable institutions in our society, and although a handful closed or merged, the trend was toward more, not fewer, colleges. For bankers, as for donors, colleges seemed to be a safe and reasonable place to invest their funds.

The path to borrowing has become more difficult now. Many colleges are now perceived by potential lenders as vulnerable, although for most colleges' constituents, it is still other colleges, not their own colleges, that are seen as at risk. Lenders are more cautious, though, and they have good reason to be.

Moody's Investors Service states,

> Most universities will have to lower their cost structures to achieve long-term financial sustainability and fund future initiatives. Universities have been restraining costs in response to the weak economic conditions since the 2008–2009 financial crises, but they have only recently begun examining the cost structure of their traditional business model. (Moody's, 2013)

Among the reasons cited by Moody's for colleges and universities to lower their cost structures were depressed family income; a drop in the number of domestic high school graduates; and the strain on nontuition revenue sources, such as state support, federal research funding, and expected weak endowment returns.

Even for those colleges that have seen their credit ratings go down, this drop has not led to their being unable to finance their building projects. Instead, any cursory glance at your favorite nonprofit college's website will likely reveal information about its new facilities that are in the planning or construction phase.

What credit rating downgrades and warnings have done is make the cost of getting credit more expensive, but the warnings have not yet propelled most colleges to rethink their edifice complexes, even when their debts are several times their endowments.

Operating Costs

Facilities cost money to build, but they cost even more in maintenance expenses over their life spans. Although donor dollars often defray part of the up-front costs, once buildings are erected it is difficult to raise additional funds for those facilities.

Donors rarely fund operating costs of facilities. They like to fund a building with their name on it. They also like to support programs known by their name, such as the Jones Family Scholarship or the John Smith Endowed Chair in European History. Of course, there are many donors who do not care about naming opportunities, but even they like to give to projects that are concrete, like a Center for the Study of Genetics or a new theater or auditorium. It is hard to excite potential donors about ongoing facility maintenance. It lacks pizzazz.

If you build facilities, however, you have to take care of them. They need to be cleaned and maintained and need heat, electricity, phones, and computers. Some need air-conditioning as well. Furthermore, regular repairs will need to be made.

If the new facilities are big ones, they will cost big dollars to build and big dollars to support. Many of the costs involve necessary expenditures to provide appropriate research laboratories or technological teaching apparatus, such as "smart classrooms," where hi-tech computers and screens can enable multimedia and interactive presentations. Other costs relate to choices made to woo particular constituencies or to enable colleges to compete in certain activities or fields. Sports arenas and student unions are in this category. Both types of facilities tend to be even more underused by most students than classrooms and other types of buildings are.

Sports arenas reflect the overcommitment to athletics at most American colleges. Pressure to build better and bigger athletic facilities assaults colleges from various constituencies. Football bowl–contending colleges need stadiums large enough to accommodate substantial crowds of paying attendees and those with complimentary tickets or else other major college teams will not play them.

But even if you are not a football college, or you are a small college that is not being pressed by your alumni to increase your athletic footprint on the campus, other forces intrude on the debate. When I was a president, the greatest pressure I experienced in athletics was from the presidents of other colleges in our athletic conference. They, or their athletic directors, kept upping the ante on the additional physical facilities we had to provide if we wanted to stay in our conference.

The demands that we heard—and that all of us finally agreed had to be met, if some schools were not to jump out of the conference and strand the rest of us—included more physical therapists at each game (our school was one of the best at complying with this), additional locker rooms, and certain types of new playing fields. Each new requirement may or may not have been justified, but there was no question that the costs were going to escalate. Some colleges could not meet those criteria.

Athletic facilities are most useful if nonintercollegiate athletes can share the space and the equipment. At smaller colleges, this often happens with the student gyms used for basketball games. But stadiums where football teams play cannot be used for too many purposes other than the games, pep rallies, and occasional concerts. If they are open air, their upkeep costs are not the same as those of buildings with roofs, of course.

But stadiums are costly to build, have huge footprints, and do have to be maintained and repaired. They may be utilized for team practices, but they rarely have much more than a small number of people in them. Much of the time these huge and costly facilities sit largely empty.

Student unions are another funding sinkhole. They cost a lot to build, they cost a lot to maintain, they generally earn little or no additional income for a college, and they suffer from significant underutilization.

At most colleges, the student union is a building that provides students with various areas, including student cafeterias and dining rooms, meeting and conference spaces, and recreational spaces such as climbing walls, where they can gather and participate in different activities. Regarding the role of the college union, the Association of College Unions International (ACUI, 2013) states,

> Traditionally considered the "hearthstone" or "living room" of the campus, today's union is the gathering place of the college. The union provides services and conveniences that members of the college community need in their daily lives and creates an environment for getting to know and understand others through formal and informal associations.

ACUI adds that student union programs "provide the opportunity to balance course work and free time as cooperative factors in education."

There is no doubt that this is a worthy and important goal. In fact, the provision of such balance is crucial for residential colleges. Most students who seek traditional colleges do so because of their expectation of college life as much more than just classes. They expect a rich blend of activities shared with friends they will make, with academics just a piece of the broader mix.

The question is not really, Should colleges offer a student union experience? The question is, Do they need to offer it in a special facility designated as "the student union"? These buildings are frequently large, and they are often virtually empty except at mealtimes, from Monday morning through lunch on Friday, eight months out of the year (just over seven months if you count two weeks off at Christmas and another week off for spring break).

There is nothing wrong with having a great student union building *ceteris paribus*. But all things are not equal if the cost of building or maintaining the student union comes out of the hides of the students, in the form of higher tuition dollars, somewhere down the pike.

The University of Utah is building a $50.4 million, 190,000-square-foot student union building that it says will be a student life and recreation facility. The facility will include a café, study spaces, "three pools, five sport courts, 15,000 square feet of cardiovascular and weightlifting space, four fitness studios, a wellness studio and climbing walls" ("University of Utah Breaks Ground," 2013).

Climbing walls are the newest amenities that schools with the money and space to install them are putting inside their student union buildings. One website of a company advertising its climbing walls says that more than 250 colleges now have them (James, 2013). In fact, although large institutions such as Virginia Commonwealth University and Temple University have new climbing walls, a lot of small independent colleges do too, including Carleton, Calvin, Hamilton, and Middlebury Colleges.

How will all of this be paid for? Well, it is partially funded with some major donor gifts. However, those gifts will not provide total support. An article about the aforementioned student union building at the University of Utah notes that "support for the center also comes from a student-approved bond, University administration and nonstudent user fees" ("University of Utah Breaks Ground," 2013).

Colleges actively promote their student union buildings on the Internet, so those with big, bold facilities obviously see an advantage in having boastworthy buildings. Texas Tech University trumpets its student union by listing on its website its many special attributes, such as the theaters (one of which has 968 seats), 21 meeting rooms, 8 study rooms, TV lounges and game areas, and the university bookstore. The student union managing director states on the site, "The Student Union provides an environment for relaxation and social interaction, opportunities for education and exchange of thought, and services for Texas Tech students, staff, faculty and our community" (Texas Tech University, 2013).

There is no doubt that colleges need to provide their students with places to eat, especially if they have students living on campus. The question to consider is not whether they must have dining halls and cafes, but how upscale they need to be.

When I was an undergraduate at the University of Pennsylvania, I used to like to eat lunch in its student union building, Houston Hall. The hall, which opened in 1896, was the first student union building in the United States. Penn was technically a coed institution at the time, although it had a College for Women. Houston Hall was really the men's student union. Women were allowed to participate in meetings at the student union that were open to them, but they were not permitted to eat in the main dining hall, which was limited to men. They could eat at the cafeteria, or in the main floor small sandwich shop. The women at Penn were provided with separate but unequal facilities on the fourth floor of Bennett Hall, a building where many classes for women were held, and where the dining services were offered exclusively for women.

While I was a regular user of spaces available in Houston Hall that my gender allowed me to access, in my years there as an undergraduate, and later as a graduate student allowed throughout the facility, I was always aware of how sparsely it was occupied except during periods of celebratory events, such as graduation, alumni weekend, and special football events.

Penn can afford the luxury of a student union building. It is one of the richest universities in America, with more than $6.8 billion in its endowment as of June 2012. But most colleges do not have Penn's wealth. According to the College Board, for the 2010–11 academic year, "Endowment assets are highly concentrated among a small number of institutions within each sector. Ten private doctoral universities hold about 43% of the total endowment assets of all private nonprofit doctoral, master's, and bachelor's institutions combined, and 10 public doctoral universities hold about 34% of the total endowment assets of public doctoral, master's, and bachelor's institutions combined" (College Board, 2013, p.28).

Colleges with smaller endowments need to consider carefully how their limited dollars can best be allocated. For those colleges—in fact for most colleges—student unions are a very poor investment. It is far more prudent to allocate their scarce surplus dollars in more practical ways, tying food service provision into already existing facilities or coupling them with other needed services in new facilities, where necessary.

The biggest negative factor about student union buildings is not the cost to build them. It is the cost to maintain them, because they earn little or no revenue and more often depend on internally generated funds to support them. For too many colleges, the largest source of internally generated funds is student tuition.

Regulatory Costs

Politicians and government agency spokespersons can regularly criticize the growing costs of tuition, but they are not free from blame for the problem. As already pointed out, a plethora of federal and state regulations confront higher education administrators. For every new regulation imposed, someone must interpret the regulation for the college and draft guidelines for how it will be obeyed. Then policies have to be established as to how the college will ensure compliance, and what the penalties will be for members of the community who fail to comply with the new regulation.

People have to be designated to monitor and oversee compliance. In addition, data need to be collected to demonstrate compliance, and annual reports compiled from the data have to be developed and sent to the appropriate government agencies.

There are dozens of state and federal regulations that every college must comply with. Just a few of the federal ones include those required by the EPA, the Occupational Safety and Health Administration (OSHA), the Clery Act (for which reports on crimes on campus must be filed), the Americans with Disabilities Act, and numerous reports required by the Department of Education. There are also state regulatory and reporting responsibilities, as well as required reports due to accrediting agencies, athletic organizations, and countless others.

There are good intentions behind all of these regulations, of course, but they do cost time and money to implement, and there are a lot of them. For colleges whose programs utilize medical, chemical, or art supplies that have some degree of toxicity, or have clinics that treat patients, regulations can be quite onerous.

Once, to erect one small new building on a small plot of land abutting water, my school in Biddeford, Maine, needed approvals from the Biddeford City Council, the Saco River Commission, the Maine Department of Environmental Protection, the U.S. EPA, the Army Corps of Engineers, and the U.S. Coast Guard, among others. We even had to go through many agency hoops when we abutted, or came close to, underground water. The point is not to belabor the difficulty in getting approvals, or the costly delays they impose, but rather to illustrate the complexity of the larger environment within which higher education institutions operate, and the growing amount of personnel necessary to oversee and manage these processes.

Some of the reports require data on enrollment, graduation, race and gender diversity, federal student loans, support of athletes, grade point averages, and much more. Others require keeping logs about the purchases and appropriate disposals of medicines or science laboratory materials. The collection of these data, and the efforts made to meet the requirements that the data are meant to substantiate, take time and effort. All of this takes personnel, and even if you give the responsibilities for monitoring and documenting compliance with the regulation to personnel already working at the college, people will have to be hired to perform the tasks the compliance folks used to take care of, but are now too busy to do. The enormous expansion of regulations in the past several decades is one of the major reasons why staff positions increased at such a high rate.

Intercollegiate Athletics

Do American colleges really need intercollegiate athletics? In America, for most of them, the answer appears to be "yes." Never mind that almost all colleges lose money on athletics. Never mind that college presidents at highly athletically competitive colleges are sometimes hostage to the athletic directors. More than a few presidents have lost their jobs, or teetered at the edge of them, over trying to fire popular coaches or athletic directors.

Most colleges in other countries do not support intercollegiate athletics. That is not because competitive sports do not have large fan bases in their countries. Just a cursory look at European soccer games makes clear that sports is big business. But that is it. It is business, not education.

Many college leaders have told me they think that probably only about 10 schools in America make money on intercollegiate athletics. When I asked one president of a large university who admitted to losing more than $10 million a year on football if he would drop the sport, he replied, "You are either in or you are out. We made the decision to be in, so we need to stay with it."

It is hard to blame him for this attitude. Even when presidents may really not want to have football programs, it is hard for them to walk away. And some really do especially want football. Most small coeducational colleges today have many more female than male students. One small private college in New England increased its male enrollees by starting a football team. The opportunity to play for the team attracted a number of male applicants. This worked for one small college but would make no difference for a larger one.

On the other hand, in the early 1990s, the new female president of the University of Wisconsin at Superior eliminated intercollegiate football as a sport. "You could count on a woman president to do that," I heard some patrons at a bar in Superior opining one night, just after it happened. The fact was, the sport was eliminated because the school was unable to find enough students who wanted to play.

Both tales reflect the difficulty some colleges have in enrolling enough male students, though. With males representing only about 46% of college undergraduates today, it is no secret that schools seek ways to attract and admit more males, including practicing what some call affirmative action for men.

Football is, however, a costly vehicle for attracting students. According to one expert on the cost of intercollegiate athletics,

> For virtually all colleges, intercollegiate athletics is not a good financial investment. In 2006, only 19 of 119 NCAA FBS [National Collegiate Athletic Association Football Bowl Subdivision] institutions realized a net profit from athletics, using a liberal definition of the term "profit." As an average for the entire period from 2004 to 2006, only 16 broke even. (Denhart, Villwock, & Vedder, 2009, p. 41)

Avid supporters of intercollegiate athletic programs will argue that the sports programs bring donors to the colleges. That may be true, but because much information about donor designation at particular colleges is confidential, it is hard to put a reasonable estimate around donor intentions with regard to athletics. Nonetheless, a lot of that donor money does not go to academic programs. It goes directly into the sports programs, which, even with donor dollars, still lose money.

One analysis of the costs and benefits of intercollegiate athletics to colleges summarized donation studies that have attempted to measure donor support due to athletics. The authors found that many of the studies drew divergent conclusions. They cited one study that looked at colleges that changed their level of intercollegiate participation but found no correlation between Division I sports status and alumni donations (Getz & Siegfried, 2010, p. 5).

Other supporters insist that the high public profile of teams that make it to the NCAA Sweet Sixteen basketball playoffs, or the football bowls, brings them enrollment bonuses, and even raises their academic reputation. Apparently, some of the public conflates athletic success with academic excellence.

Colleges with big-time athletic programs spend a lot more on athletes than they spend on other students. According to a study by the Delta Cost Project, "Athletic departments spend far more per athlete than institutions spend to educate the average student—typically three to six times as much" (Desrochers, 2013, p. 2). The study also noted that in FBS institutions "median athletic spending was nearly $92,000 per athlete in 2010, while median academic spending per full-time equivalent (FTE) student was less than $14,000 in these same universities" (p. 2).

The study pointed out that the enrollment bump some associate with winning teams rarely lasted more than a year or two. It also found that although there was some evidence that state legislatures may provide larger appropriations to public institutions that participate in NCAA Division I programs, visibility, rather than success, may be the driver.

Whatever the value of football bowl athletic programs, most colleges lose money on the enterprise and often spend not just funds, but considerable time and energy on them as well. Furthermore, they distort the presumed academic values that undergird institutions of higher learning.

A recent study by Inside Higher Ed found that salaries of college football coaches had increased at much higher rates than salaries for faculty at the same colleges. The study showed that coaches' salaries in the Southeastern Conference were more than eight times that of faculty. In that conference, the football coaches' salaries increased almost 130% from 2005 to 2011, to an average of nearly $7 million each, whereas faculty salaries grew just 15.5%, to an average of just under $82,000 (Hirko, Suggs, & Orleans, 2013). That very big difference does reflect the market, of course, but it is a sad statement about the values of the colleges paying their coaches' salaries that even their most vaunted faculty can only dream about.

At least some collegiate athletic team coaches face job risks somewhat similar to those faced by adjunct faculty. An in-depth story recently revealed the difficult financial and emotional struggles of an itinerant assistant basketball coach who had shuffled through 12 coaching jobs in 16 years (Wolverton, 2013).

And while few of a college's nonathletes derive much benefit, other than as voyeurs at the intercollegiate games, while their tuition and tax dollars are expended on football and basketball players, the players also are exploited. They are sought after and admitted to their colleges not so they can be educated, but so their skills can contribute to stronger teams for their institutions to field. Some schools have relatively high rates of graduation for their athletes, within six years (not counting students who transfer or opt to leave to sign with professional teams), but many NCAA Division I colleges have abysmal rates.

There are powerful financial incentives for coaches to win games and championships, and only modest ones for improving the academic performance of their players. As U.S. Secretary of Education Arne Duncan and Tom McMillen wrote in an article for *USA Today*, "These incentives for football and basketball head coaches were dwarfed by bonuses for performance on the field or court. Academic incentives averaged $52,000 per coach, while athletic incentives averaged $600,000 per coach—a lopsided ratio of 11-to-1." They added, "When many states are reducing funding for higher education, it is hard to justify such skewed priorities and runaway athletic spending" (Duncan & McMillen, 2013).

College athletes are at risk of more than just not graduating. The public has only recently become aware of the injuries that they face, and of the limited protection available to cover the costs of care for those injuries. Usually the colleges have health care policies that, coupled with parents' policies, cover the care of an injury when it occurs. The NCAA provides some coverage if the medical claims exceed $90,000, but if the claim is not that high or the student leaves the team or the college the ongoing costs are not covered (Pennington, 2013).

The bottom line for intercollegiate athletics is that very few students, very few players, and even fewer institutions benefit from the activities. College presidents, in private, frequently bemoan the primacy of intercollegiate athletics at their schools, and some presidents have even written books and articles criticizing this national problem, but usually after they have stepped down from their presidencies.

A handful of colleges have reduced the role of athletics. In their book *The Innovative University,* Christensen and Eyring (2011) describe the positive changes that have taken place at Brigham Young University–Idaho, where intercollegiate athletics was eliminated. Now Spelman College is eliminating intercollegiate athletics in favor of fitness programs. More colleges are sure to move in this direction, especially private ones. For some, it will be economically necessary. Others will be able to do it because their boards of trustees will accept it.

It will be harder for public colleges with highly competitive teams because of political pressure. During my time at state-aided Temple University, I saw legislators and other political powers wooed with free tickets to football and basketball games. They were invited to lunches with the university president at the university's luxury suites at the football stadium, or to dinners prior to the basketball games.

These invites did not guarantee political support, of course, but they also did not cause the loss of such support. The care and cultivation of legislators is a necessary art that must be practiced by the senior staffs of state colleges. Public colleges also try to stay on the good side of municipal authorities, who vote on local taxes and must be dealt with for zoning and construction approvals.

Too many college presidents are beholden to their athletic directors or major coaches, to some extent. Most of us have known presidents who lost their jobs or came close to losing them because the state governor or a key legislative leader, or a powerful member of their board, sided with an athletic powerhouse coach in a dispute, rather than the president.

While I was at the University of Minnesota, the athletic director traveled to another university because he was dissatisfied with his position at Minnesota. The governor apparently persuaded the president of the university to join him in meeting the athletic director and offering him sweeteners to stay at Minnesota. Rumors at the time suggested that the governor pressured the president. According to a press report, the athletic director "received a rousing welcome Thursday night when he returned to Minneapolis." The report added that the governor and the university president "joined the Gopher pep band and cheerleaders," who greeted the athletic director at the airport (AP News Archive, 1995).

Another athletics story involves one of my own experiences with athletics at my former university. In 1996, Westbrook College merged with the University of New England. Both had previously been independent institutions in southern Maine. Amid all the anger and hullaballoo about the merger, particularly from Westbrook alumni, there were also numerous difficult decisions to be made about how to integrate two very different institutions. There could only be one dean of a merged College of Arts and Sciences, one director of admissions, one dean of student services, one head librarian, and one director of athletics. Except for the athletic position, codeans and codirectors could have been appointed, if we had so wished. But the athletic conferences to which the teams belonged stipulated that there could be just one director of athletics. The other person would have to settle for being the assistant director.

Westbrook was the far smaller school, with just one college unit and about 260 students total. The school with which it merged had a medical school; a College of Arts and Sciences; and several graduate programs, which were to become a third College of Health Professions. Now it has dentistry and pharmacy colleges as well. At the time of the merger, the Westbrook athletic director was also the coach of men's basketball and women's basketball. He was well liked by the sports press and had winning records.

As the president of the newly merged institution, I had to decide which of the two coaches to appoint to head the merged athletic programs. Some parents of students on one of the sports teams began trying to help me make the right decision by letting me know that they would withdraw their sons or daughters from the school if I did not appoint the Westbrook coach as the coach for the merged teams. "How did you find out about this," I asked the mother of one of the athletes, who lived in another part of the country. "The coach told us you might not choose him," she said.

As a relatively new president, having served for just a year before the merger, I had found it beneficial to seek advice from my predecessor, Hedley Reynolds, at times when tough decisions had to be made. "If the coach is making calls and giving you this much trouble now, just imagine what will happen once you officially make the appointment," Dr. Reynolds sagely told me.

I took his advice and paid with some negative remarks by several sports reporters, but I was freed from being under pressure from my own athletic staff during the 11 years I served at the University of New England. The high point of our athletic program, for me, came in 2003, when our school won a prestigious award from the NCAA and *USA Today* for having the highest student-athlete graduation rate—100%—in the nation in Division III.

We may not have been the kind of athletically successful school the NCAA or *USA Today* was hoping for, though. It may be that they were looking for an athletic powerhouse that also had a strong academic record. Notre Dame won the award for the NCAA Division I that same year. Perhaps *USA Today*, sponsor of the award, was seeking a somewhat similarly athletically well-known small college and was disappointed when the school that won for Division III, and the runners-up, were small, less known colleges, because the award was eliminated a year after we won it. The award to the University of New England sits today in a showcase outside the college gymnasium.

Buried in the Budget

Intercollegiate athletic programs frequently lose more money than faculty committees and boards of trustees know. The athletic staff is clever about how it uses funding, and senior administrators who support them are complicit in hiding true costs. Here are some of the ways this is done.

While some colleges allocate the costs of athletic scholarships to the athletic budget, others list the costs under general scholarship support. For football, with its 85 full scholarships per team for students playing for Division I teams, that adds up to a lot of money. The free room and board provided may also be accounted for under the same heading. This is so patent, though, that those colleges that want honest cost accounting can generally figure out these costs.

The room and board costs are high at many of the colleges. Male athletes on football and basketball teams tend to be big men. They eat a lot more food than the average student. Watching the players line up all the platters and drinks for lunch alone is an awesome experience. The caloric count can be staggering. Though the team may be charged for the average cost of meals, the true costs are far more. Furthermore, if they choose to live off campus after their first year, student athletes can receive a check each month equal to the amount the college charges for room and board, even if they can find cheaper accommodations.

Tutoring can be a substantial cost because most athletes on top-ranked college football and basketball teams are admitted with far lower academic qualifications than most other students at their institutions. The cost of such tutoring is sometimes subsumed under the academic budget.

NCAA Division III schools do not award athletic scholarships, but they are not free from many of the other costs of intercollegiate athletics. They still must have facilities that their athletic conference affiliates deem appropriate. They still must hire coaches and assistant coaches for many of the varsity sports programs. And they still must pay for uniforms and equipment; travel to games; and sundry other expenses, including referees and physical therapists for games.

Other Costs

There are other costs for athletics. At small colleges, announcements are made on game days to all faculty reminding them that athletes in their classes must be dismissed early because of the game. Spring break dates at one large state college in New England have been set at the behest of the baseball coach, who takes his team south for practice, because cold weather prevents early practice sessions in his area.

Teaching faculty also get notes asking them to reschedule exams for athletes who will be traveling on test days. Some colleges pressure faculty to go easy in grading key athletes. I have never been at a college where I experienced such pressure, but allegations about such pressures are rife.

What are the costs in institutional integrity when students who cannot meet the admission standards of a college are admitted over more qualified applicants simply because they are athletes? Consider, too, the sense that other students in a class get when they see an athlete being treated with favoritism. What about the messages students receive when they learn that crimes committed by athletes, such as sexual assaults, are allegedly covered up by institutional leaders?

And what about the tolerance for coaches who bully their charges, such as University of Indiana coach Bobby Knight in the past, and lately Rutgers University basketball coach Mike Rice? Rice was fired, but only after secretly taken cell phone pictures of him hitting and kicking student athletes became public.

Rutgers has been heavily criticized for keeping Rice even after senior officials knew about his abuse. A *New York Times* article said, "College sports analysts noted that the video of Mr. Rice first surfaced just as Rutgers was engaged in sensitive negotiations with the Big Ten, when the university would have been especially wary of attracting negative attention of any kind" (Eder & Zernike, 2013, p. A1). For Rutgers, apparently being in the Big Ten athletic conference was deemed more important to its reputation than managing itself in a way that enhanced its reputation for academics and integrity. When Rice was fired, he received a $475,000 severance payout.

There are other costs for some athletic programs that few people are aware of. *New York Times* op-ed columnist Joe Nocera (2013) recently exposed what he called the "military prep school scam" (p. A19). The United States' army, navy, and air force academies operate preparatory schools, which Nocera says cost taxpayers about $25 million a year. Although created for other purposes, the prep schools serve a significant number of athletes whose academic credentials fall below admission standards for the academies. In the case of the Naval Academy, more than one third of the students in the prep school in 2011 were its recruited athletes (p. A19).

Who Pays for Intercollegiate Athletics?

We know that almost all colleges that offer intercollegiate athletics lose money on it. So how exactly do they cover the costs? If you have a big enough program to be in the NCAA Division I, some of your funds will come from NCAA revenue. In 2011–12, NCAA revenue was $871.6 million. The NCAA attributes about 81% of all its revenue to media agreements, basically the broadcasting of games. The rest of its income comes largely from ticket sales for championship games (NCAA, 2013, p. 12). The NCAA estimates that the median negative net generated revenue of its member colleges in the FBS was almost $12.3 million in 2012.

In 2011–12, the NCAA distributed about $503 million to Division I conferences and member institutions (NCAA, 2013). For those colleges with revenue losses in athletics, what helps them meet the expenses for their programs?

Some of the costs are defrayed by ticket sales at other than Division I championship games, but this is small potatoes at all but the football bowl schools. Many of the less competitive colleges give free or low-cost tickets to their students, and complimentary tickets to donors and other supporters.

Some costs are partially defrayed by donations to the athletic programs. Boosters and other team fans may give large gifts to the programs. These often are tied to specific uses, though, such as scholarships for athletes, facilities development, or sweeteners for senior athletic staff salaries.

State subsidies for public colleges provide a fair amount of the funding for intercollegiate athletics at baccalaureate colleges and at universities. For the most part, community colleges do not spend their precious dollars on expensive athletic outlays, and that is a major reason why community colleges cost a lot less to support and can charge a lot less to attend.

The money that comes from state subsidies is taxpayer money. It is not money that just happens to be available. When a public college develops its budget and seeks state support for funding it, part of what has been figured in is the athletic budget. When the state accepts that budget, it is saying that the taxpayers of the state are committing to supporting the salaries of the coaches and athletic directors, as well as all the other costs associated with fielding intercollegiate athletics.

But no matter how much money a state gives toward the budget, nowadays it is rarely the major supporter of the institution. The rest of the support for the athletic budget has to come from somewhere, and where it comes from is student tuition dollars and student fees.

A study by the Delta Cost Project found that for Division I colleges athletic costs increased at least twice as fast as academic spending, on a per-capita basis, between 2005 and 2010. In addition, whereas student fees provided just 7.6% of the athletic budget for colleges in the FBS of the NCAA, in other subdivisions more than 70% of those budgets came from student fees and institutional and state support (Desrocher, 2013, p. 8). One reason for the wide difference might be that FBS teams come from very large schools, which can spread their costs among many more students than would be the case for smaller schools.

Perhaps the most scandalous thing about the intercollegiate sports budget is that much of the money to support the programs is not coming from revenue generated by the teams, either through ticket sales or through broadcast revenue. Many of the dollars are coming from the tuition that all the other students, who are not on these teams, pay to get their education.

Think about it. Tuition is high. Budgets are strained. Athletics is losing money, but it is fully funded. Where else could the money be coming from? Of course, if you are a state college, you can claim the dollars are part of your state allocation. But if the dollars were not given to support money-losing football and basketball teams, it could be used to lower tuition.

For a college with 20,000 students, that $12 million loss could be used instead to lower tuition for every single student, by about $600 per year. And because many students receive some kind of aid, the actual savings for the rest of them could be greater than $600. That is not enough to bring tuition down to manageable levels for most students, but it would certainly be a healthy start.

In fact, if other costs of intercollegiate athletics were either eliminated or not spent in the first place, the savings would be even greater. The costs of stadiums, and the opportunity costs of such investments, mean that less money is available for other needed educational expenditures.

At independent colleges that are not bowl contender schools and that lack state subsidies, all of the costs of athletics are borne on the backs of the students. Colleges say that their intercollegiate athletic programs are for their students, but at most schools, it is a small percentage of the student body that actually benefits firsthand from these investments. Instead, what is really happening is that a large number of students are transferring their borrowed tuition dollars to a small number of students who are playing on the teams.

So students who go into deep debt in order to finance the education they need to earn their college degree pay more than they need to in order to underwrite the costs for providing competitive sports programs for other students, many of whom are there primarily in the hope of getting professional sports opportunities, rather than academic degrees. Many of those college athletes will not even make it to graduation.

Add to that the fact that the football bowl schools spent more than six times as much on their athletes as they did on their other students, whose tuition and fees were partially subsidizing the athletes. Other colleges spent three to six times as much (Desrochers, 2013).

It does not feel fair.

Graduate Programs

There is a generally accepted belief in higher education that undergraduate programs help to subsidize graduate studies. For the most part, this is true. But its applicability depends on the particular graduate programs involved.

Graduate study is very expensive for both students and colleges. Some professional programs, such as business and law, may be self-supporting, or even cash cows at times, but many arts and sciences graduate programs collect little tuition to support themselves.

PhD programs are more expensive than many other graduate programs. Classes are generally offered in small seminar formats, and professors offering doctoral classes often have reduced teaching loads in order to serve as dissertation advisors and especially as dissertation supervisors. These are frequently the most highly paid faculty in their respective departments.

Many doctoral students have full tuition scholarships. Even though a number of them may teach several undergraduate courses, the savings they generate are rarely enough to compensate for their costs, especially if the courses would otherwise have been taught by adjunct professors.

Medical school education is also expensive, but the reason is different. In general, it relates to the low teaching load of the research faculty at most American medical schools, and to the costs of administering hospitals and clinics. American medical school faculty researchers are substantial recipients of biomedical grants, but the costs of managing research facilities is also very high.

For-profit medical schools in the Caribbean, which do not support research programs or hospitals, are big moneymakers. They turn profits because they take in large numbers of students who pay high tuition. Research is not on the agenda, and scholarships are rarely offered to applicants from other than the host nation.

One large cost they do have is paying for clinical placements in U.S. hospitals. The third and fourth year of medical school is spent in hospitals, under the supervision of doctors who agree to work with the schools and their students. An article on the arrangements the offshore medical schools make with New York hospitals said that the schools "typically pay hospitals $400 to $450 per student per week for clinical training" (Mangen, 2010). The article also noted that most American medical schools pay little or nothing for clinical placements, and that if they did pay such fees, they would have to significantly raise tuition.

Law schools, unlike doctoral programs and American medical school programs, have long been regarded as the cash cows of academia. Tuition at many law schools is well over $40,000 per year. Scholarships are provided, but the bulk of the students pay full tuition.

Costs to deliver the curriculum are low, compared with the costs of some other graduate programs, particularly those in the sciences. Many classes are taught in large lecture hall formats, so teaching costs are held down, even though law school professors rank among the most highly compensated faculty nationally. Although law professors may do research, the schools do not need to provide science laboratories for them.

There are far too many law schools in the United States for the number of available jobs requiring law degrees. Surely the American Bar Association and the law school establishment have known this for a very long time. It constitutes a serious breach of academic ethics to not only allow but encourage too many students to enroll in programs for which there are too few job opportunities, especially when those programs can cost more than $100,000 and three years of a person's life. It has been done to make money for the law schools, their faculties, their host institutions, and the organizations to which they pay dues and fees. It should stop.

The University of Maine School of Law, which is the only law school in that state, wisely responded to the changes in market conditions. In the spring of 2013, the dean told the school's foundation board members that he planned to cut back the size of the next entering class if necessary, because the school did not want to accept students it deemed less qualified in order to fill a class. In the end, the class size did not have to be trimmed.

There are other graduate programs that are sometimes cash cows. At least they may appear to be so to some of the colleges that invest in them as ways to help balance the budget. Graduate education degrees are the most prolific ones offered, partly because they are cheap to offer and have a large potential clientele of schoolteachers and administrators who need additional coursework to meet continuing education requirements, or to be eligible for higher-salaried positions in their states.

Many of the four-year baccalaureate colleges that have expanded into master's-level graduate programs have begun their ascents with education degree offerings. These programs have often been mounted by hiring just one of two faculty members, in addition to those already on deck in the undergraduate education programs, with strengths in areas such as special education or administrative leadership.

Another common add-on graduate program is business administration. There are strong business programs and there are weak ones, with the weak predominating. Many smaller college business programs are not accredited by the Association to Advance Collegiate Schools of Business (AACSB). That does not necessarily make them poor programs, but many could not qualify because their graduate business programs are not sufficiently rigorous in quantitative areas, an important consideration for advanced business degree holders.

Education, business, and generic management programs grew at nonprofit colleges over the last two decades for several reasons. First, they grew because they were low cost to provide. Most of these programs could be entered into and offered with little up-front investment because laboratories and other specialized facilities and equipment were not needed.

Second, there was a steady stream of students available to enroll in them, such as teachers required to take continuing education courses to maintain their certifications. Business and management programs flourished because so many people saw an advanced business degree as a ticket to upward mobility in the business world. The students who enrolled in these programs assumed that less rigorous business degrees were as valuable as ones that demanded great rigor, although most were not.

Third, for many of the colleges that went into these graduate areas, the bulk of the students enrolling in the programs were older and, consequently, did not need or could not qualify for internally provided financial aid. Therefore, even if the programs charged less for these classes than the rate the colleges charged for undergraduate tuition, these graduate programs still often returned positive cash flows to the institutional bottom lines.

For example, Simmons College, whose students at the undergraduate level are all women, has coed graduate programs. According to an article in the *Boston Globe Magazine,* the graduate programs at Simmons netted more than $24 million in excess of costs to the college's bottom line. One reason is that whereas 81% of the college's undergraduate students receive financial aid (or discounts) from the school, only 20% of graduate students do (Marcus, 2013). Simmons offers good-quality graduate programs, but not all schools do.

Although many graduate programs were relatively inexpensive to add on to four-year colleges, because laboratories were not required, expensive equipment was not needed, and specialized accreditation was unnecessary, the ease of entry has meant that there is plenty of competition for students. Few of the programs are distinctive enough or of high enough quality to stand out from the pack of imitators in the nonprofit sector. Whereas once these programs were seen as unique in their local communities, potential students can easily make price comparisons with the colleges just on the other side of town offering almost identical programs.

Worse yet for schools offering these graduate programs, the for-profit world has discovered the value of these programs. Although most for-profit colleges do not offer graduate programs, those that do are offering them at very competitive prices. The graduate programs most frequently available at for-profit colleges are graduate business offerings, followed by graduate teaching programs.

The proliferation of programs, and the seeming acceptance of them, has already led to changes. Some public and independent colleges are starting to cut back on graduate program offerings. Willamette College, in Oregon, has taken a very bold step. It plans to close its Graduate School of Education.

Willamette's president, Stephen Thorsett, said that state and accreditation requirements have propelled education programs "towards greater standardization and uniformity, and reduced the value the market places on distinctiveness or even program quality."[1]

Although the faculty in the program disputed the need to close the programs, Thorsett pointed out that the

> low barrier to entry has led to an explosion in the number of local, regional and online MAT-degree programs in the Willamette Valley, at public, independent and for-profit institutions, in the midst of a global economic climate that does not support, now or in the foreseeable future, commensurate growth in employment opportunities for new teachers.[2]

Other thoughtful higher education leaders are likely to make similar decisions. The colleges that cut back on graduate programs for quality control reasons, because the programs cannot be sustained at levels they deem appropriate for the institutions, will be far better off than those who eventually close their programs because they have withered away.

Quality graduate education is a critically important component of higher education. Even though some graduate programs have been low cost to offer, much of graduate education is expensive to deliver. It is also necessary in an advanced society. But we offer more of it than we need in many programmatic areas. This is evidenced by the fact that too few graduates of many of our doctoral programs are able to find full-time employment in their chosen fields. That is why there are so many adjunct faculty in the marketplace, and why their compensation levels are so shameful.

Graduate education is popular with faculty because it gives professors the opportunity to work with advanced-level students, some of whom will become their peers. For some, it gives them assistants to work on their projects or jointly write papers. For others, it provides potentially talented graduate students to do studies the professors can add their own names to as supervisors.

For colleges, gaining approval from their accreditors to offer graduate programs allows them to change their designations from "college" to "university." Strong and vital graduate programs provide our society with the future thinkers and leaders we will need.

But most graduate education remains expensive to offer. Many colleges are going to have to cut back on these programs. Institutions will have to assess which of their programs are strongest and pare back those that do not place most of their graduates in appropriate positions.

The costs of many graduate programs are borne on the backs of undergraduate students, whose tuition is used to support the fellowships the graduate students are receiving. Given the need to hold down undergraduate tuition charges, colleges need to start expecting graduate programs to become more cost effective, or more self-supporting.

"Using undergraduates to finance graduate education is going to get tougher, except in a few cases," according to Judith Eaton, president of the Council for Higher Education Accreditation (CHEA). She adds that "money is necessary, but not sufficient, to produce quality."

Endowment Issues

College endowments are funds held by a college that the college invests so that a regular amount of income is earned for the school. An endowment is composed of holdings of money and property, most of which have been given to the institution by donors.

Typically, substantial numbers of individual gift holdings within endowments contain stipulations as to how the income generated by the particular funds may be used. Colleges invest the funds within their endowments to derive income that they then can use for present expenses.

Endowments are composed of several parts. One part represents funds that were given or committed with stipulations that are legally required to be met, such as a gift specifying that the income generated each year be awarded as scholarships to students from a particular high school or county or pursuing a particular program.

Another part of the endowment is the quasi-endowment, which is not really an endowed fund. Colleges may choose to place internally available funds within the quasi-endowment. In a year when a college has revenue in excess of its expenditures, its governing board may add some of that surplus to its quasi-endowment, which means that the funds will be treated as endowment funds until or unless the governing body determines how and when it will be spent.

Legally, these funds are unrestricted because boards can release them. The rest of the funds in the endowment represent other monies that have been added in, or gifts with no restrictions.

Colleges with very large endowments can and do use a share of them to fund student aid. Alan Brinkley, former provost of Columbia University, told me that any student whose family income was under $60,000 did not have to pay tuition at Columbia because aid above federal financial aid is provided by the college from its endowment. Columbia's endowment was more than $7.6 billion as of June 30, 2012 (Wolfson, 2012).

Columbia has a reputation as a university that is generous with financial aid. In its most recent fund-raising campaign, Columbia specifically sought to raise nearly half a billion dollars for financial aid. The school actually succeeded in raising nearly double that amount.

Brinkley said that he thinks the inequality in America is one of the biggest problems we face as a nation. He is right, of course, but the endowments of large universities simply perpetuate the huge division between the have and have-not institutions, as well as the population in general.

It would be wonderful if Harvard (with its more than $30 billion endowment), Princeton, and even Columbia spent the bulk of their endowment income on providing free education to students from poor families. Of course they do provide free education for the small percentage of low-income students they admit. But much of the endowment scholarship money, which is just a small percentage of the total endowment income, is used to offer enrollment package sweeteners to highly desired candidates, who frequently compare scholarship and fellowship aid offers before making final decisions about where they will attend.

Instead of raising tuition, the richest colleges could lower tuition, by spending more of the unrestricted parts of their endowments. In fact, in some parts of the nation, state-elected officials are suggesting that their public colleges do exactly that. At hearings in Wisconsin in May 2013, legislators raised questions about the $1 billion balance being held by the University of Wisconsin System, of which about $648 million was unrestricted. One state senator commented, "Here we have accounts of tuition being squirreled away at the same time you raised tuition. What was your intent?" (Kiley, 2013). Among the explanations given by system officials was the need to have reserve funds to cover several months of operation, in the event of operating shortfalls, cash needs, or to deal with contingencies such as unanticipated emergencies. Legislators had a lot of concern about the fact that much of the unrestricted balance, "$414 million, according to the legislative audit—consists of revenue from student fees, which the system has been increasing at a rate of about 5.5 percent a year in recent years" (Kiley, 2013).

The University of Maine System has also been the target of criticism over its endowment because some critics feel that although its reserves have grown, the funds that enabled the growth should have been used in ways that would have lowered or at least held down tuition increases. The system, which includes seven universities spread across the state of Maine, has seen its reserves doubled to $177 million over the last four years. It argues, as the University of Wisconsin System did, that its reserves are necessary to provide for emergencies, capital needs, and unanticipated expenses (Christie & Schalit, 2013).

The separate universities in the University of Maine System also have accumulated funds. The largest of these is at the University of Maine, the state's land-grant university in Orono. Its endowment had assets totaling more than $193.4 million in 2013.[3]

More state governments are likely to raise questions about the unrestricted holdings in the endowment portfolios of their publicly funded colleges. Asking tough questions and putting pressure on senior public higher education officials will not by itself change anything. But the questioning suggests a new awareness and concern about the issue.

If a college has an excess of revenue over costs that it is able to place in its endowment in a particular year, that excess may well have been largely funded by taxpayers and student tuition and fees. It is fair for legislators to argue, as some have, that tuition charges should not be raised when previous tuition dollars received have still not been spent.

Legislators are adept at playing political gamesmanship, to be sure. Some make statements to demonstrate for the hometown constituents that they are in the taxpayers' corner. Others, on the opposite side of the aisle from the governor, may just be seeking to embarrass the state administration's appointees. It is likely, though, that in an era of tight state budgets more questions will be asked in more legislative chambers and executive branches of state government about the growing wealth amassed in the uncommitted parts of public college endowment holdings.

Colleges do need some security around their funding obligations. Most colleges cannot accurately predict their enrollment for the coming year until after students have registered and paid for their fall classes. They are correct in arguing that they need excess funds to provide a cushion for unexpected expenses or problems. Especially given the ups and downs of the stock market in recent years, the interest income that they can anticipate to use toward scholarships or chaired professorships, or any other obligations, cannot be ascertained with certainty.

Furthermore, highly academically competitive public universities may look with unbridled envy at their sister independent institutions, with their multi-billion-dollar endowments. Top public colleges see the premier private colleges with whom they compete as having much more money available to fund new and exciting ventures. The lack of a similar funding source to draw on can be seen as a competitive disadvantage.

Colleges cannot have it both ways, though. If you want to feed at the public trough, even if it provides only a small proportion of your annual funding, you have to accept publicly imposed requirements.

Realistically, legislative pressure on public colleges will not have a great impact on tuition costs because most of the public colleges in America do not have large enough endowments to direct toward holding down tuition and fee charges. At a minimum, an increased focus on the availability of unspent dollars, which could be allocated to minimize raising tuition, is likely to make it harder for public colleges to impose high tuition hikes without risking cuts to their state allocations.

Although not all American colleges have large endowments, some have enough funds to support their programs for a long time. As of June 30, 2011, 70 colleges had endowments of more than a billion dollars. (National Center for Education Statistics, 2012). Harvard University, with its endowment of more than $30 billion, could manage for a long time without raising any additional dollars. Keep in mind that it still would generate tuition and fee income, as well as grants and other sources of funds, along with interest income on whatever portion of its endowment remained in any given year. Its 2012 operating budget of $4 billion could probably be covered for more than a decade.

Whereas many colleges ought to use a large portion of their endowment income to reduce tuition costs, in the case of Harvard, perhaps a better solution would be to encourage its donors to give to needier schools. Harvard is not going to do this, of course, but its thoughtful donors ought to take more note of need than of buttressing the endowment of the richest college in the country.

When students from my alma mater call me to ask for donations, I say yes once every four or five years. The rest of the time I tell them our college is very well funded, and I am choosing to give to colleges and other nonprofit organizations that need the money more than Penn does.

Our federal government could encourage nonprofit organizations, including colleges, to plow more of their endowment resources into the reduction of student or service costs. One of the easiest ways to do this is to change federal tax laws so that they help prevent the salting away of present-generation funds to build and benefit institutions far into the future, rather than using them to ameliorate present needs.

One way to do this would be to reduce the tax exemption for gifts to nonprofit 501C-3 organizations. Although this might hurt worthy causes and would not necessarily lead to endowment spending, such a policy has had advocates in Congress in recent years (Strom, 2010). Another tactic would be to require college and other nonprofit endowments to spend a higher percentage of their endowment assets each year or else pay taxes on the endowments, as private foundations must do. An even more radical approach would be to impose graduated payout requirements based on the number of months of expenses that could be supported by the assets. Perhaps the best strategy would be to stagger the percentage of tax reduction a donor could receive based on the relation of the organization's operating budget to the size of its endowment.

In a thoughtful article in the *Fordham Law Review*, Sarah Waldeck (2009) argues that "particularly with respect to skyrocketing tuition and a growing institutional wealth gap . . . policymakers (should) modify the charitable deduction for gifts to universities with mega-endowments" (p. 1795). She notes that institutions with ratios in the top 10% of endowment size to operating budget had "more than a ten-year reserve" (p. 1808).

Although colleges can claim that large endowments are bulwarks against downturns, and provide ballast if loans are needed, Waldeck (2009) points out that endowments are not the only financial assets colleges own. "An endowment does not include the value of a university's physical assets, which can be used as security on a loan to help carry an institution through financial difficulties" (p. 1808)

The extraordinarily large endowments of a relatively small number of colleges also cause a major dislocation in higher education. The presence of big endowments allows these colleges to continually fund newer and better facilities, programs, and other enticements for students and faculty. This in turn leads to the arms race in higher education, as the rich schools set the pace for what all the other schools will try to emulate, on whatever scale of activity they can stretch their resources to afford. This is usually done by increasing tuition.

If we want a country that is not divided by a higher education caste system, we need to find a way to moderate the worst instincts that are involved in building the biggest endowments and hoarding the most money. We ought to require that more of it be spent and less of it be put away for "someday."

Research Costs

Although we may not like having to recognize the reality that it is necessary to lower research costs, it is a change that is coming, no matter how much we rail against it.

Basically, the fact that faculty conduct research is what makes learning from them worthwhile. The best education comes from learning that everything we think we know will one day be disproven by a better theory or example of why the universe works the way it does. Whether it is in science or medicine or art, we are always about understanding how we know, and what we know. Education, through a research-based model, helps us confront the nature of continually changing information.

When students learn from professors who are engaged in research, they learn about and understand scientific method. For a health professional, for instance, it is important to know that what they have learned about the reasons for or treatment of a disease may be outmoded. They must be open to understanding that old knowledge continually gets superseded by new knowledge.

There are two reasons why major research efforts will become reduced at all but the most elite private universities and the public land-grant institutions, and even for them, they will change in notable ways. The first reason is the increasing specialization of research, which drives the costs of much research ever higher, requiring not just one specialist but, rather, teams of researchers with specialties that support each other. The second reason is that it is becoming more difficult to obtain research dollars. Cutbacks by federal granting agencies, even if reversed in the short run, are ensuring that colleges will be unlikely to see the kinds of increases in research dollars experienced in the past. In addition, there are now many more universities and research centers competing for the increasingly scarce dollars.

The best way for most colleges to be able to support the costs of research projects at their institutions will be for them to partner with other colleges, laboratories, hospitals, and nonprofit research centers, sharing some personnel and costs. In the health professions fields, there are already a number of such joint ventures taking place, to connect medical schools with hospitals in tighter relationships, even when they are not both owned by the same institutions. They will not be merging, but rather collaborating in their laboratories.

One good example of tripartite collaboration involves the Spartanburg, South Carolina, campus of the Edward Via College of Osteopathic Medicine, which is building laboratories jointly with the Gibbs Cancer Center, at the Spartanburg Regional Healthcare Center. The medical school will provide important faculty researchers to work with Gibbs Center researchers at the hospital-based facility.

Additional Issues That Beset Public Colleges

A major difference separating public colleges from independent ones is the public expectation that a public institution will offer programs needed by the community or state or nation even if the program is very expensive to deliver. For example, veterinary medicine is a very costly program to provide, but we need people trained as veterinarians.

Because the veterinary medicine degree programs are so cost-inefficient, the programs are highly subsidized. Veterinary schools are very expensive to run, with their requirements for laboratories and clinics where large-animal surgery, among other topics, can be studied.

Most of the schools of veterinary medicine in the United States are at public universities. The University of Pennsylvania, an independent institution, offers the degree, but it receives substantial state support for continuing to do so.

For public colleges, the average published tuition prices are a lot lower than the published tuition prices for independent colleges. The reason is that public colleges are the recipients of state or local dollars. Even though in many states the amount of support relative to expenses has stayed flat or declined, public institutions still depend on their state subsidies.

And no matter how parsimonious the allocation, or how tight the budget is in a given year, for public colleges there is always the hope for future increases at the public trough. Administrators, staff, students, or clients are enlisted, efforts are made to sway political representatives to support the institution's needs, and if funds are not made available, internal constituents view it as the fault of government.

Government funding supplies public officials with the ability to impose controls on tuition rates. Legislators, hearing from constituents, or wanting to face reelection contests where they can take credit for holding down tuition, are active critics of rising charges on students. As an example, the Florida legislature has laws governing not only how much tuition can be raised, but how much other student fees can be raised, in any given year.

There are four trends creating growing dissension between states and the colleges they fund, according to Aims McGuinness (2011), a senior associate at the National Center for Education Management Systems: escalating demands, severe economic constraints, higher education's "inherent resistance to change," and the instability of state political leadership (pp. 139–140). The escalating demands are being driven by increases in the applicant pools, especially when state funds do not increase to meet the increases in enrollments. This is particularly the case for many community colleges, which have seen heavy waves of increases in students applying for admission. These colleges are supposed to provide access for most of their applicants, but without increases in funding, some are unable to stretch the resources they are allocated.

Both two- and four-year colleges have been increasing their tuition and fees faster than inflation, just as the independent colleges have been doing, particularly as a result of flat or modest increases to their state allocations. In addition, faculty and staff complain that their salaries have not kept up with those of their colleagues in the independent sector.

The substantial subsidies that public colleges once received from their states have fallen dramatically in recent years, not in terms of the total state dollars allocated, but the share of the college budgets covered. For example, in Virginia each four-year college and university received approximately 30% of its budget from the state in 1981. By 2010, the average level of support was down to 11% (State Council of Higher Education for Virginia, 2009).

Colleges with this little support are more appropriately described as state related rather than as state supported, a designation Pennsylvania has used for its relationship to the University of Pittsburgh and Temple University. However small the share of state support, the dollars are still large. For Pitt and Temple, state support amounts to more than $135 million per year for each of them (Southwick, 2013).

The resistance to change is endemic in almost all of nonprofit higher education. The only way for much change to occur in public higher education, which is more change resistant than the independent college sector, is if state governments start to demand changes.

The final issue that McGuinness notes, the instability of state political leadership, is true of all political levels of governance. Gubernatorial elections can bring new leadership initiatives and directions in state support and demands from state-funded colleges. And political leaders can respond to the growing awareness of the gaps between what college programs promise and what they can demonstrate they are able to deliver of their students by tying state funding for colleges to demonstrated goal attainment.

State System Lack of Control

In some states, public institutions are coordinated through the imposition of statewide governing boards. There may be a governing board overseeing all of the community colleges in a state, or all of its four-year colleges, or all of its research universities. Some states have these oversight boards for all three sectors, and some for only one or two of them. Where they exist, the primary purpose is usually to rationalize the allocation of budgets and services, and to ensure similar policies and compliance with state regulations.

Some state systems not only wield more power than others, but are able to use that power in a positive way. American colleges and universities have a strong tradition of institutional autonomy, according to McGuinness (2011, p. 145). Even where they are part of systems, those systems are more often coordinating boards than controlling ones. Few of them have the authority to function as rationers of resources. Some community college system boards and leaders do exercise fairly strong control. For four-year colleges, and especially universities, end runs around their systems are the name of the game.

In a large number of systems, though not all, individual colleges each retain their own boards that set their own college's policies within the general set of policies established by the system board. The local board is also the source of political support and lobbying dollars for the local college.

Making meaningful change is vastly harder when colleges each have their own local boards because they can come up with so many ways to circumvent changes, including pointing out that another college in the system is slack about compliance. Last year I heard a system chancellor say that having local boards is a recipe for doing nothing.

There are also substantial differences among states in how they manage enrollment costs. Regarding efficiency outcomes, consider the cases of public uses of state higher education dollars in Maine and California. Maine enrolls most of its public college students in its two most expensive to operate institutions, the University of Maine and the University of Southern Maine. By contrast, California limits access to the University of California System institutions, which are high cost to operate, to the top 12.5% of its high school graduates and placing most of its students in community colleges and the California State System, which cost less to run.

California is a much larger state than Maine in population, so its students have a lot more choices. California is five times as large as Maine in geographic area, but 29 times larger in population size. The people in Maine live disproportionately in the southern part of the state, where one of the two largest colleges is located. The other is in the center of the state. The state has only seven colleges in the University of Maine system. Though there are frequent discussions about the high costs of maintaining small colleges in the more remote parts of the state, legislators have been understandably reluctant to close those colleges, particularly due to the impact it would have on commuting students.

Political Lobbying and Electoral Pressure

In the run-up to budget adoption, state-supported and state-aided colleges often take verbal beatings. They get bullied and tarred for obscure sins of omission and commission. They listen to proposals to cut their budgets by amounts that could seriously reduce their ability to offer their present levels of services.

This is political theater. The threats are often substantially overstated, designed to allow particular legislators to tell hometown constituents how they fought to reduce college expenditures. But they are threats, and even if the final budgets do not cut as deep as those initially threatened, in recent years, there have been significant cutbacks.

Colleges are not hapless in the face of budget-slashing proposals. They have learned to play the political game too. They bring well-respected board leaders to hearings. They develop political strategies to energize their supporters to contact their own representatives. They alert their students and faculty and staff to the possibility of lost jobs and programs. In essence, they mount a political campaign.

In many states, public colleges each hire their own internal lobbyists, along with well-connected external lobbyists, to make sure that key legislators and officials understand their needs and are supportive of their requests. At legislative hearings, the fight for shares of the higher education budget is often seen as a zero-sum game, where your college must fight what a sister institution wants in order to get its own requests approved. Much lobbying by campuses takes place at state legislative hearings. Public colleges campaign for their own new buildings and expanded resources. Some state colleges also use legislative hearings to try to hold back expansion efforts of colleges they see as competitive to their own institutions. These lobbying efforts can cost a lot of money.

Unionization, Pensions, and Deferred Costs

Another reason why public higher education is hard to change is that most public colleges have unionized faculty, whereas most independent colleges do not. Most state colleges have faculty unions as well as staff unions. Union rules, like tenure policies, although not necessarily intended to do so, often impose barriers to change.

Measuring the effects of faculty unionization in higher education is very difficult because of the wide variation in the cultures and economies of different communities and institutions. As one article on this issue noted, dealing with faculty unions could hinder college administrations, "but it also might be that dealing with dysfunctional administrations makes faculty members more likely to form unions" (Schmidt, 2013).

It is because of a Supreme Court ruling, *National Labor Relations Board v. Yeshiva University*, decided in 1980, that the majority of independent colleges do not have unionized faculty. The ruling asserted that Yeshiva's full-time faculty were managerial employees and therefore not covered by the National Labor Relations Act. That decision has enabled many private colleges to use the courts to beat back unionization efforts.

At least 60 private colleges are unionized. The Yeshiva decision does not prevent them from allowing unions to form. The ruling also does not protect colleges from unionization if their faculty do not have management-type responsibilities. It also cannot prevent part-time faculty from unionizing, nor is it likely to be able to prevent unionization at for-profit colleges unless they adopt the nonprofit model of faculty management of curriculum, grading standards, hiring decisions, and other shared governance rights that most nonprofit college faculty enjoy.

The faculty have these same rights in public colleges too, but the governing bodies of many of those systems or states have chosen to approve faculty union rights. One of the big and costly rights that faculty, both unionized and nonunionized, have won in public colleges is generous pension funding.

For most of private higher education, pension plan policies have been based on defined contributions, similar to pension norms in the business world. Under a defined contribution plan, typically an employer contributes money to an employee's pension based on either matching what the employee puts in up to a fixed ceiling or stipulating the contribution based on a percentage of the employee's salary. In other words, the amount to be contributed is stipulated.

In many public colleges, the same policy exists. But in some states, faculty and other staff, as state employees, enjoy defined benefit pension plans. A defined benefit plan means that what the employer guarantees is a fixed amount of income to an employee after retirement. It is usually based on some combination of an employee's earnings and years of service.

This is the type of pension policy in place in many local and state jurisdictions for police and firefighters, and often for schoolteachers and other public employees as well. In some places, this could be equal to 80% of the average of an employee's three highest earning years. It is this type of defined benefit plan that is now crippling the budgets of so many states.

When asked what major steps public colleges could take to compete more effectively and to become more affordable, one former public system chancellor told me, "We need to reduce contributions to pensions." His other key recommendation was to change layoff and retirement rules, to give the colleges more flexibility if they are going to hold down tuition increases or compete with for-profit colleges.

Although a few states have approved right-to-work laws, these do not prevent unionization of faculties. What right-to-work laws do prevent is a requirement that all faculty or staff in a unionized group have to join the union or pay fees to it in order to keep their jobs.

Notes

1. S. Thorsett in a letter to Willamette faculty and staff June 6, 2013.
2. Ibid.
3. University of Maine Foundation 2013 Annual Report, p. 3.

References

American Association of University Professors. (2013, May 29). *1940 Statement of principles on academic freedom and tenure.* Retrieved from http://aaup.org/file/principles-academic-freedom-tenure.pdf

AP News Archive. (1995, February 3). *Sports shorts.* Retrieved from http://www.apnewsarchive.com/1995/Sports-Shorts/id-03f2c4edeceb4037b86c0d-d063d0e64c

Association of College Unions International. (2013, April 26). *Role of the college union.* Retrieved from http://www.acui.org/content.aspx?menu_id=30&id=296

Baum, S. (2012). *Trends in college pricing 2012.* New York, NY: College Board Advocacy and Policy Center.

Baumol, W. J., & Bowen, W. G. (1966). *Performing arts, the economic dilemma: A study of problems common to theater, opera, music, and dance.* New York, NY: Twentieth Century Fund.

Bennett, D. L. (2009, June 26). Bureaucrat U. *Forbes.* Retrieved from http://www.forbes.com/forbes/2009/0713/opinions-college-tuition-teachers-on-my-mind.html

Blumenstyk, G. (2011, April 2). Colleges scramble to avoid violating federal-aid limit: For-profits' tactics to comply with 90/10 rule raises questions. *The Chronicle of Higher Education.* Retrieved from http://chronicle.com/article/Colleges-Scramble-to-Avoid/126986/

Christensen, C. M., & Eyring, H. J. (2011). *The innovative university: Changing the DNA of higher education from the inside out.* San Francisco, CA: Jossey-Bass.

Christie, J., & Schalit, N. (2013, April 24). University of Maine system cuts staff, programs while reserve fund grows to $177 million. *Bangor Daily News.* Retrieved from http://bangordailynews.com/2013/04/24/education/university-system-cuts-while-reserve-fund-grows-to-177-million/

College Board. (2013). *Endowment assets per FTE student, 2010–11.* Retrieved from https://trends.collegeboard.org/college-pricing/figures-tables/endowment-assets-fte-student-2010-11

Denhart, M., Villwock, R., & Vedder, R. (2009, April). *The academics athletics trade-off.* Washington, DC: Center for College Affordability and Productivity.

Desrochers, D. M. (2013, January). *Academic spending versus athletic spending: Who wins?* The Delta Cost Project. Washington, DC: American Institutes for Research.

Duncan, A., & McMillen, T. (2013, March 22). Want to change college athletics? Financially punish coaches. *USA Today.* Retrieved from http://www.usatoday.com/story/sports/ncaab/2013/03/20/arne-duncan-tom-mcmillen-march-madness-education-coach-salaries/2004835/

Eder, S., & Zernike, K. (2013, April 3). Rutgers leaders are faulted on abusive coach. *New York Times,* p. A1.

Getz, M., & Siegfried, J. (2010, May). *What does intercollegiate athletics do to or for colleges and universities?* (Working Paper No. 1005). Nashville, TN: Vanderbilt University Department of Economics.

Green, J. P. (2010, August 25). *Colleges feeding administrative bloat.* Goldwater Institute. Retrieved from http://goldwaterinstitute.org/article/colleges-feeding-administrative-bloat

Harvard endowment rises $4.4 billion to $32 billion. (2011, September 22). *Harvard Magazine.* Retrieved from http://harvardmagazine.com/2011/09/harvard-endowment-rises-to-32-billion

Hirko, S., Suggs, D. W., & Orleans, J. H. (2013, April 27). *Athletics in the academic marketplace: Using revenue theory of cost to compare trends in athletic coaching sala-*

ries and instructional salaries and tuition. Paper presented at the annual conference of the American Educational Research Association, San Francisco, CA.

James, F. (2013, August 20). *Obama's college-cost tour is a chance to get past climbing wall.* Retrieved from http://www.npr.org/blogs/itsallpolitics/2013/08/19/213605532/obamas-college-cost-tour-climbing-walls-or-complexities

Kaminer, A. (2013, April 24). College ends free tuition, and an era. *New York Times,* pp. A1, A19.

Kezar, A., & Maxey, D. (2013, May/June). The changing academic workforce. *Trusteeship, 21*(3), 15–21.

Kiley, K. (2013, April 26). Reserve judgment. *Inside Higher Ed.* Retrieved from http://www.insidehighered.com/news/2013/04/26/wisconsin-systems-budget-reserves-become-target-lawmakers

Leontiades, M. (2007). *Pruning the ivy: The overdue reform of higher education.* Charlotte, NC: Information Age Publishing.

Longanecker, D. A. (2008, November). *Mission differentiation vs. mission creep: Higher education's battle between creationism and evolution.* Western Interstate Commission for Higher Education. Retrieved from http://wiche.edu/info/gwypf/dal_mission.pdf

Mangen, K. (2010, December 12). Students from Caribbean med schools head for New York, angering some local programs: The trend angers some medical educators, who say their trainees are being crowded out of clinical rotations. *The Chronicle of Higher Education.* Retrieved from https://chronicle.com/article/Students-From-Caribbean-Med/125681/

Marcus, J. (2013, April 14). Why some small colleges are in big trouble: Money is tight. Competition is brutal. Are some Massachusetts schools on the road to ruin? *Boston Globe Magazine.* Retrieved from http://www.bostonglobe.com/magazine/2013/04/13/are-small-private-colleges-trouble/ndlYSWVGFAUjYV-VWkqnjfK/story.html

Martin, A. (2012, December 14). Building a showcase campus, using an I.O.U. *New York Times,* pp. A1, B4.

McGuinness, A. C., Jr. (2011). The states and higher education. In P. G. Altbach, P. J. Gumport, & R. O. Berdahl (Eds.), *American higher education in the twenty-first century: Social, political, and economic challenges* (pp. 139–169). Baltimore, MD: Johns Hopkins University Press.

Moody's. (2013, January). *Outlook for entire US Higher Education sector changed to negative.* Global Credit Research report 16. Retrieved from https://www.moodys.com/research/Moodys-2013-outlook-for-entire-US-Higher-Education-sector-changed--PR_263866

National Association of College and University Business Officers (NACUBO). (2002, February). *Explaining college costs: NACUBO's methodology for identifying the costs of delivering undergraduate education.* Washington, DC: Author. Retrieved from http://about.usps.com/who-we-are/postal-history/state-abbreviations.pdf

National Association of College and University Business Officers (NACUBO). (2013). *The 2012 NACUBO tuition discounting study.* Washington, DC: Author.

National Center for Education Statistics. (2012). *Digest of Education Statistics, table 411: Endowment funds of the 120 colleges and universities with the largest endowments, by rank order: 2010 and 2011.* Washington, DC: Author. Retrieved from http://nces.ed.gov/programs/digest/d12/tables/dt12_411.asp

The National Collegiate Athletic Association (NCAA). (2013). *Revenue and Expenses: 2004–12, NCAA Division I Intercollegiate Athletics Programs Report.* Indianapolis, IN: Author.

National Labor Relations Board v. Yeshiva University, 444 U.S. 672 (1980).

Nocera, J. (2013, April 9). The military prep school scam. *New York Times,* p. A19.

Pennington, B. (2013, April 5). In a moment it can all be gone. *New York Times,* pp. B11, B15.

Russell, A. (2010, October). *Update on the community college baccalaureate: Evolving trends and issues.* Washington, DC: American Association of State Colleges and Universities.

Schmidt, P. (2013, April 5). Universities benefit from their faculties' unionization, study finds. *The Chronicle of Higher Education.* Retrieved from http://chronicle.com/article/Universities-Benefit-From/138353/

Southwick, R. (2013, June 30). *What's in the 2013–14 state budget deal: Highlights of the $28.37 billion plan.* Retrieved from http://www.pennlive.com/midstate/index.ssf/2013/06/whats_in_the_2013-14_state_bud.html

State Council of Higher Education for Virginia (SHEV). (2009, September 1). *The erosion of state funding for Virginia's public higher education institutions.* Richmond, VA: Author.

Strom, S. (2010, December 2). Nonprofits fear losing tax benefit. *New York Times.* Retrieved from http://www.nytimes.com/2010/12/03/business/03charity.html

Texas Tech University. (2013, April 26). *Student union & activities.* Retrieved from http://www.depts.ttu.edu/sub/

University of Utah breaks ground on new $50.4 million George S. Eccles Student Life Center. (2013, April 25). *Deseret News.* Retrieved from http://www.deseretnews.com/article/865578950/University-of-Utah-breaks-ground-on-new-504-million-George-S-Eccles-Student-Life-Center.html?pg=all

Waldeck, S. E. (2009). The coming showdown over university endowments: Enlisting the donors. *Fordham Law Review, 77*(4), 1795–1835.

Wolfson, L. (2012, October 15). Columbia University endowment has 2.3% investment return. *Bloomberg News.* Retrieved from http://www.bloomberg.com/news/2012-10-15/columbia-university-endowment-has-2-3-investment-return.html

Wolverton, B. (2013, June 3). Bounced around: After 12 coaching jobs in 16 years, Elwyn McRoy takes one last shot. *The Chronicle of Higher Education.* Retrieved from http://chronicle.com/article/Bounced-Around/139581/?cid=wb&utm_source=wb&utm_medium=en

Zemsky, R., Wegner, G. R., & Massy, W. F. (2005). *Remaking the American university: Market-smart and mission-centered.* New Brunswick, NJ: Rutgers University Press.

4 How the For-Profits Do It

For-profit colleges are businesses. They need to raise enough income to cover expenses and generate profits. Some small for-profit colleges earn only modest returns, but all for-profit colleges seek profits that will benefit the owners and investors.

Many of the for-profit colleges are owned by very large corporations. In early 2010, before it had to start scaling back its offerings, the University of Phoenix operated programs at more than 200 campuses and offered more than 100 college degree programs. In 2010 there were almost 600,000 students enrolled in the various campuses (University of Phoenix, n.d.).

Publicly traded colleges are governed by boards that have a legal fiduciary responsibility to their shareholders. Whatever else they may do, they must sooner or later show a profit from their activities. Profit, rather than public service, must be their primary focus, or they will not survive in the business world. This does not mean that for-profit colleges will not do a good job. It is in their corporate interest to serve their students well, to build a strong, positive reputation for the quality of their programs and grow by attracting more students.

How do colleges make a profit when so many nonprofit colleges cannot break even without donations or subsidies? What is it that for-profits know that nonprofit colleges don't know?

First of all, not all American public and independent colleges lose money, nor do they lose money every year, before adding in donations, grants, and subsidies. There are some nonprofit organizations in America whose present endowments are so large that they could fund their operations for long periods of time without exhausting their funds. On the other hand, most nonprofit colleges have accrued sizeable long-term debt but do not face annual deficits, at least after donations and subsidies.

The reason that for-profit colleges are growing so quickly in this decade is that an opening has been made for them, through the failure of the traditional public and independent colleges sector, to adequately meet the needs of Americans seeking higher education.

The high debts that students accumulate in college, the low graduation rates, the difficulty in turning degrees into good jobs, the limited hours and seasons that coursework is offered, and the failure to meet the educational needs of working Americans have all conspired to force many of those seeking educational credentials to opt for the proprietary colleges, with their greater willingness to meet the students where they are, in terms of their course needs, their time availability, and their physical locations.

There have been proprietary schools in America for more than 200 years. For much of their history, postsecondary proprietary colleges offered one- and two-year career education programs, such as secretarial science, nursing, dental hygiene, home economics, or trade training.

These institutions were usually called junior colleges if credit for some of their completed coursework could be transferred to four-year colleges, or technical colleges if most of their coursework was not eligible for transfer credit. In the 1950s, some of the proprietary schools were accused of fraudulent accounting practices involving student aid, and of using misleading advertising to entice students to their programs (Honick, 1995).

The development and widespread growth of community colleges slowed the growth of proprietary schools. As community colleges have offered more career-oriented programs, "The historic function of the proprietary school has shifted away from an exclusive emphasis on preparing students for postgraduate employment, toward offering courses that also emphasize general competencies" (Hyslop & Parsons, as cited in Lee, 1996, p. 3).

Now single-campus proprietary schools are giving way to multicampus and multimodal for-profit conglomerates. Now, as before, there are concerns as to whether these providers are largely bottom line oriented, rather than quality focused. Now, as before, there are widespread criticisms of the ways that students are aggressively recruited to the colleges.

One higher education policy expert has noted that within the proprietary sector, "There's no doubt that the worst for-profits are ruthlessly exploiting the commodified college degree. But they didn't commodify it in the first place" (Carey, 2010).

A report to the United States Senate Committee examining student enrollment data from 30 for-profit colleges showed that from 54% to 80% (depending on the college) of the students who enrolled in those colleges' degree programs in 2008–9 left without a degree by mid-2010 (U.S. Senate Health, Education, Labor, and Pensions Committee, 2012, p. 24). Because such a large proportion of their students have been dropping out, deep in debt, with little ability to pay back their loans, Congress has been investigating the fact that students at for-profit colleges are responsible for 47% of all student federal loan defaults in 2008 and 2009 (U.S. Senate Health, Education, Labor, and Pensions Committee, 2012).

One likely reason is that some colleges compensated recruiters by giving them commissions based on how many students they enrolled. These recruiters may have encouraged applicants to enroll in programs for which they were inadequately prepared or promised them unrealistic career outcomes.

Now federal financial aid is in danger of being withdrawn from the colleges. Several institutions lost their eligibility for federal financial aid because they violated the Higher Education Act Amendments of 1998, which caps the percentage of a for-profit college's revenue that may come from federal government financial aid at 90%.

For-profit colleges are highly dependent on their students' access to federal dollars. Students at for-profit colleges received about 25% of all federal Pell Grants and loans in 2009–10, even though they represented only about 13% of all college students (U.S. Senate Health, Education, Labor, and Pensions Committee, 2012, p. 24). According to *The Chronicle of Higher Education*, the University of Phoenix collected more than $5 billion from government student aid. Five other large providers of for-profit college programs each collected around $1 billion through federal aid dollars (Kingkade, 2012).

Accrediting agencies are being pushed by Congress and the U.S. Department of Education to ensure that the for-profits are not luring students into programs with false advertising and promises of future jobs and earnings that are unrealistic. The accrediting agencies are also being asked to monitor for-profit colleges to ensure that enough of their students are graduating. That could be a big stick—colleges lose their federal aid dollars if they lose accreditation.

To quell the criticisms and maintain accreditation, several for-profit college corporations have already begun the process of improving recruitment, and moving away from clearly false promotions of their programmatic offering outcomes. John McKernan, former president and chair of the board of Education Management Corporation (through August 2012), the second largest provider of for-profit colleges, told me that for-profit colleges should be given the ability to say no to students whom their counselors believe are taking on too much debt. John McKernan, who remains on the board, said in response to default issues that some of the for-profits have proposed requiring institutions whose student loan defaults are above an acceptable level to share in the costs of those defaults "so they have skin in the game." The nonprofits do not have their own skin in the game, and that removes much of the pressure for change in their sector.

Education Management Corporation has four divisions: the Art Institutes, Argosy University, Brown Mackie College, and South University. The Art Institutes, which specialize in design, media arts, fashion, and culinary arts, has more than 50 locations.

The company enrolled more than 130,000 students in 2012 and had more than 24,000 full-time, part-time, and adjunct faculty and other staff (Education Management Corporation, 2013a). It had assets of almost $3 billion as of June 30, 2012 (Education Management Corporation, 2013b).

McKernan is one of the savviest people in the country about what is on the horizon in higher education. Part of the reason has to do with the fact that he has bridged both the nonprofit and for-profit sectors and has a wide vision of issues impacting multiple sectors.

He was elected the governor of Maine for two terms, from 1987 to 1995, and knows a lot about many aspects of higher education. He served two terms in the Maine House of Representatives, where he first got elected at age 24, and later was elected twice as a member of Congress, before becoming governor. His wife, Olympia Snowe, is a former long-term U.S. senator from Maine. In 2013 he became the president of the U.S. Chamber of Commerce Foundation.

A man who is thoughtful and knowledgeable about both for-profit and not-for-profit education, McKernan has had significant responsibilities in both arenas for many years. Even now, along with his high-profile corporate position, he still provides public service in higher education in the state of Maine, as chair of the board of the Maine Community College System.

He sees no conflict in his two positions, because he believes that community colleges are different from other nonprofit colleges, and less vulnerable to outside competitive forces, because they have a cost structure and subsidies that make them quite cost-effective for students. For the rest of public and private nonprofit colleges, the cost is high and the governance unwieldy.

For-profit colleges will continue to expand, McKernan believes, both because they are very flexible and because they can make timely decisions from the top. He also points out, "The next generation of college students will be more adept at using online learning, and the online products available to them will be much better."

The governance structure is a key to the ability of the for-profit sector's expansion. According to McKernan,

> We can make more top-down decisions, and we can make them quickly, if we must. We are more responsive to market needs, and to our faculty staffing needs. We can be more precise on salaries, on teaching loads, on course scheduling, and have more flexibility on academic programs we want to

initiate or need to terminate. There is a lack of flexibility in traditional higher education.

When asked about the closing of programs, McKernan noted that his company invests significantly in the programs it offers—it expects them to last a long time.

What the for-profits can do is make rapid responses to needs. They are agile and flexible. They can change quickly to meet emerging market needs. They have managerial control, and are able to exercise cost containment. For the most part, they use rental facilities for their programs and have no residence halls to support. They outsource and can unbundle their services. They mainly use adjunct faculty, have no tenure, and except under rare circumstances do not offer athletics.

Furthermore, interest in the kind of programs many of them offer is growing. As the president of for-profit Ashford University told me, "The market for career-related programs will be stronger over the next 10 years."

Rapid Response Time

In a private conversation, the president of a regional accrediting agency told me that a public college system administrator said that it would take one of his schools about two and a half years to gear up for a new program, at a minimum. And that is usually just for the program approval stage. After that come system approvals in some states, following established hiring protocols, and waiting for new program leaders to do national searches for their start-up faculty, under the institutional or system guidelines. Then they have to wait for the newly hired folks to show up the following semester or year.

By comparison with the several years it takes to bring a new program to fruition at a public or an independent college, the turnaround time for a highly competent for-profit school to develop and implement a new program can be as fast as four to six weeks. A for-profit's decision-making function is far more efficient than that of the nonprofit model. Even if it takes a year to plan and implement a new program, that is substantially much less time than almost any nonprofit college would need.

Richard L. Pattenaude, the president of for-profit Ashford University, told me that in the for-profit world of higher education "the sense of urgency is palpably different" than in the nonprofit world. Pattenaude spent much of his career leading public higher education institutions, before joining Ashford.

Ashford has a sense of urgency because in 2012 the Western Association of Schools and Colleges (WASC) denied accreditation to the school.

Ashford, which was enrolling about 90,000 students, most of them online, with less than 1,000 on its one traditional campus, needs to be accredited in order for its students to receive federal financial aid.

Bridgepoint, the company that owns Ashford, quickly hired Pattenaude, a respected higher education leader who had previously served as chancellor of the University of Maine System, to help make the changes necessary for its programs to be considered worthy of accreditation. Pattenaude told me that Ashford was in the process of "focusing on quality as a key strategy." This would be necessary now because "quality will be more important, given increased transparency," he added. Shortly after our conversation, Ashford received initial accreditation from WASC.

Timing is not everything, of course, even in the world of business, but early entrance into a field can give a business or college a definite advantage over later responders. It is essential to be able to start new programs quickly, and equally essential to be able to cut back on or eliminate a program that can no longer place its graduates. Ease of exit is every bit as important as ease of entry in the marketplace.

Colleges with tenured faculty can find it almost impossible to close a program over the short term. Faculty committees will urge continued study of the issue, and members of the program scheduled for elimination will argue that tenure protects their rights, even though most college bylaws stipulate that even tenured faculty can be let go if their programs are reduced or eliminated. Nonetheless, the traditions of our higher education culture make the process protracted and painful.

At Temple University, in 1982, with the university facing significant financial problems, 52 tenured faculty members, in programs that were severely underenrolled, lost their tenured positions. Most of them were then offered buyouts or nontenured administrative positions. Only four faculty members declined all offers. The faculty fought for and got Temple University placed on the American Association of University Professors (AAUP) censure list. It was not removed from censure until 1992, when a rapprochement was reached among those involved in the disagreements.

To reach the agreement, Temple trustees approved a position that declared such layoffs would not occur in the future unless the school faced a financial exigency or an entire department or academic program was being shut down. The AAUP defines *financial exigency* as an "imminent financial crisis which threatens the survival of the institution as a whole." It must threaten the entire institution, and not be able to "be alleviated by less drastic means" (AAUP, 2013a).

By contrast, for-profit college corporations can address market needs quickly and directly. As one for-profit leader told me, "We can make top-down decisions. We can be more responsive to markets, even to the needs of our faculty. In addition, we can be more precise in faculty compensation." Most of all, he said, "We have more flexibility to start and to terminate, if we need to."

Training for Market Needs

Whereas public and independent colleges have traditions that favor dispersed centers of decision making, for-profit colleges have owners or managers who can make and usually enforce their decisions. While the nonprofit schools have multiple constituencies to protest or tie up decisions for long periods of time, for-profit colleges have one constituency, the owners.

As with all colleges, for-profit college leaders must obey the laws, the requirements for accreditation, and other approvals that may be necessary for their students to qualify for federal student aid, or licensure in the professions for which they are studying, and for the colleges to have the right to offer programs in the states where they provide instruction.

The landscape on which for-profit colleges operate is continually shifting. The job market in the United States responds to local demand as well as international economic ups and downs. When demand for a particular type of skilled employee is greater than the supply, trade schools and colleges jump in to help provide training to meet employer needs.

For-profit colleges pride themselves on being job-market sensitive. Certainly, much of their career focus is on job-related degree programs in areas such as business, art, and health professions. Some publicly traded for-profit companies have purchased mom-and-pop-type for-profit schools and reoriented them from underperforming technical trade programmatic areas to more market-hot areas, such as allied health programs.

The University of Phoenix (2013b) website states that it offers associate's, bachelor's, master's, and doctoral degrees, as well as certificate programs. It lists its major areas of offerings as business, criminal justice, education, nursing and health care, social sciences, technology, and continuing education.

The University of Phoenix (2013a) Division of Nursing webpage claims that 41,000 nurses have graduated from its schools. It offers LPN (licensed practical nurse) through graduate nursing programs. The site also states that the university has 1,000 faculty teaching criminal justice courses and 1,400 faculty in its nursing program. Of course, many of the faculty are part-time and may be teaching only one course.

In spite of the fact that for-profit schools have been set up to meet job market needs, many of them do not do very well. Just as our public and independent colleges often prepare students for career opportunities they frequently cannot access, either because the training is inadequate or because the market for the particular field is too small for the number of students being trained for it, so do for-profit colleges, but some are doing it in much less acceptable ways.

It is one thing to admit more students to teacher education programs than are likely to be able to get teaching jobs in their regions. It is much more troublesome when a college builds its recruitment program on implied promises of strong career placements while knowing that there are far too few jobs in the particular field for which the college is offering training.

In 2010, the Accrediting Council for Independent Colleges and Schools asked the Career Education Corporation to "show cause" why its college should retain its accreditation. A number of the corporation's programs were not able to place at least 65% of their graduates in the field for which they had trained them. This is a problem for many for-profit institutions, which put a lot of their dollar expenditures in the up-front activity of marketing their programs and recruiting new students at the apparent expense of ensuring that there are enough opportunities to place them appropriately.

Increasingly, there are allegations that the schools knowingly recruit and accept more students than they are able to place. In 2010, the Career Education Corporation offered to pay $40 million to settle a class-action lawsuit filed by some of its former students. The litigants accused one of the corporation's schools of misleading students about their job prospects. In the lawsuit, students claimed that the college reported placement rates of between 75% and 96% for its culinary-arts and baking programs. It did not disclose that most of its graduates' placements were in minimum-wage culinary jobs for which the graduates did not need degrees (Field, 2011).

Recent investigations by Congress, focusing on the reasons for high dropout rates and low federal student loan repayment rates, have noted that the for-profit sector, especially many of its large corporate providers, seem prone to the problem of overpromoting the career opportunities of their programs and underreporting the likelihood of successfully attaining the positions for which they claim to prepare their students.

Cost Containment

A publicly traded education corporation leader, who previously worked in nonprofit colleges, put the difference between the two types of management best. "They work with a sharper pencil," he told me. He also said of the for-profits, "Our ability to be more efficient allows us to control tuition costs."

Managerial Control

There is little real managerial control in public higher education. At most independent colleges, the tradition of shared governance also holds sway, although a small percentage of lower-tier colleges may observe it more with lip service than reality. A vote of "no confidence" by the faculty is usually enough to end a college president's tenure in the office.

Shared governance means that the faculty participates in many of the crucial decisions made in their college. The AAUP Committee on College and University Governance statement of 1920 called for shared responsibility among governing boards, administrations, and faculties in "personnel decisions, selection of administrators, preparation of the budget, and determination of educational policies." It has been supplemented over the years with the additions of faculty governance and academic freedom; budgetary and salary matters; financial exigency; the selection, evaluation, and retention of administrators; college athletics; governance and collective bargaining; and the faculty status of college and university librarians (AAUP, 2013b).

Some faculty appear to believe that almost any decision is properly one that they should participate in and that, furthermore, deviation from a representative faculty group recommendation is apostasy. When I was serving as a university administrator, my onetime denial of tenure to a faculty candidate, after the tenure committee had voted to recommend the awarding of tenure, was greeted with anger and alarm, as if I had violated a long-agreed-to contract. I told the faculty committee members that my decisions were not rubber stamps, or they would not be necessary, and reminded them that they had previously come to me with questions before making their recommendations about marginal candidates to see how I might view those potential recommendations. I also assured them that I respected and valued their input and only rarely acted against their advice. Even then, I did so because I had information about the candidate that might not be available to the committee. In fact, in the aforementioned case, some students had brought serious confidential concerns to our dean.

In other cases, deans, provosts, and presidents might need to deny tenure, even to well-qualified candidates. Tenure is a lifetime contract, in essence, because the AAUP standard requires that a faculty member with tenure cannot be terminated except for cause or financial exigency, with both standards defined so that they can rarely be met.

One reason an administrator might need to deny tenure to someone is that a department or program already has enough tenured faculty to meet its needs. Another reason is that enrollment in a program is falling and the program can no longer enroll enough students to justify additional faculty hires, especially tenured ones, with their lifetime contracts.

Despite the expectation of faculty for shared governance, faculty generally believe that university presidents have vast powers, including the ability to somehow "hide" large quantities of monies from the prying eyes of staff.

When I was a faculty member at Temple University, a colleague on one of our arts and sciences college committees seriously charged that the president's office was secreting tens of millions of dollars in hidden accounts, in order to deceive the faculty about the true value of resources available for faculty salary increases. Temple University was then, and remains, a state-aided university, which means that its records are open to public inspection. The full budget is easily accessible on Temple's website.

One area of contention between faculty and administration in higher education is the presumed growing use of business models of institutional management. A particular sore point is the creeping use of business terminology, which many faculty dislike. A new president of a proprietary college told me that even his college faculty had requested that the president commit to making the college "more academic." When asked for specifics, faculty said that they objected to the use of the term *corporate*, in a policy labeled "corporate travel policy."

Throughout higher education, college presidents sense that they have little real power. One nonprofit college president is reputed to have said to colleagues, "When I send out a directive to faculty, they consider it a request for a meeting."

Years ago, I was tapped as an assistant to the then president of Temple University. A faculty colleague I bumped into on the way to my new office let me know how unimportant my new position was. He also reminded me how far I had fallen from grace, as a faculty member selling out to the administration. "As far as I am concerned," he informed me, "your job now is to ensure that we get the supplies and services we need to do our job, and keep out of our way."

One major incursion on college presidents' power is the process in place for search committees. Hiring requirements at traditional nonprofit colleges include an expectation of open searches for all academic or academic-related positions. These committees are usually chaired by faculty or other academic leaders. Usually there are protocols in place that specify how advertising is to occur and the guidelines to be observed.

Most searches, even for senior leaders, presume that a search committee will represent the constituencies the person hired will work with or for. For example, a committee conducting a search for a dean might consist of three faculty members who will serve under the new dean, one administrator from another part of the institution, a student, a staff member, and either an alumnus of the program or perhaps a trustee.

Although senior administrators often ask to be given three or four finalists' names unranked, as the result of a search, faculty do not always give administrators what they ask for. In many cases, they make it perfectly clear what the order of preference is and sometimes state who the only accept-able candidate is, from their point of view. An unsatisfied administrator can choose to reopen a search or capitulate.

Having to hire administrators such as deans through delegation to a search committee can seriously undermine the ability of a senior execu-tive to make hires based on the candidate's commitment to the executive's vision or plans for the institution, or even the comfort level between senior administrators who will need to work closely together. Faculty on search committees frequently weigh scholarly contributions, respect for faculty, and willingness to maintain the status quo within their own units as important signals of administrative appropriateness. Senior executives look for budget management skills, vision, work habits, and evidence of the ability to make and execute tough decisions. The two ways of assessing candidates may not always be in conflict, but if they end up leading to the same outcomes, more often than not it will be accidental and fortuitous.

In the state of Florida, under its Sunshine Law requirement, all public college searches are done in public, including even the most senior positions in the institutions. State laws even prohibit trustees from having any private conversations about candidates. Search committees for college presidents are required to publicly reveal the names of candidates being considered.

This deters many people from applying, especially those who are still employed in positions they do not wish to leave until after they have signed a new contract. When your local newspaper carries a story about you being a candidate for a position at another institution, your supervisors or trustees may decide to let you go, even though you may not end up being hired by the Florida public college in whose search you participated.

Searches as well as all other matters that the board members discuss, including institutional programmatic issues, must be discussed only at publicly noticed meetings, where the comments are all publicly aired and recorded. Board members cannot mention any issues they might later vote on to any other person on the board unless at such a publicly noticed meet-ing; otherwise, they will be in violation of the law. This is an admirable standard theoretically but results in decision making that is slow, not always fully informed, and sometimes more contentious than necessary because the parties in disagreement could not privately work things out. Another prob-lem is that trustees sometimes are loathe to ask questions they have because they fear putting potentially litigable issues on the table when the discussion is open to the entire public.

For-profit institutions do not have these problems. They can make deci-sions at the top, put them into place, and require compliance. They can hire the people they want, and they can part with them when they wish to. They can keep their plans confidential, and they can expose their intentions at the most auspicious times for their businesses, rather than the earliest moments on, as state colleges must do.

But the freedom of for-profit colleges to govern as they wish runs afoul of some of the most cherished ideals and expectations of our model of higher education. Appropriate autonomy of key decision makers, over their own arenas of influence, is a crucial accreditation standard. Governance, and how it is managed, is looked at for every institution, in every institutional accreditation. Most agencies according specialized accreditation also expect some reasonable level of autonomy for the programs they examine relevant to decision-making authority within the unit under consideration.

For example, the American Osteopathic Association (AOA) Commission on Osteopathic College Accreditation (COCA) requires, under Standard Two, its governance, administration, and finance standard, that the College of Osteopathic Medicine (COM) and/or its parent institution develop and implement bylaws that clearly define the governance and organizational structure that enables the medical school to fulfill its mission and objectives. Further, the responsibilities of the COM's administrative and academic officers and faculty must be clearly defined and the dean of the medical college must have responsibility and authority for fiscal management of the medical school (AOA COCA, 2013).

In general, accrediting agencies want academic units to have responsibility for their academic programs to ensure academic quality. This is the norm in nonprofit higher education, where boards of nonprofits are expected to set policy, while paid professionals oversee the operations and programs. This norm is violated in the for-profit model, where the freedom to manage can also allow the freedom to manipulate, misuse, abuse, or otherwise distort the academic mission. I once visited a for-profit college right after the owner had effectively fired all the members of the board of the college. Such an action was within the legal purview of the owner. The question is, Is this a practice that can be consistent with good governance of a college?

The questions revolving around governance and the independence of boards of for-profit colleges are troubling and have not yet been satisfactorily resolved. I recently asked the president of a successful small proprietary professional university what it was like to work for owners, after years of working in the public higher education sector. "I'm in denial," the president said. "I try to think of them as the founders, rather than the owners."

Regional accrediting agencies are taking a harder look at governance issues now. In March 2013, the University of Phoenix learned that its accreditation status was in jeopardy because of governance concerns. The North Central Association of Colleges and Schools Higher Learning Commission placed the university on probation, due to concerns about lack of autonomy of the university from the control of Apollo Group, Inc., the parent holding company of the University of Phoenix.

There are two levels of sanctions that the Higher Learning Commission can impose. "Notice" is often the first step. According to the Higher Learning Commission's guidelines, "An organization is placed on notice if it is found to be pursuing a course of action that could result in its being unable to meet one or more Criteria for Accreditation" (Higher Learning Commission, 2013, p. 79). The other, more serious sanction is "probation." "Probation is a public status signifying that conditions exist at an accredited institution that make it no longer in compliance with one or more of the Commission's Criteria for Accreditation." If an institution does not provide "clear evidence of its progress toward ameliorating those conditions" within a specified time, the commission may withdraw the institution's accreditation (Higher Learning Commission, p. 81). The Commission may also require an institution to show-cause why its accreditation should not be removed.

Regarding the case of the University of Phoenix, the Higher Learning Commission stated,

> Specifically, the review team concluded that the University of Phoenix has insufficient autonomy relative to its parent corporation and sole shareholder, Apollo Group, Inc., to assure that its board of directors can manage the institution, assure the university's integrity, exercise the board's fiduciary responsibilities and make decisions necessary to achieve the institution's mission and successful operation. (Fain, 2013)

Apollo officials responded, "We believe that it is neither remarkable nor improper for a parent corporation to exercise appropriate influence over its wholly owned subsidiary" (Fain, 2013).

The University of Phoenix accreditation status was changed in June 2013, from "probation" to "notice," which still is a very serious charge that the corporation must deal with.

Rented Facilities

Most of the major for-profit corporations, though by no means all, own few of the facilities where they offer instruction, except for either recently bought campuses, or designated campus "show places," used to highlight and add gloss to the corporate brand. As Ashford president Pattenaude told me, "Except for one small campus, we don't carry overhead for bricks and mortar. We don't use our funds to support residence halls, parking lots, and gymnasiums."

The practice of renting facilities is one of the major differences between the ways that for-profit and nonprofit colleges use their funds. Traditional colleges build campuses and own the buildings and facilities on them. Colleges can and do rent some off-campus facilities to supplement their classroom, laboratory, or office needs, but these are usually time-limited efforts to deal with short-term needs, or to span the time between needing more operational space and building and completing new facilities.

Occasionally, a nonprofit college trapped for funds might work with an outside developer whom they contract with to provide a residence hall for some of its students, but this is often the only externally owned facility likely to be part of the campus, or to be considered as more than a short-term emergency solution.

Like many others, I had thought that rental facilities were used by for-profits in order to have quick egress when necessary. In other words, if an area's educational opportunities became saturated, or stopped making a profit, the corporation could fold up its tents in that area and move to a more promising location, without incurring huge sunk costs. Not so, according to Governor McKernan. He says that the renting of facilities is a strategic choice. So I asked him how long the leases are that his corporation typically contracts. I expected 3- to 5-year terms with good "escape" or sublet options, but that apparently is not the norm for the company. Instead, the leases are frequently for 10 years with the right of two 5-year renewals.

Why do this? Why would a for-profit company want to tie itself down with long leases? According to McKernan, when Education Management Corporation opens a location, it does so after extensive market research, and as a result, very few of its locations ever close. "We expect to be there a long time," he states.

Then why not buy the facilities? This is a financial decision, according to McKernan. A building is a major investment. Paying rent requires less upfront dollar investment and is allocated over time, whereas purchasing buildings ties up cash or adds to indebtedness. "We put our money in advanced technology, rather than buildings," McKernan added.

Another surprise involved the other contractual obligation to which most owners renting to Education Management Corporation must agree. Because the company opens programs that it expects will succeed, it asks its landlords to give it the right of first refusal for any openings that occur in the rental property. This allows the corporation to have the means to expand its offerings, if programs grow.

What the company does not want is to run a successful college at a site and then find its landlord refusing to renew its lease. Good management

includes hedging future bets that allow exits when necessary but also guarantee the opportunity to continue in place, where that makes sense.

When I mentioned to McKernan how frequently I saw the University of
Phoenix signs strung across building facades at business parks in major cities,
he said that the Apollo Group, Inc. (of which the University of Phoenix is a
subsidiary) rents many of its facilities near major thruways. "A million cars a
week go by their signs," he noted.

No Residence Halls

Most for-profit colleges do not provide residence halls for their students.
With the exception of the handful of campuses for-profit corporations have
taken over that already had established residence halls, the colleges have neither wanted them nor needed them.

The quintessential student for a for-profit college is nontraditional. If
the students are older, they are likely to already have a place to live. If the
students are younger, they are likely to be less affluent and living with family, rather than on their own. Many of the students are working and going
to school part-time, so they are not usually interested in living in college
residences.

Although many colleges do break even or turn a small profit on their
residence hall rentals, relative to the annual operating costs, the sunk investments are substantial and take years, if ever, to be recovered through the modest annual profits. By the time the buildings are paid off, if not long before,
they need to be replaced with more modern, cost-efficient, and amenity-rich
facilities. Most nonprofit colleges have deep backlogs of deferred maintenance projects.

For-profit schools avoid the deferred maintenance problems by not
building residence halls, and by renting rather than building other college
facilities. The corporate colleges also do not concentrate their programs in
areas that require huge capital expenditures, such as research laboratories or
football stadiums.

Outsourcing and Unbundling

Two tendencies prevail in our nonprofit colleges that force up costs and
minimize control. One is to have almost every required service be done by
campus staff. The other is for faculty and students to oppose the devolution
of any program or service presently provided by campus employees to an
outside provider. Opposite ways of providing these services are outsourcing
and unbundling.

Outsourcing

It took a long time for colleges to get to a place where most of them could allow outside vendors to deliver some of their services, such as run their bookstores or staff their cafeterias. Students using commercially managed college bookstores today would have a hard time imagining the bitter and protracted debates their schools went through to make the move from in-house to outside book store management in the 1970s and 1980s. It would be even harder to imagine the fights that took place when national food service vendors were brought in to replace college-managed kitchen help on many campuses.

Today, it is not unusual to find colleges giving outside firms the authority to offer some campus services, although severe conflicts still often occur when an external vendor is allowed to replace an in-house provider.

Outsourcing and unbundling are strategies used to separate functions from having to be provided jointly, by a unitary organization or through a unitary process. *Outsourcing* is the term used for contracting a business process to an outside organization, instead of staffing it with one's own employees. For-profit colleges are far freer to use outsourcing than public and independent colleges are. Therefore, they can allow other companies to deliver many of those outsourced services more cheaply and efficiently than the college can deliver them. Businesses use outsourcing for a variety of reasons, including lowering costs; increasing staffing flexibility; providing access to experts; and minimizing managerial problems such as labor disputes, regulatory issues, taxation concerns, and seasonal and emergency coverage needs.

In recent decades, the public has become aware of the outsourcing of many business services to remote locations. For example, your call to check on your airline ticket may be answered by a responder in Argentina or the Philippines who has been trained to speak in American-accented English. We may not all like this, but we tolerate it because we recognize that it is done to hold costs down. In addition, the clothes you buy may have been assembled in Hong Kong, but the separate parts may have been stitched in Nepal. And the X-rays taken of your twisted ankle may be read overnight by an orthopedic physician in India.

Most businesses outsource the majority of services they need so that they can concentrate their activities on honing the delivery of their core product or service. Public and independent colleges' core services are providing teaching and cocurricular life activities for their students. They have been more reluctant than for-profit colleges to contract out other services to third parties.

I was a young professor when my then university decided to outsource its bookstores. There was widespread criticism from faculty and students at the time, who protested that the commercially owned bookstore company being brought in could not be relied on to carry certain texts and other books faculty might desire to order unless it was profitable for the company to do so. Today, most colleges outsource their bookstores, and a majority of colleges outsource the management of their cafeterias and dining halls. Some colleges outsource computer services. A small but growing number are contracting out the cleaning and maintenance of their college facilities.

Interestingly, even some academic courses are being offered by third parties, who split fees with an accredited college, for programs the third party either markets or produces for larger audiences than the nonprofit college is able to attract on its own. For the program to be acceptable to accrediting agencies, however, the college faculty must oversee and approve the academic content of the courses.

Unbundling

Many businesses use bundling as a sales strategy. For example, fast-food establishments often offer promotions featuring a burger, french fries, and a soda at a special price, lower than it would be if the items were purchased separately. Other companies may package two pillowcases with two sheets. Still others, such as cable television service providers, bundle a number of stations, including ones you do not want along with ones you desire, in the sets of offerings they present to their customers.

Unbundling, on the other hand, involves separating a service or set of products into their component parts. Whereas everything about a particular product or service historically may have had to be constructed by the same person or same unit, the ability now exists to unwrap the packaging and allow the parts to be developed in different places and by different people.

Unbundling college offerings can empower a provider to have one set of academics offer classes, another set give and grade examinations for the classes, and still another group evaluate whether students have learned what they needed, or what an industry or profession requires of them.

Unbundling can also refer to other ways that institutions can separate or specialize in how they offer services and products. Anya Kamentz (2010) points out that "books can be freed from the printed page, courses freed from geographical classrooms and individual faculty, and students can be free from enrolling in a single institution" (p. xi). She adds that institutions that focus on just one particular discipline will increasingly be able to find interested applicants.

Higher education is ripe for unbundling, some suggest. There are three legs on the higher education stool: teaching, research, and service. Arthur Levine (2013) was quite prescient when he wrote that unbundling would occur because only teaching "is universally profitable to colleges and universities.

Research is sort of like NCAA football. It is only profitable to a very small number of schools. Everyone else loses money" (p. 5). He went on to say that new "providers" who would enter the market would only be interested in the teaching leg, and added that there would be a reduction in the number of physical college campuses.

One higher education leader gave me an example of how teaching could be unbundled. First you divide the tasks involved in developing, teaching, and assessing a course. Next you have industry gurus tell you what they need a job prospect in a professional field to know. Then you hire curriculum specialists to design what has to be covered.

After that is done, you can hire a world-class faculty member to offer the course. You can also hire specialists in assessment to design ways to measure performance and outcomes. Faculty are content specialists, this leader pointed out. They are not necessarily good judgers of learning outcomes, nor are they experts in testing and assessment.

I suspect that many of us have had brilliant professors who did not write good examination questions or were not always able to help us with issues we had trouble understanding. Unbundling may seem complicated, but, in fact, it allows each step in the learning process to be managed by specialists in those discrete steps. We do not have to see them working to benefit from their efforts. And whether or not we approve of this disaggregation of teaching and learning processes, they are bound to increasingly be used in the market, as purveyors of higher education seek ways to measure and document their efforts and achievements.

As we have seen, for-profit colleges have indeed entered the market, offering teaching services. The market is growing, and along with that growth has come the realization that various kinds of bundling and unbundling may yet be proffered through both the for-profit and nonprofit sectors. Several for-profit colleges, and at least one nonprofit, the University of Southern New Hampshire, are already in the process of developing models of teaching and assessing that use cutting-edge techniques to unbundle their course offerings.

Adjunct Faculty

"There is a buyer's market for faculty," a for-profit college president told me. As long as doctoral programs produce more graduates than the market can absorb in full-time college positions, surplus faculty labor will be available. Such a surplus creates a vast opportunity for institutions that want to use that surplus labor.

One for-profit system president shared his company's model for how faculty will be utilized. One example he offered was the use of a four- or five-person team composed of faculty who might teach history courses. The team of history faculty will agree on outcomes, metrics, rubrics, and textbooks for the courses they will offer. A course designer will then help to develop each course. The course material will be comparable regardless of who teaches it. A video and technical expert will help plug it into the delivery system. Finally, an assessment expert will develop the tools for evaluating the effectiveness of the course, the faculty member teaching it, and the success of the students who took the course. This is a real example of how for-profit colleges are unbundling the delivery of college courses.

This model can work because the faculty are not employed full-time and are not tenured, so they cannot argue against nor prevent such a disassembled method of course development from being applied in their program areas. For-profit colleges benefit from the fact that their faculty lack managerial control over the full presentation and assessment of their courses, and that most of the faculty are not full-time employees.

One of the major areas where for-profit colleges have lower costs than their nonprofit competitors is their faculty. Most of the for-profit colleges use part-time faculty, saving them the costs of benefit packages and allowing them to hire their teaching staff at costs far below what full-time faculty would earn.

Sadly, the for-profits have availed themselves of the part-time faculty that our traditional colleges have already exploited. First they exploited them by offering them graduate programs from which they were unlikely to find appropriate career opportunities. Then they used that same pool of graduates as part-time teachers, to help lower the institutional cost of providing undergraduate classes.

Traditional colleges used to use mostly full-time faculty, with a smattering of part-time supplemental faculty. In recent decades, that has changed so dramatically that overall about half of all faculty at nonprofit colleges and universities are part-time hires (Coalition on the Academic Workforce, 2012). These part-time faculty combined with the full-time contingent (or temporary) faculty represent more than three of every four faculty members.

That still provides a lot more generous sprinkling of full-time faculty than many of the for-profits use. For example, at the time when Ashford University was denied accreditation in 2012 by the WASC, it had only 56 full-time faculty out of a staff of 2,514 faculty and 875 instructional staff. By contrast, the university had 2,305 staff working in enrollment services. According to the accreditation team report, "The team was concerned that this does not suggest an optimum alignment of institutional resources with stated mission and priorities" (Fain, 2010).

In addition to their use of part-time or adjunct faculty, few, if any, for-profit education companies offer tenure. Whereas colleges with tenure systems find it difficult and sometimes close to impossible to do rapid programmatic turnarounds, colleges without tenure are free to move programs and personnel to reflect market needs.

No Athletics

Another large cost advantage that for-profit colleges have is that they do not support intercollegiate sports. They do not give athletic scholarships and they do not build stadiums. They do not lose huge sums of money, because they need to justify any losses they experience by showing how they otherwise profit from them, a standard intercollegiate athletic programs would be hard pressed to meet.

If you have no intercollegiate athletic programs, you do not lose hundreds of thousands or millions of dollars. Even small colleges with part-time coaching staffs must still pay for a coach and at least one assistant coach for almost every varsity team. Add to that the cost of equipment, gym or field facilities, players' outfits and gear, team travel costs, and athletic trainers and physical therapists to be available at games.

If you have no intercollegiate athletic programs, you do not have to provide training rooms and fields and stadiums in which to play the sports. You do not have to worry about the integrity of your athletic programs, and you are not beholden to your coaches or athletic directors.

Of course, for-profit colleges serve a lot of older, working adults, a market group more interested in gaining job credentials than in supporting intercollegiate sports athletes at their schools. There can be an occasional exception, however, as when a for-profit company buys a college that was previously a nonprofit and inherits athletic fields and arenas. It may decide to let them be used for a while.

As for-profit companies grow and improve, we can expect to see enhanced provision of some social activities where appropriate, in order to improve a brand's competitive position. Whatever activities are offered, however, will have to be demonstrably related to either attracting students or increasing income. One for-profit institution, Grand Canyon University, has already moved in this direction by becoming a member of the NCAA.

Grand Canyon is a for-profit Christian university whose stock is traded on the stock exchange. Like Liberty University, which is nonprofit, Grand Canyon has grown largely through its online programs. Grand Canyon has almost 25,000 students.

When asked why a for-profit college would want to join the NCAA, several for-profit college company executives were perplexed. One for-profit leader responded, "My best guess is that they plan to use any publicity they generate to enhance the reputation of the rest of their offerings. They bought a nice campus. Most of their programs will be located off the campus, though. I can't see a big benefit for them."

Someone else, not an educator, proffered a different possible reason. This person is involved in state-of-the-art media. "Some colleges could make money from athletics, if the cable companies carry more of their games. Restaurants and bars that feature constant playing of games could lead to more revenue for some schools," he said.

In fact, cable TV fees for sports networks keep rising. Subscribers to cable services generally have to pay for sports channels they may not want or use, just as students have to pay for intercollegiate teams on which they do not play. Because there is a lot of discussion now about potentially reining in the ability of cable companies to require purchasing packages of channels, instead of the customer just selecting preferred channels, the profits of providers could go down, and if so, the returns to colleges would then also likely decrease.

All in all, though, few for-profit college corporations invest in intercollegiate athletics. Most of them simply do not find it profitable to do so.

For-Profit Colleges and Cocurricular Activities

Whereas many of the smaller mom-and-pop-type for-profit colleges may provide some on-campus activities, many of the larger, corporate ones do not. Their models are built on the efficient delivery of course content, not on the development of healthy and well-adjusted future citizens.

Of course, no colleges are able to effectively socialize all of their students to healthy norms. Unfortunately, we often are witness to news reports of violent incidents, including mass killings, taking place on American college campuses. Yet most residential colleges, and certainly faith-based and elite independent colleges, do strive to produce ethically honorable graduates. Honor codes are but one symbol of this cultural effort.

Campus-based for-profit colleges may make efforts to develop cocurricular activities, for accreditation purposes or to increase their competitive position, but when they do, it is more likely to spring from profit-motivated concerns than from corporate social responsibility commitments.

The term *cocurricular*, as used in the academy, means programs and activities that are extracurricular, which are provided by a college to enhance the overall environment of the college experience. These activities include participating in clubs, such as a French club, a hiking club, or an issues-oriented club. They include athletic activities and theater programs, as well as dances and other social activities. They are especially directed toward residential students, with an eye toward keeping them healthy, involved, and happy while matriculating at the college.

These activities are important ones. They may help a student develop friends and a sense of purpose, while they integrate the student into the fabric of campus life. Although not all cocurricular expenditures made by nonprofit colleges may be warranted, some for-profit schools offer some extra activities as a way of helping students bond to the college, in the hopes that this will help with retention. More such services are likely to be offered in the future.

Limits to For-Profit Higher Education Expansion

A number of for-profit education corporations have faced some withering criticisms for some of the tactics they have employed to attract students, and even more criticism for their inability to graduate most of their students, while leaving many of them deeply in debt with no degrees to show for their efforts and money.

For-profit colleges will improve what they are doing. There is a lot of money to be made in offering higher education services. Those companies that do it best for reasonable costs will thrive in the marketplace. Profit is a powerful incentive. As corporations seek to improve their brand reputation, some of the improvements they make will necessarily benefit their students.

Because they have the promise of becoming extremely successful, and making a great deal of money for their investors, they are likely to continue to grow. One reason is that they are needed by the millions of potential students who cannot find the programs they need being offered by most nonprofit colleges at times and in ways that are accessible for them. Another reason is that quite a few of the larger for-profit companies are making significant investments in developing improved teaching methods and student support systems. Some are building assessment tools much more sophisticated than most colleges use today. With those tools, the firms will refine how and what they offer to students, to make their programs of study as outcome oriented as possible.

Some for-profits are buying the campuses of failing nonprofits in order to have a campus face to showcase their brand, or to offer to those who want a campus-based learning experience. Other efforts are under way too. In fact, some savvy for-profit colleges are borrowing strategies from the nonprofit sector to look as much as possible like the college your parents attended.

Strayer University, which has more than 100 campus locations, has announced that it will provide what it calls a "graduation fund" to "cover up to 25 percent of the cost of an undergraduate degree for dedicated students" (Strayer University, 2013). The way this will work is that for every three classes a new student successfully completes Strayer will allocate an award that will entitle that student to take a future class cost free. Of course, this is really a discount, but it is an extremely smart one. The discount does not kick in until a student completes three courses. All too many students at for-profit schools drop out after the first one or two courses. This discount also does not apply up front, but after the fact. It is similar to the marketing difference between selling a sweater for half price and offering a buy-one-get-one-free deal, which ensures that every buyer of a sweater spends at least the full price of one sweater before the discount kicks in.

Maybe nonprofit schools could learn from this and offer half-price tuition for the second year of classes, for students who satisfactorily complete their first year. That would also be a 25% reduction, but colleges do not do that. Instead, many front-load their discount awards, offering the biggest savings for the first year, with the hope that those who attend will stay, even as the net price goes up.

Strayer also announced that it was freezing its tuition through the 2014 school year. Strayer, with 50,000 students, is obviously using marketing tools similar to those used in other profit-making sectors, to ensure that it holds on to its present numbers as it seeks to grow. Nonprofits would do well to try new marketing strategies themselves, instead of continuing to depend on the same old tired front-end discounts.

DeVry has also begun offering scholarships and discounts for some of its programs. Other for-profits are likely to follow, as competition among themselves as well as with growing online nonprofit college programs heats up. Nonprofits such as Liberty University and Western Governors University charge a lot less for some of their online offerings than many of the profit-seeking corporations do. According to an article in *The Chronicle of Higher Education*, "[the for-profit college sector] that was once a major disruptive force in higher education is being disrupted itself" (Blumenstyk, 2013).

There is another possibility for the future of some for-profit schools that could be very troubling. Not all are going to be successful. Some will fail because of the current negative publicity. Others will fail because they will not be strong enough or have high enough quality to prevail in the marketplace, as competition grows.

One potential solution being proposed for failing for-profit colleges is to change to nonprofit status. A for-profit college could transition to tax-exempt status and be eligible for tax-exempt gifts, both of which could improve its bottom line. A presentation at an annual meeting of the trade association of for-profit colleges explained just how to make such conversions (Halperin, 2013). This is not an entirely new strategy, though. In the past, there were always some proprietary colleges that made the transition to nonprofit status.

Critics worry that some of these conversions could allow these colleges to reap the benefits of nonprofit status while maintaining the perks and privileges that come with private ownership, by being a for-profit wolf in nonprofit clothing. There is in fact plenty to worry about if for-profits start converting to nonprofit status. The biggest issue is the possibility that these colleges could be managed the way some tax-exempt charities are, with lots of donations coming in to support the executive leadership and fund-raising operations, and too few dollars spent on the issues for which the charities solicit support. As one critic wrote, "The concern is that some of these sharp operators may attempt to use their newly-transformed non-profit colleges as private piggy banks, or use their new status to continue selling predatory programs to vulnerable students—veterans, single mothers, immigrants, low-income people" (Halperin, 2013).

To prevent the abuse of tax laws and education standards, accreditation agencies and state licensing departments are going to have to be very vigilant, particularly in exploring any links that any newly converted nonprofit colleges retain to for-profit subsidiaries or holding companies.

References

American Association of University Professors. (2013a). *Financial exigency, academic governance, and related matters.* Retrieved from http://www.aaup.org/report/ financial-exigency-academic-governance-and-related-matters

American Association of University Professors. (2013b). *Governance of colleges & universities.* Retrieved from http://www.aaup.org/issues/governance-colleges-universities

American Osteopathic Association Commission on Osteopathic College Accreditation. (2013). *Accreditation of colleges of osteopathic medicine: COM accreditation standards and procedures.* Retrieved from http://www.osteopathic.org/inside-aoa/ accreditation/predoctoral%20accreditation/Documents/COM-accreditation -standards-effective-7-1-2013.pdf

Blumenstyk, G. (2013, June 16). Nonprofit colleges compete on for-profits' turf. *The Chronicle of Higher Education.* Retrieved from http://chronicle.com/article/ For-Profit-Colleges-Consider/139851/

Carey, K. (2010, July 25). Why do you think they're called for-profit colleges? *The Chronicle of Higher Education.* Retrieved from http://chronicle.com/article/Why -Do-You-Think-Theyre/123660/

Coalition on the Academic Workforce. (2012, June). *A portrait of part-time faculty members: A summary of findings on part-time faculty respondents to the Coalition on the Academic Workforce Survey of Contingent Faculty Members and Instructors.* Retrieved from http://www.academicworkforce.org/CAW_portrait_2012.pdf

Education Management Corporation. (2013a, May). *About EDMC: Celebrating more than 40 years of delivering quality higher education to the communities we serve.* Retrieved from http://www.edmc.edu/About/Default.aspx

Education Management Corporation. (2013b, May). *Education Management Corporation reports fiscal 2013 third quarter results.* Press release. Retrieved from http://investors.edmc.edu/phoenix.zhtml?c=87813&p=irol-newsArticle&ID=1813993&highlight=

Fain, P. (2010, July 10). Rise of the accreditor? *Inside Higher Ed.* Retrieved from www.insidehighered.com/news/2012/07/10/profit-ashford-university-loses-accreditation-bid

Fain, P. (2013, February 26). Possible probation for Phoenix. *Inside Higher Ed.* Retrieved from insidehighered.com/news/2013/02/26/university-phoenix-faces-possible-probation-accreditor

Field, K. (2011, November 21). Job placement problems could cost some career education colleges their accreditation. *The Chronicle of Higher Education.* Retrieved from http://www.chronicle.com/article/Job-Placement-Problems-Could/129862/

Halperin, D. (2013, February 11). If a for-profit college becomes a non-profit, is that good? Not necessarily. *Huffington Post.* Retrieved from http://www.huffingtonpost.com/davidhalperin/if-a-for-profit-college-b_b_2661788.html

Higher Learning Commission. (2013, November). *Commission policies affecting institutional affiliation.* Retrieved from http://policy.ncahlc.org/

Honick, C. A. (1995). The story behind proprietary schools in the United States. In D. A. Clowes & E. M. Hawthorne (Eds.), *New Directions for Community Colleges,* (No. 91, pp. 27–40). San Francisco, CA: Jossey-Bass.

Kingkade, T. (2012, September 28). For-profit colleges collect $32 billion, 3 lose federal aid eligibility for failing 90/10 rule. *Huffington Post.* Retrieved from http://www.huffingtonpost.com/2012/09/27/for-profit-colleges-lose-federal-aid-90-10_n_1920190.html

Lee, L. (1996). Community colleges and proprietary schools: Conflict or convergence? In D. A. Clowes & E. M. Hawthorne (Eds.). *New Directions for Community Colleges* (No. 91, pp. 5–15). San Francisco, CA: Jossey-Bass.

Levine, A. (2013, May 26). *Privatization in higher education, 2001.* National Governor's Association Online. Retrieved from http://www.nga.org/files/live/sites/NGA/files/pdf/HIGHEREDPRIVATIZATION.pdf

Strayer University. (2013, May 7). *Strayer University launches "graduation fund" to address college affordability and promote graduation.* Retrieved from http://www.strayer.edu/news/strayer-university-launches-%E2%80%98graduation-fund%E2%80%99-address-college-affordability-and-promote

University of Phoenix. (n.d.). *Fact sheet: An overview of Phoenix activities.* Retrieved from http://www.apollo.edu/content/dam/apolloedu/pdf/Apollo-Group-UOPX-Fact-Sheet.pdf

University of Phoenix. (2013a). University of Phoenix: Division of nursing. Retrieved from http://www.phoenix.edu/colleges_divisions/nursing.html

University of Phoenix. (2013b). University of Phoenix hompage. Retrieved from http://www.phoenix.edu/

U.S. Senate Health, Education, Labor, and Pensions Committee. (2012, July 30). *For profit higher education: The failure to safeguard the federal investment and ensure student success* (Majority Committee Staff Report and Accompanying Minority Committee Staff Views July 30, 2012). Retrieved from http://www.help.senate.gov/imo/media/for_profit_report/PartI.pdf

5 What Nonprofit Colleges
Must Do

Most colleges will survive the shakeout that is coming if they develop and use smart strategies. Some of them, already in straitened circumstances, will not be able to last as independent institutions. Some will close. Some will meet their fiscal obligations by selling their campuses and facilities to for-profit providers, just as many hospitals have done. Some will merge with or become branch campuses of larger nonprofit colleges, a process that is already under way. A previously independent College of Podiatry became part of Temple University several years ago, and the Franklin Pierce Law Center became the law school for the University of New Hampshire.

Smaller or vulnerable state colleges whose enrollments are flat or declining are candidates to be reconstituted as branches of larger, more viable campuses. For a decade, three of Maine's state colleges in remote parts of the state have been proposed for mergers that might put them all under one administration, or merge them with other campuses. They are far from the towns and major population centers, in a state with fewer than 1.4 million people and vast unpopulated regions that make it hard for people to travel to where the larger colleges are located. Maine also has an aging population. It has the highest median age in the nation and one of the lowest proportions of young people. Its college-age population is shrinking, so there will be fewer students for most of the state's colleges unless they can attract many more students from outside of Maine. While they search for ways to do this, for-profit and out-of-state nonprofit colleges are increasing their efforts to poach in Maine's potential student pools.

One strategy that the small Maine state colleges are using is to try to attract more students from other states, from Canada, and from islands in the Caribbean. If these colleges are successful at attracting out-of-state students, then taxpayers will have to ask how much of their hard-earned dollars should be used to at least partially underwrite students whose families pay taxes in other jurisdictions. Students from outside a state usually pay higher rates, but some do get financial aid, and all benefit to some degree from the fact that the institution is subsidized by taxpayers.

Many states require their publicly funded medical programs to favor in-state applicants or to admit some fixed percentage of them. This happens with some other expensive-to-offer programs too. But if a large cohort of students from elsewhere is necessary to enable a college to fill its classes so that it may continue to serve some students in its own backyard, is that a compelling reason for supporting the need to do so with public dollars? It is a public policy question that states have not yet asked.

In Maine and elsewhere, as reality intrudes, many colleges will have to adjust their size, tuition, governance, or approach to higher education in order to stay in business, let alone to flourish. The following set of recommendations provides options for altering the way colleges offer their programs to keep the institutions healthy and relevant.

Focus on Outcomes

A college that wants to thrive has to focus on outcomes. Most of higher education, especially accrediting agencies, used to focus on inputs. Inputs are the resources an institution has, such as the number of faculty, the size of classrooms, the proportion of distinguished scholars teaching at the college, and the comprehensiveness of its programs.

Outcomes concern what happens to students as a result of the education they receive at the college. The regional institutional accrediting agencies have wisely made the leap from looking at inputs to investigating outcomes.

When a college is undergoing a review, the accrediting team will look at finances to make sure the institution is fiscally sound. Academic programs will be examined to be sure that students taking particular majors, such as economics, are offered enough upper-level courses to be able to complete their programs of study and graduate on time.

Catalogues and websites will be explored to see if the information students receive is consistent across the college. Attention will be paid to learning resources, such as library and laboratory support, and to policies enabling students to appeal decisions they may consider unfair.

But the newest area of concern, which has been growing for more than a decade, is to put more stress on the outcomes of the education students are provided at a college than on the inputs. The new focus is sharply on assessment and continuous quality improvement.

Assessment is a process in which a college determines what its goals are and then explores measures that let it know if those goals are being met.

This requires reaching agreement on goals and finding ways to measure their attainment.

Colleges can provide evidence of the quality of their programs by evaluating retention and graduation rates, the success of graduating students in being accepted to professional and other postgraduate programs, licensure passage rates (for programs such as nursing), and other outcomes. Good assessment yields knowledge about what is working and what is not working, and the reasons for the outcomes. Continuous quality improvement occurs as colleges use the findings from their measurements to explore ways to improve performance and put those improved processes and programs into place.

According to Judith Eaton, president of the Council for Higher Education Accreditation (CHEA), the most important goal accreditation reviewers seek is assurance of student learning. For accreditation agencies this translates into colleges putting greater emphasis on outcomes, providing evidence of student learning, and offering that evidence by having greater transparency.

Evidence and transparency are the keys to successful efforts to be accredited today. Reviewers have four concerns:

1. How do colleges measure student learning?
2. How do colleges evaluate the programs they offer?
3. How do colleges use feedback from their evaluations to improve their programs and processes?
4. How do colleges share information about their learning outcomes, such as graduation rates, licensure passage rates, and job placements, with the accrediting groups and with their prospective students?

Accrediting commissions are not the only groups asking for this information. The federal government is pushing for transparency, with the Department of Education and Congress each seeking more assurance that the dollars they invest in higher education are being appropriately used and the intended outcomes reached.

One accrediting agency president told me that her accreditation commission members, state and federal monitors, and the general public all support more transparency and want colleges to provide more information to the public. "The only pushback is from the college and university presidents," this higher education leader said.

Focus on Customer Service

"The for-profits have gone through the first phase of their existence. They have been like cowboys riding in the Wild West," one critic told me. But there is one thing they are doing right, according to him: "They have taught those of us in the nonprofit sector the importance of customer service."

Students need to be the number one priority, and they need to know it. College has to be all about serving students before any other considerations are on the table. One easy and important way to serve students is to give them full-time faculty, who are focused on teaching and will be available throughout the semester to help them.

Students deserve to have full-time faculty teaching their classes unless a course is highly specialized, an outside authority is brought in as an adjunct professor in order to provide specialized expertise, or a practitioner is utilized to provide real-world issues and experience. Otherwise, the use of part-time and temporary faculty is abusive to the students as well as the faculty.

The part-time faculty at our two- and four-year colleges teach a high percentage of the classes that students take in their first two years of undergraduate work. Though the students are paying to get taught by the professors whom the college lists in its catalogs, both the students and the part-time instructors are getting cheated. The professors are getting cheated because they went to graduate school, studied, and postponed earning a living until they could become professors like their mentors. Most of them will not get to have regular, ongoing, full-time employment as college professors, nor will they earn decent or dependable livings, as long as they are contingent help. The students are being cheated because they want and deserve the professors whom their colleges deem worthy enough to offer full-time positions. Their adjunct instructors are only able to put in limited hours at each of the colleges where they teach, while trying to string together enough classes to make ends meet.

In addition to lacking job security, part-time faculty generally lack office space, secretarial support, a campus-provided computer, or even a campus phone or phone number. How can students access these adjuncts except at highly limited office hours in a room shared with six to eight or more other adjuncts often with other students or faculty sitting in the same tight quarters? In fact, a study by the Higher Education Research Institute at the University of California, Los Angeles and the Center for the Future of Higher Education found that more than a third of part-time faculty do not even have access to a shared office, let alone a private one (Hurtado, Eagan, Pryor, Whang, & Tran, 2012, p. 11).

Interestingly, Harvard is asking its vast network of well-educated and well-placed alumni to become involved in mentoring students for the online courses it is offering. For a course in the humanities, The Ancient Greek Hero, Harvard sent out an e-mail inviting alumni who had taken the course at the college to volunteer as mentors and discussion facilitators. Where are the Harvard faculty who ought to be doing this? Doesn't Harvard have enough money to pay them?

Build Cocurricular Life

The ability of a college to deliver a quality on-campus experience will remain as an advantage in the marketplace. There will always be potential students seeking a traditional college experience. Most of them will be young, and just out of high school. They will have parents who are in a position to pay for their undergraduate college costs, or they will be students who qualify for substantial scholarship support.

For these young people, young enough, talented enough, or rich enough to be able to attend residential campuses, cocurricular offerings will be an important draw. The services and facilities provided may not have to be lush, but they will have to be good enough to draw students for whom many colleges will be competing.

Throwing money into facilities would be a disastrous policy for the majority of schools, though. Facilities will not be the big differentiator between those that make it and those that do not. The cocurricular investments will need to be made in student services, the kind of services that help the students to learn, make friends, feel welcome at their college, and have rewarding activities.

There is already a fly in the ointment, however. Just as residential colleges become more reliant than ever on differentiating themselves via the quality of the on-campus experience they are able to provide to students, a new entrant in the marketplace is hoping to redefine how it can compete in this territory. It intends to offer a totally different residential and cocurricular life to its students.

The Minerva Project, a new for-profit venture, plans to offer only online classes but have its students living together, first in San Francisco, where the company is headquartered, and then in dormitories in major financial capitals around the world. Minerva has raised about $25 million in start-up funds, and Lawrence H. Summers, former president of Harvard and former U.S. Treasury secretary, is the chair of its advisory board. It plans to recruit its students from around the globe.

Minerva hopes to become a top-tier university, committed to outstanding teaching. To demonstrate that commitment, and to honor strong teaching, Minerva plans to award an annual prize of $500,000, for "extraordinary, innovative teaching" (Lewin, 2013). The classes offered will be online discussion-intensive seminars. According to Ben Nelson, Minerva's founder, the students "will have the same qualifications, grades, extracurricular activities that Ivy League Universities look for, and an intellectual hunger and thirst" (Lewin, 2013).

So, the future of higher education is clearly going to be full of hybrid models, as every player seeks to define an approach that works, a brand that is positive, and a method of bringing in enough revenue to meet the costs of the package of goods and services it plans to offer. There is no one safe model for ensuring success.

Develop a Brand

One important thing that savvy nonprofits can learn from the profit-making sector is the importance of developing and building a brand. It may sound too commercial for the tastes of many academics, and in some ways it is. However, what is essential about having a branded image is the idea that a school must excel at something. Whatever that something is, if it is a desirable enough attribute, the college should hone it, explain its benefits, and market it.

"We think about our brand all the time," the president of Southern New Hampshire University told me. "Because we compete in an online course market space, all of our television ads say, 'Not for Profit.'" He said that he wanted potential enrollees to know that profit was not a motive for his school, especially given the recurring news about the noncompletion rates and high debt loads of for-profit program dropouts. "The public is more educated now about problems with for-profit colleges. A lot of students who call us now ask, 'Is this a real college?' They mean, are we a nonprofit kind of college."

Every college needs to measure what it is doing and see where its strengths are. Then it needs to ask if it has the ability to concentrate on and increase in its areas of strength. For example, if a college has a terrific theater program, it may want to stress that strength. If it is not able to expand the program because it cannot either train or provide enough opportunities for its students to be in audience-attended shows, perhaps it could build related programs, such as set design, advertising art for theaters, or theater and other nonprofit organization management. Similarly, some colleges have excellent nursing programs but cannot expand them because they are limited by the number of trainee positions the hospitals in their region are willing to extend to the programs. They might choose to supplement their strong nursing programs with related health care programs where there is still room to grow.

The effort to build brands is absolutely contingent on a college's willingness and ability to measure and transparently document its outcomes. You cannot sell how strong your journalism or mechanical engineering program is unless you can show how well its graduates are doing—not some cherry-picked graduates, as has been the norm for more than a quarter of a century, but instead, an honest assessment of how a reasonable proportion of the graduates have done. Consumers of educational services are getting smarter. The consumers of the future will expect detailed outcome information before plunking down $150,000 or more for four years of tuition and board.

Eliminate Intercollegiate Athletics

The worst thing about intercollegiate athletics is not the cost, although eliminating costly athletic programs would save colleges a good deal of money and enable them to lower tuition costs. The worst thing is the distortion they cause in the mission and purpose of higher education. "Scholarships" are awarded to students who are not scholars, whereas many bright and scholarly students go unsupported, or inadequately supported. Many athletes are admitted who would not otherwise qualify, in effect taking seats that will be denied to more academically qualified applicants. Top athletes at highly competitive colleges often get room and board as well, something very few scholars are able to receive. In addition, at many schools, athletes are encouraged to take "easy" courses designed for them, and a level of personal tutoring that few other students can access is provided to help them study and learn.

All this is bad enough. But we all know that there is more. The films taken of Rutgers' men's basketball coach Mike Rice pushing and slapping students is only the latest embarrassment by coaches in college sports. Even with the video evidence of his abusive behavior, he still got a severance pay allocation of nearly half a million dollars.

College athletes are regularly in the news too. Colleges often try to cover up abuses and crimes by first-string athletes, in order to appease their coaches or keep the students playing in order to keep their teams competitive.

Colleges say that they offer these competitive sports for all of their students, but only a handful actually get to play, and with rare exception, these are not walk-ons; they are recruits. Of the thousands of students who may attend a college, maybe several hundred in all get to compete in intercollegiate athletics.

Urging colleges to eliminate intercollegiate sports feels a bit like Sisyphus, forever rolling a boulder up a hill only to have it roll right back down. Small victories may come, though, even if they occur largely because some schools will not be able to afford those programs as budgets tighten.

The first college to publicly proclaim that it will eliminate its intercollegiate athletics program is Spelman College, in Atlanta. On November 1, 2013 Spelman's president, Beverly Daniel Tatum, announced that intercollegiate athletics would be eliminated at the end of that academic year. Tatum said that rather than spending nearly $1 million on just 4% of Spelman's students, she would redirect the money "toward a campus wide fitness and wellness initiative that she sees as crucial to her students' health and overall well-being" (Grasgreen, 2012). Spelman has led the way in very publicly moving its intercollegiate athletic expenditures from funding a small number of athletes to fitness programs for all its students.

Although another college, Brigham Young University–Idaho, eliminated intercollegiate athletics in 2000, it did so as part of a major transition. The school had been a two-year institution, Ricks College. It transitioned to a four-year college, Brigham Young University–Idaho. As part of the process of change, a decision was made to eliminate intercollegiate athletics in favor of intramural sports programs, where students at the college play only other students from the same school, for fun and exercise, rather than for revenue and media exposure. (Clayton Christensen and Henry Eyring [2011] wrote a book about the experience.) Spelman College and Brigham may be among the first colleges to take such actions, but they will not be the last.

Most colleges that already participate in intercollegiate athletics will find it hard to opt out without considerable pressure to do so. For most schools, the pressure comes from the opposite direction. But if there is continued economic pressure on college budgets, other small colleges are bound to follow suit.

What small colleges really need are robust intramural sports programs. Because most students at most colleges do not participate on intercollegiate teams, it may prove less disruptive to make the switch to intramural than many college leaders believe. Certainly, it could be a substantial money saver, as college budgets tighten.

Lots of sensible people argue that athletic programs at our colleges have become drivers of the institutions, instead of accessories to support their fundamental purposes. In a letter to the editor of the *New York Times*, one critic of athletics at colleges wrote, "The real problem is that universities should be in the business of education, not mass entertainment." He added that if universities wanted to be entertainment purveyors, they should "continue reducing their faculties and switching to online courses in anticipation of joining the N.F.L. and the N.B.A. instead of just serving as farm teams" (Alter, 2013, p. A18).

Reduce Spending on Facilities

One state governor has already taken an action to force colleges in his state to rethink the dollars they are spending on facilities construction. Governor Terry Branstad of Iowa vetoed funding for three large construction projects planned for the state's three largest universities. He said that the reason he did this was that he wanted officials to recognize the changes that are taking place in the way people learn, such as online education, "rather than have a lot of buildings that are going to sit empty in future years" (Boshart, 2013).

As important as this message is for public colleges, it is even more important for small independent colleges. They need to focus on maintaining or reducing their building footprints, rather than continually trying to expand them. They must turn their capital investments away from facilities and utilize their dollars more effectively on programs and delivery.

One of the most crucial lessons that nonprofit colleges can learn from for-profit education corporations is to rent rather than buy. There are many willing potential business partners who will put up facilities if colleges offer leases of 10 years or longer. Sometimes it may not be easy or feasible to find the right partner, especially for a college in a rural area, where there may not be other potential users for a landlord to fall back on, if a college ceases to renew a lease. For the most part, however, leasing frees an administration from needing to borrow and go into debt for an additional facility. It also frequently holds down the costs of frills and furbelows that might otherwise be added, because, after all, it is just a rented facility. Furthermore, renting is more likely to force a reckoning of the costs and benefits of utilizing a building. Colleges rarely ask, "Do we really need to keep this building open?" unless a building is an eyesore, is falling apart, or is in the path of new construction.

Colleges also need to become more insistent on offering classes at a wider spectrum of times. They need to consider starting earlier in the morning, remaining open later at night, or offering more programs on weekends, especially for working adults. And why can't there be six-day programs, with some classes running Mondays, Wednesdays, and Fridays, and other sets of classes running Tuesdays, Thursdays, and Saturdays? That one change would provide 20% more classroom space immediately, without changing anything else.

Finding new and better ways to minimize the overexpansion and underutilization of facilities should be a continual focus for institutional leaders.

Differentiate Faculty Roles

The concept of faculty role differentiation has actually been around for at least 25 years, although it has been implemented only sporadically. A college faculty that is built on a model of faculty role differentiation can alter or adjust the mix of responsibilities different members of the faculty are expected to undertake. The basic idea is to be able to vary responsibilities of individual faculty members in relation to their strengths or productivity.

This means each faculty member should be initially assigned the same number of credit hours to teach, with reductions in teaching loads based on grant activities or special assignments. Special assignments can include chairing a department or serving in a collegewide role that requires a considerable time commitment. Grants allow faculty to "buy off" class time, replacing it with grant work whose dollars compensate the college, allowing it to hire replacements to teach the courses.

The number of credit hours that a faculty member is normally required to teach varies across the spectrum of institutions, of course. For many community colleges a normal workload may consist of four or five three-hour classes offered each week, each semester, with one semester of work offered in the fall and a second semester in the spring. For a research university, the load likely would be 12 hours per semester, with reductions in teaching loads based on additional research or grant activity, or service. At elite universities such as Yale or Princeton, the load for a distinguished faculty member might be as low as teaching just one or two courses each year.

At many research institutions and other colleges, a typical workload expectation would be similar to that of the policy in place at the University of Colorado Boulder, where faculty are expected to put 40% of their effort into teaching, 40% into research and scholarly effort, and 20% into service. In calculating teaching time, not just actual classroom activity is measured. Preparation time, office hours for advising students, and time for grading papers or tests are also added in.

Service can mean committee work, or special activities undertaken for a faculty member's department, college, or the university as a whole. It includes advising students, sitting on tenure review committees, being a faculty representative to a board of trustees committee, or mentoring new faculty.

Most faculty members work very hard. They are committed to their fields of expertise, and frequently to their students as well, although as Zemsky and Massy (1990) have pointed out, faculty tend to be more beholden to colleagues who specialize in the subdivisions of the fields of interest than in their institutions or students.

A number of higher education leaders have told me that redefining faculty workloads is absolutely essential to making colleges more efficient and more able to hold down tuition costs. Right now, at most colleges, faculty who become full professors are likely to have lower teaching loads than their peers, because it is assumed that they do serious research, which led to their promotions to full professor in the first place.

Once awarded, though, a full professorship is not taken away, even if the bearer of the title no longer does publishable research or outstanding creative work. Even if the professor is a poor teacher, does little service, and no longer creates, the workload and title do not shift.

Colleges need to change their workload rules. They can mandate changes, of course, but most of them don't. They seek faculty support for the changes, and it is rarely given. And even when support is given, the changes are rarely implemented, because if a professor refuses to accept them lawsuits get threatened, the holiness of tenure gets pronounced, and many a wishy-washy administration will just give in.

What needs to be done is to assign everyone a reasonable workload, and then allow course reductions for proven activities, such as actual hours spent as department course advisors, actual service on major committees, and research or creative work that is either funded or broadly recognized as excellent by appropriate specialists in one's field.

Some colleges are already making incremental changes in workload arrangements, by altering the conditions only for new hires. Faculty who are already at the institution are grandfathered into their prior arrangements. This is a relatively easy fix to adopt. Its major flaw is that it can take years, even decades, for meaningful change to occur, at a time when the luxury of waiting may be extremely costly.

Eliminate or Phase Out Tenure

Tenure is a big elephant in the room in terms of college faculty costs and inflexibility. Administrations need the ability to redirect resources in order to prevent waste, discontinue outmoded or no longer needed programs, and meet emerging needs.

Tenure prevents the judicious use of financial resources by tying the hands of administrators. Tenure supporters argue that tenure can only be withdrawn based on cause or financial exigency. Cause is assumed to mean charges brought against a faculty member. Lack of need for a program is not considered exigency.

It is difficult for colleges to have scheduling flexibility if they have tenured faculty because the only circumstance allowing for laying off professors is the threat of bankruptcy or closure of entire programs or schools. Yet having programmatic flexibility is essential for efficient and effective management, and ultimately, for many colleges, it is necessary for survival. It is also extremely difficult to fire faculty with cause. Even faculty who dislike a colleague or recognize the poor teaching, plagiarism, or mental instability of one of their own circle the wagons to protect tenure when it is threatened, even in cases of gross malfeasance.

What colleges must do is alter the terms of employment so that faculty who fail to meet reasonable standards can be parted with and programs that obsolesce or become too costly to sustain can be discontinued.

The easy way for college leaders to do things is to change the terms of employment going forward. Just as in the case of adjusting workload policies, new faculty could be hired with no expectation of tenure. Leaving tenure in place for grandfathered faculty would saddle many colleges with rigid and inflexible staffing patterns for a long time into the future, though. If colleges do eliminate tenure, they must be careful to put in place standards for judging how faculty who are hired with contracts that do not include tenure will be evaluated, reappointed, promoted, or let go.

One great benefit of the tenure system is that it provides a frequently rigorous, though onetime, assessment of the qualifications of a candidate to be made a permanent employee, based on the standards of the particular institution. There is a clear up-or-out process. Even if faculty being reviewed for tenure are good teachers or researchers or are well-liked department workhorses, if they are judged not quite good enough for a lifetime position, they can be let go under this process.

Without tenure, some institutions might never sever their ties to merely adequate faculty. Why go through the unpleasantness, they might decide, unless they must. In general, in higher education, it appears that many of the colleges without tenure are not ranked as high as those schools that do have it. In fact the president of the Franklin W. Olin College of Engineering, which does not offer tenure, said he had some initial trepidation about whether the college would exercise sufficient care in hiring professors because the appointments were seen as less permanent (Stripling, 2011).

Of course, since that time, more colleges, especially new ones, have elected to offer contracts rather than tenure. Others have chosen to blend their retention systems by offering tenure-track positions to smaller proportions of their faculties, or to limit tenure more tightly in some units than in others.

This has certainly been the case with some medical schools. In an article on tenure in medical schools, Bunton and Mallon (2007) state, "Although tenure systems remain well established in medical schools, the proportion of faculty on tenured or tenure-eligible tracks has continued to decline over time" (p. 281). They also note, "Changes in the financial guarantee associated with tenure have transformed the fundamental concept of tenure at many medical schools, and the percentage of schools that have lengthened the probationary period for tenure-track faculty has steadily increased during the past 25 years" (p. 281).

In the case of medical schools, the drop in tenure is largely due to the uncertain world of medical research funding, and the high cost of employing medical doctors. Similar changes in the share of college instructors on tenure are occurring across all of higher education, but for a different reason. An article in *The Chronicle of Higher Education* stated that the U.S. Department of Education found that only 31% of college instructors were tenured or on tenure track in 2007 (Basken, 2010). This was undoubtedly due to the increased use and abuse of adjunct faculty.

Adjunct faculty can be hired by both for-profit and nonprofit colleges because there are so many unemployed and underemployed prospective instructors in the market. As the web editor of *Washington Monthly* pointed out, "Between 2005 and 2009 American universities spit out 100,000 new doctoral degrees, for 16,000 open jobs. No wonder colleges aren't offering tenure to their instructors. They don't have to" (Luzer, 2013).

The market for instructors will change, of course. Fewer students will forgo income for 7–10 years, or more, if there are not going to be jobs for them. Additionally, fewer second-tier PhD programs will continue to exist as student numbers shrink or colleges find themselves unable to sustain the expenses of the programs.

In a normal market, few people will give up a decade of earnings to prepare for a career that is likely to be unattainable. PhD programs have survived and proliferated because faculty teaching at the institutions offering those programs have encouraged prospects to take them, knowing the small likelihood of success graduates would face.

Responsible faculty and their academic leaders need to confront the damage that is being done to a generation of dissertation writers. Scaling back or eliminating less successful programs is a moral necessity, not just an economic one.

Scaling back won't solve the tenure dilemma, though, only the adjunct one. For colleges that eliminate tenure, as they increasingly must, it needs to be replaced with a contract system containing much of the same assessment properties as tenure has without the lifetime contract. Rigorous standards of academic capability must still be used, and faculty who do not measure up will still need to be let go after reasonable evaluation periods.

For those who worry about the loss of protection of academic freedom, tenure is no longer really necessary for that purpose, especially in the non-profit sector, where academic freedom is still a major standard for according respect, just as freedom of the press is in the news world.

Furthermore, in our highly litigious society, it is very hard to fire people with grounds, let alone without grounds. And with so many faculty members able to fall within the rubric of some category or another of groups that are discriminated against, administrators venture into the area of pink slips very gingerly.

I once had someone who was dismissed from a program because of sexual misconduct sue me, claiming that his problem was the result of an emotional problem, and that I was therefore discriminating against him

based on his disability. There was also the case of an older internal applicant who claimed age discrimination when he was denied a position he
had applied for. The position advertisement had mentioned that a PhD
was preferred. The applicant, who lacked graduate credentials, noted that
the ad did not state that graduate work was a requirement rather than a
preference. The Human Rights Commission he appealed to ruled in the
institution's favor.

Senior college officials know that before anyone is let go, especially a
faculty member, there generally must be evidence of efforts to counsel the
person and clearly lay out what the person must do to continue holding his
or her position. In addition, paper trails of evidence of misfeasance, malfeasance, or just plain not measuring up must clearly document any case likely
to engender a lawsuit.

Outsource Nonacademic Services

Any projects or services that a college cannot provide at better quality and
more cheaply than external providers should be outsourced. Outsourcing is
a great way to provide what students and faculty need at a given time, while
maintaining maximum flexibility for the future. For too long, too many colleges have tried to provide all of their own services, at higher costs than third
parties could provide them and often at lower quality.

Consider services that clean buildings. They have down to a science just
how many brooms, bottles of detergent, and rolls of paper towels they need
to supply for a given square footage of space with different usage patterns,
and they are able to purchase those supplies in greater bulk, for all their customers, than individual colleges can. They can better control water leakage,
management services, and personnel replacements. They do not have to tie
compensation levels to other salaries in the institution, but rather to similar
workers in other types of places.

In emergencies, they have specialized personnel, specialized knowledge,
and specialized equipment to provide, because they are more likely than a
stand-alone college to have had experience handling a similar emergency
somewhere else.

Moreover, there can be more opportunity for upward mobility for the
staff in these outside provider companies. Cleaning staff personnel cannot
normally expect to get promoted to faculty status, but within cleaning companies, they can move up into midlevel management, if they are conscien-
tious and capable.

This is not to say that outside providers will necessarily be good employers, only that the possibility is there. How supportive a firm is of its personnel

and how good a job that personnel does for a particular college are matters of selection and negotiation.

When services that are outsourced are perceived as inadequate, college constituencies are prone to blame it on the switch from internal to external providers. Often, the truth is that the level of service is far more dependent on the level of dollars expended and the requirements demanded than on who provides it.

Bookstores, food services, facilities maintenance, fleet maintenance, and information technology services are all areas that have experienced some degree of a transfer of management from colleges to outside providers. Others, often done only temporarily, include student recruitment management and capital campaign management.

Utilize Technology Effectively

Virtually every expert on higher education who was interviewed agreed that to continue to thrive colleges must offer some online courses. In particular, it will be imperative that colleges find ways to encourage their own students to take the college's own online courses.

A study by Babson Survey Research Group found that almost 70% of chief academic leaders now say that online learning is crucial to their long-term strategy (Allen & Seaman, 2013, p. 4). However, effective utilization of technology requires more than simply providing advanced Internet services or offering classes online, although these are both crucial pieces of necessary technological requirements for colleges now.

If you access Google or any other search engine for almost any kind of information about higher education, you are likely to find boxed ads at the top and bottom of the page, or all along the sides of the page, placed by large, for-profit colleges, such as Strayer, Walden, or the University of Phoenix. A handful of nonprofits, especially the successful businesslike Liberty Online University, also appear, but in general, nonprofit schools have not yet joined the aggressive ad-placement efforts of the corporate education providers.

Ad placement on search sites is a rapidly expanding business. I recently learned just how slick and manipulative it has become as a source of funding for news media, for example. As newspapers and magazines find subscriptions declining, and ad revenue falling below levels that can sustain print media, publishers have put more news, and especially more soft news, such as opinion and essay blogs, on their sites.

For breaking stories, at one major newspaper site, stories run with several different headlines to appeal to different potential audiences. A screen compares readership on all articles and simultaneously tracks one story with two or three headlines to see which header draws relatively larger audiences. Then the less effective leads are replaced with new ones, and the process is repeated, sometimes for the life of the story.

One entrepreneur has even developed software that allows advertising agencies to bid on ad placement, based on specific desired criteria, in milliseconds, so that the ads may change as a page is refreshed. This technique enables deep-pocketed advertisers to quickly move their allocated dollars to the most likely potential receptive audiences as quickly as stories develop and move them away as interest wanes.

The colleges that can present their offerings with such immediacy create market advantages for their programs, with which smaller, less well-funded, or technologically unsophisticated schools can barely hope to compete. As viewers see the once unknown names of these advertised colleges over and over, in multiple venues, the college names become recognizable and begin to develop the kind of sheen or respectability that any successfully advertised product ultimately wants: an imprint of the importance and success of the branded product in the mind of the recipient.

So far, most public colleges have not diligently tried to attract students on the web, other than through burnishing their own websites, which for some smaller schools is still a work in progress. Profit-seeking colleges have developed very savvy sites, which quickly propel any prospects linking on to them to start inputting personal data, in order to get custom-tailored responses to the users' interests.

Until quite recently, public colleges have been especially unaggressive in pursuing enrollees through technology. Many do not use this enrollment technology well, even when they are underenrolled, and even when they need to increase their numbers in order to remain separately governed in the face of some state efforts to merge less efficient campuses or make them branches of larger colleges. Often the colleges want to be more effective but do not know what to do and lack the skilled personnel who could put such efforts in place.

There are several barriers to effective utilization of online programs. For one thing, nearly half (44.6%) of all academic leaders surveyed for the Babson Survey Research Group study believe that it takes faculty more time and effort to teach online. In addition, only 30% of chief academic officers believe that their faculty accept the legitimacy of online education. Finally, a significant share of academic leaders have concerns ranging from the ability of online students to be disciplined learners, the retention rate of online programs, and acceptance of online degrees by potential employers (Allen & Seaman, 2013, pp. 5, 6).

One exception is Georgia Institute of Technology, which is offering a three-year master's degree in computer science whose courses students will be able to take entirely online. Georgia Tech is partnering with Udacity and AT&T, to offer the programs, which will cost less than $7,000, the university claims. Presently, the average cost of an online computer science master's degree is almost $25,000, according to research cited by *Time* (White, 2013). Georgia Tech's degree will cost less than one third as much and will have the advantage of offering credentialing from one of the most respected engineering colleges in the nation. According to Asa Sphar, vice president of recruitment and profiling at tech recruiting company CSI Executive Search, LLC, "Georgia Tech's announcement probably is a game changer that will have other top-tier universities that offer degrees in computer science scrambling to compete" (as cited in White, 2013).

Reduce Staff

Colleges need to reduce administrative levels and positions. They need to reduce the distance between faculty and deans, and between entry-level and senior nonacademic staff. There has been an explosion of growth in college staffing, and although some of the positions may be crucial to retain, it is also crucial to return to less steeply tiered and less hierarchical organizational models. Certainly, finding acceptable and effective ways to deliver academic programs with fewer nonacademic staff will be essential if the growing costs of a higher education are to be rolled back.

Shorten the Curriculum

Because of program inflation and degree inflation, many college programs have grown unnecessarily long and expensive. Even our traditional four-year baccalaureate degrees may be longer than they have to be for some programs and students.

Now, a growing number of colleges are recognizing this reality and working on finding a variety of ways that the length of time in college programs can be shortened. Most such efforts involve having students take classes year round, which reduces their time out of the paid workforce. Such programs prevent students from having work or internship experiences during the summer, but the trade-off is still a positive one.

These are intellectually lazy approaches to the problems, however. What is most desirable is to redesign programs so that they require fewer months or years of study. Over the years, additions to programs grow in order to keep the content relevant to a changing environment. This happens in almost all fields of study.

What happens less frequently is cutting back on courses that are no longer essential for understanding or functioning well in the discipline in question. A couple of factors account for this. First, faculty who specialize in and teach the courses that are declining in importance do not easily cede what they have committed their professional lives to studying and what they may believe is still of great importance. Second, the pressure to raise the barriers to entry in many professional fields often militates against the pressure to eliminate longtime, but no longer essential, classes.

There really ought to be sunset law–type requirements for courses. Sunset laws require that certain agencies, benefits, or laws expire by a fixed date unless they are reauthorized. To be retained as part of a department-approved curricula, a course should have to be reapproved every seven years or so. Reapproval should be contingent on a successfully argued proposal focused on demonstrating why the subject retains higher relevancy than some of the other courses offered by the program.

To be fair, most nonprofit academic programs do have curriculum committees that monitor their fields and examine proposed new courses or requirements. Some are basically just pro forma, merely checking out requests for approval for special offerings.

Others, however, really do the hard work of asking themselves where their field of study is heading, whether or not they are meeting their students' needs as well as they could, how well prepared they are to provide training that reflects future needs, and how they can do a better job.

The latter approach is the one that is necessary throughout higher education. Most colleges have academic plans that study their overall approach to their academic mission on a broad scale, including topics such as semester versus quarter schedules; core curriculum requirements; academic reporting lines (such as which collegiate units' departments are placed within which collegiate units); and major changes in approaches to grading, outreach expectations, research requirements, and external relationships.

What is needed now are deep explorations into how lean we can be in our requirements, and our consequent costs, to take no more students than we believe can be placed in jobs in the fields of study we offer, and in the time it takes to give them excellent preparation for both those jobs and the life skills they will need.

The problem of offering three-year degrees is that historically the minimum criterion for a student to graduate has been 120 credits of college work. That is what is required by most colleges for a bachelor's degree. What is the magic in 120 credits anyway? Just because it has been used for a long time doesn't necessarily justify it now. There are programs that may need more credits, and some that need fewer. The requirements for general education credits, typically called the common core, can remain the same for all programs once an appropriate amount of liberal arts study time is agreed upon. This is possible because a bachelor's degree signifies not just the aggregation of a set of skills in a specialized field, but, at the very least, a broad acquaintance with the whole spectrum of knowledge.

Getting a college degree in a particular field could be adjusted to provide the specialized studies, on top of the general education requirements, that are necessary in that field. The time spent in coursework need not, and probably should not, be the same for every discipline a college offers.

Few colleges and few disciplines have actually explored how to shorten the requirements for graduation by redesigning them into fewer courses or shorter lengths of time of study. This effort requires opening up the entire set of offerings for examination. It asks for a future rather than past orientation to the field of study. It demands a commitment to setting aside one's personal conflicts of interest in the quest for the right blend and approach.

Given the dramatic decline in law school applications, a number of law schools are already being forced to look at options they can undertake to protect the integrity of their programs, reduce potential debt for their students, and remain competitive and viable. Many law schools are cutting back on the size of the classes they will admit. They are doing this less to shrink the pool of excess graduates above market needs than to protect the quality of their programs, but it is a good thing for them to be doing because it helps to accomplish both goals. With a shrinking applicant pool, a law school has to dig down deeper into that pool in order to maintain class size. By admitting less qualified students (by whatever particular criteria it has traditionally used), the school risks having a lower percentage of its graduates pass the state bar examination, thereby risking its accreditation status.

Quite a few law schools are also looking at ways to differentiate themselves from the pack of schools, or to make their own schools more affordable by shortening the length of time to achieve the degree. Law schools at Drexel University, Pepperdine University, and the University of Dayton are planning two-year programs. Brooklyn Law School and Northwestern School of Law currently offer this option. All of them require the full range of courses, just at an accelerated time frame.

Even President Barack Obama has weighed in on the topic. During a town hall–style meeting at Binghamton University, the president said, "I believe that law schools would probably be wise to think about being two years instead of three years" (Lattman, 2013).

Medical schools are considering shortening the curriculum too, with some looking at real change. Presently, medical students with debt graduate with an average debt of $225,000. They spend eight years in college, and then another three years as residents. For many medical specialties, the residency periods can be far longer. Not only is there debt to pay off, but 11 or more years of foregone income, the length of time these students spent in baccalaureate, medical, and residency programs.

The American Medical Association (AMA) has undertaken a major campaign to help medical schools explore new ways to educate medical students. It has awarded 11 medical schools across the country $1 million each for five-year projects exploring ways to "close the gaps between how medical students are trained and health care is delivered" (AMA, 2013). Among the programs funded are ones exploring competency-based progression, total student immersion in the health care system, and a three-year technology-enabled program.

As tuitions rise, with consequent rises in debt loads, medical educators are giving a lot of thought to ways to make medical education more affordable. Few nations require such long periods of training for their physicians, and many of those nations provide very good health care for their citizens. If Germany, Sweden, France and countless others can produce competent doctors using shorter training periods, why can't we explore doing the same thing?

For several decades, at least some medical schools have allowed strong candidates who have completed all the requisite science courses to enter their programs at the end of their junior year of college, although the number of such students and programs is small. More recently, Lake Erie College of Osteopathic Medicine has created a small three-year, instead of four-year, medical school track for students who are willing to commit to becoming primary care physicians. In addition, New York University (NYU) is now experimenting with cutting a year off its four-year program to shorten the time in medical school. NYU is trying this for the same reasons the profession as a whole is looking at the issue: Costs and debts are rising, while clinical resources are contracting.

Less costly and less time-consuming ways have to be found to provide future doctors for our nation. Unless we do this, we could face a crisis in the provision of health care for our nation. As fewer physicians opt to go into sole practices because of the complexities of managing electronic records and third-party payment collections, most doctors will work for hospitals or clinics in the future. And as hospitals tighten their belts, or are taken over by for-profit corporations, physicians will be likely to earn less in return for management services and more security. That will make it ever more difficult for them to pay off huge debts.

At the same time, we face a future in which our health care needs will expand more rapidly than the supply of physicians is likely to be able to do. A growing population, an aging population, and an increasingly obese population will require more doctors, but the ability of medical schools to expand while maintaining quality is not going to be sufficient to meet those needs unless significant changes can be made in the present model of training.

References

Allen, I. E., & Seaman, J. (2013, January). *Changing course: Ten years of tracking online education in the United States: Executive summary.* Babson Park, MA: Babson Survey Research Group and Quahog Research Group, LLC.

Alter, S. (2013, April 15). Letter to the editor. *New York Times,* p. A18.

American Medical Association (AMA). (2013, June 14). *AMA awards $11M to transform the way future physicians are trained* [Press release]. Retrieved from http://www.ama-assn.org/ama/pub/news/news/2013/2013-06-14-ama-awards-11-million-change-med-ed.page

Basken, P. (2010, August 23). Medical colleges shrink tenure as their teaching hospitals grow. *The Chronicle of Higher Education.* Retrieved from http://chronicle.com/article/Medical-Colleges-Shrink-Tenure/124105/?sid=at

Boshart, R. (2013, June 24). Branstad cautions against overbuilding at regent campuses. *The Gazette.* Retrieved from http://thegazette.com/2013/06/24/branstad-cautions-against-overbuilding-at-regent-campuses/#sthash.3XSghAtX.dpuf

Bunton, S. A., & Mallon, W. T. (2007, March). The continued evolution of faculty appointment and tenure policies at U.S. medical schools [Abstract]. *Academic Medicine, 82*(3), 281.

Christensen, C. M., & Eyring, H. J. (2011). *The innovative university: Changing the DNA of higher education from the inside out.* San Francisco, CA: Jossey-Bass.

Grasgreen, A. (2012, November 1). Beyond sports. *Inside Higher Ed.* Retrieved from http://www.insidehighered.com/news/2012/11/01/spelman-eliminates-athletics-favor-campus-wide-wellness-initiative#ixzz2RFGYZG5Q

Hurtado, S., Eagan, K., Pryor, J. H., Whang, H., & Tran, S. (2012). *Undergraduate teaching faculty: The 2010–2011 HERI Faculty Survey.* Los Angeles, CA: Higher Education Research Institute at UCLA.

Lattman, P. (2013, August 23). Obama says law school should be two, not three, years. *New York Times.* Retrieved from http://dealbook.nytimes.com/2013/08/23/obama-says-law-school-should-be-two-years-not-three/

Lewin, T. (2013, April 22). Yearly prize of $500,000 is created for faculty. *New York Times.* Retrieved from http://www.nytimes.com/2013/04/22/education/minerva-project-announces-annual-500000-prize-for-professors.html?_r=0

Luzer, D. (2013, January 24). *The decline of academic tenure.* Retrieved from http://washingtonmonthly.com/college_guide/blog/the_decline_of_academic_tenure.php

Stripling, J. (2011, May 15). Most presidents prefer no tenure for majority of faculty. *The Chronicle of Higher Education.* Retrieved from http://chronicle.com/article/Most-Presidents-Favor-No/127526/

White, M. C. (2013, May 21). The $7,000 computer science degree—and the future of higher education. *Time.* Retrieved from http://business.time .com/2013/05/21/the-7000-computer-science-degree-and-the-future-of-higher -education/#ixzz2UiOhD6Bt

Zemsky, R., & Massy, W. (1990). Cost containment: Committing to a new economic reality. *Change, 22*(6), 16–22.

6 Case Studies, Opportunities, and Challenges

According to Stephen Shannon, president of the American Association of Colleges of Osteopathic Medicine (AACOM), the use of for-profit online services will continue to grow if its providers can find ways to successfully deal with gainful employment issues. Dr. Shannon is a broad thinker who has helped to bring together various major medical education organizations to jointly confront significant issues they all face. He notes that content delivery is already being provided to medical students in a variety of modes. For example, the American Association of Medical Colleges (AAMC) is already using YouTube to offer some training modules.

AACOM already includes among its member medical schools one for-profit school, Rocky Vista University, which is accredited by the American Osteopathic Association (AOA), and has apparently done a good job of training its medical students. Rocky Vista's graduates have been meeting or exceeding the median for passing their national examinations and residency placements (Commission on Osteopathic College Accreditation, 2013, p. 4).

With respect to the use of online training, Shannon states there are many potential valuable uses, such as the ability to deliver some training, on subjects such as parasitology, to thousands of students at a time through online modules. At the same time, he cautions that "integration of knowledge and the process of coming to decisions about diagnosis happen best in classroom or small group settings." Shannon also says that online programs can deliver some health care material very well, but they still lack the ability to "integrate knowledge and critical thinking."

There are several models of online higher education programs that can be offered to prospective students. Powell (2008) suggests that these are the direct model, the community model, and the subscription model. In the direct model, the Internet allows an education company to reach its course buyers directly. It can offer a "virtual product, virtual delivery agent, and virtual process" (p. 61). This is the standard, fee-based online course offering.

The community model, based on user loyalty, makes its money partly on the sale of related products or services, the way many promotional business presentations offer low-cost tickets to hear speakers whose speeches extol books and products available at the presentation. Low-cost online courses may enhance their profit margins with the added sales of auxiliary products.

Under the subscription model, a fee for service is paid, generally for the level of service desired, similar to a television cable subscription. Apple offers a yearly subscription service under which customers can take as many courses on using Apple applications as they desire at Apple Stores for a whole year. It is a great value and very popular. StraighterLine offers what can be called a subscription, or modified-subscription, model for online courses.

Schools Successfully Using Technology

In spite of the tough times facing higher education, a few nonprofit colleges are flourishing. For the most part, these are schools that entered the online teaching world early and have invested considerably in honing their programs and delivery methods. Liberty University and Southern New Hampshire University have seen considerable growth in their online programs.

Smaller online programs, such as the ones at the University of New England (UNE), have also benefited. Most of these successful programs have created programmatic surpluses that the colleges then used to expand both online and campus services and facilities, plumping up their physical campuses from assets created by their online programs.

Liberty University

Liberty University, a Christian institution founded by Rev. Jerry Falwell, whose son Jerry Falwell Jr. is now the president, is located in Lynchburg, Virginia. The university, now more than 40 years old, has about 12,500 students at its Lynchburg campus, but another 90,000 students are taking its courses online (Liberty University, 2013b).

Liberty University Online is an amazing success story that has helped to build and propel the entire institution. According to its website, the school now offers 151 undergraduate, 54 graduate, and 1 post-master's degree programs at its Lynchburg campus, and 57 undergraduate, 100 graduate, 3 post-master's, and 6 doctoral degree programs through Liberty University Online. Students from more than 95 nations take Liberty Online courses. *The Chronicle of Higher Education* listed Liberty University as having the fastest growing college enrollment in the nation from the fall 2001 term to the fall 2011 term (Almanac of Higher Education, 2013).

As late as 2005, Liberty University had only about 3,800 online students. The astonishing growth of its online enrollment since then has propelled the school to a place where its 2013 net assets were more than $1 billion, according to its audited financial statements for June 30, 2013 (Liberty University, 2013a). Although Liberty Online has seen amazing growth in its yearly online student enrollment since 2005, some leaders at the university expect its enrollment to begin to level off over the coming decade. "Let's say that while we expect continuous growth, we will be building continuous quality improvement," one administrator told me.

One reason the online program is so strong is that significant resources have been allocated to the support of Liberty's information technology programs. According to two sources, the university's information technology (IT) department had a staff of more than 400 full-time people working in it. One source said, "They work on IT 24/7, 365 days a year." He added that the university was not looking to make money, but to reach out to advance its mission and vision. "They really market their product line of courses to churches and evangelicals across the globe."

U.S. News & World Report (2014) has ranked Liberty the 89th best regional college in the South. On the other hand, because Liberty teaches creationism along with evolution and has a Center for Creation Studies, many scholars still look askance at its academic offerings. Its programs are regionally accredited. For its adult students on campus, there is also the issue of its positions on sexuality.

The school's own website notes its exceptions to policies of nondiscrimination. To be accredited by the American Bar Association, the School of Law at Liberty University had to pass a higher bar on nondiscrimination than its other component schools. The site states that

> in its employment practices, the School of Law does not discriminate on the basis of sexual orientation, but does discriminate on the basis of sexual misconduct, including, but not limited to, non-marital sexual misconduct, homosexual misconduct, or the encouragement or advocacy of any form of sexual behavior that would undermine the Christian identity or faith mission of the University. (Liberty University, 2013c)

It further states:

> This policy statement is neither intended to discourage, nor is it in fact applicable to, any analytical discussion of law and policy issues involved in the regulation of sexual behavior, or to discussions of any recommendations

for changes in existing law. Discussions of these matters are both practiced and are welcomed within our curriculum. (Liberty University, 2013c)

However one feels about the strictures under which students or faculty are admitted to the university family, the fact is that Liberty has found a path to success that combines its faith-based missionary fervor with a similarly strong outreach effort with its online programs. All one has to do to verify that effort is to look up Liberty University on Google. Many of the first 20 or 30 listings are basically ads placed by Liberty. In fact, online searches for college education topics frequently show ads for Liberty at the top of the web page.

Liberty entered the mass online market early and made a huge commitment to developing, supporting, and sustaining the technical support necessary to grow the program. One source suggested that several key board members with strong business IT backgrounds pushed or promoted the concept. An IT person said that a former chief information officer pushed the online developments because he was committed to changing the way that content is delivered.

Now Liberty's online program is strongly in place, giving the institution an edge in an arena that is already very competitive, and will grow even more so over the coming decade.

Southern New Hampshire University

Half of the people interviewed for this book asked me if I had spoken to Paul LeBlanc, the president of Southern New Hampshire University (SNHU). That is because educators in the know believe that Dr. LeBlanc is building imaginative and future-oriented online programs at the independent university he is leading.

The university has one of the four or five largest nonprofit online programs in the nation. It has grown from about 2,400 on-campus undergraduate and graduate students, plus about 3,000 other students taking an assortment of off-campus programs in 2003, to nearly 30,000 students by mid-2013, with 26,000 of them online. The institutional budget was about $15 million for the 2003–4 academic year. For the 2012–13 year it was $128 million. LeBlanc expects to approach the $200 million threshold for the 2013–14 year.

SNHU was a small college that was largely unknown outside its region until LeBlanc came there. Its central campus in Manchester, New Hampshire, began life as a for-profit business training school in the 1930s. It wasn't until the 1960s that it was approved by the state to offer associate's degrees and then bachelor's degrees. It became a nonprofit institution in 1968.

LeBlanc became the president of SNHU in 2003. Prior to coming to the university, he had headed Marlboro College in Vermont. He also had business experience, having served as vice president for new technology at Houghton Mifflin Company. Known as an authority on the use of technology in education, he has transformed his university into an exciting, cutting-edge educational institution that has received awards and accolades for its vision and performance. *The Chronicle of Higher Education* listed it as the fifth fastest growing private master's-level college in the nation from 2001 to 2011 (Almanac of Higher Education, 2013).

The college has five campuses; four are spread across southern New Hampshire, and one is in Brunswick, Maine. According to its website, it offers more than 180 undergraduate and graduate degree programs, many of them online. *U.S. News & World Report* (2013c) says of the school, "The prevailing conventional wisdom at Southern New Hampshire University (SNHU) has always been that there are no limits to what students can achieve. As an institution, there are seemingly no limits to what SNHU can achieve as well." That observation is demonstrated in a number of strategic efforts the school has initiated that are light-years ahead of what most other nonprofit colleges are doing. "We are so data driven," LeBlanc says, explaining how the university assures quality control over the new ways it is presenting a college education. "We measure everything. We do it by program, by region, by costs, by students."

The university's online programs have had high retention of their students, something that has eluded for-profit online college course providers. LeBlanc credits the retention to SNHU's strong advising model. "We only have each advisor work with 100 students for the first six courses they take online," he said. The ratio is increased to 300 students per advisor after students have completed those six courses.

"Our retention from entry to completion is about 55%," he said, a remarkable rate for online offerings. LeBlanc pointed out that the institution also benefits from the fact that it hires very good people and continues to train them. He added that many of them come from the for-profit world and thus have a strong customer service orientation and a sense of urgency.

LeBlanc has pioneered the use of competency-based degrees. A competency-based degree is one that allows a student to demonstrate mastery of an area and receive an associate's degree when 120 competencies are achieved. This may seem like the old credit-for-life-experience programs, but in fact, it is very different. It is not based on what students claim they have learned, but on what they can demonstrate they have competence in, a higher standard.

LeBlanc has hired and then trained people to serve as advisors to students in competency-based programs. In April 2013, the U.S. Department of Education approved SNHU's competency-based initiative to be covered under Title IV. It is the first time the department has approved the direct assessment of learning for federal aid eligibility. The New England Association of Schools and Colleges (NEASC), the university's regional accrediting agency, has already approved it too, based on a "history of trust" along with its demonstrated academic solidity, according to LeBlanc.

The university's innovation in untethering an associate's degree attainment from the amassing of credit hours through classes taken is titled College for America. The College for America plan is built on the concept of moving "away from seat time and credit hour definitions of learning," and moving funding "from inputs to outputs" (LeBlanc, 2012).

The program is aimed at nontraditional students, especially working adults who lack confidence in their potential college skills. They can start anywhere, at any time. It is planned to be low cost, at $2,500 per year, which could be funded with financial aid or company reimbursement. The goal of the program is to have students learn at their own pace and be able to demonstrate mastery of a competency, rather than a course. Each individual competency is designed to meet the needs of one of three competency clusters: foundational skills (communication skills), personal and social skills (personal effectiveness), and content knowledge (business essentials).

A student needs to demonstrate mastery of 120 competencies in order to receive an associate's degree. Substantial advising and mentoring is intended to be provided. There are no grades and no required seat time. "If it can be demonstrated in a clear and rock solid way that a student has achieved competency, it shouldn't matter how they get that knowledge," LeBlanc says.

Credit hours, the traditional standards for determining academic degree attainment, have generally been based on an hour of class time taken three or four times a week in a 14- or 15-week semester, with laboratory and studio sessions typically requiring more than one hour of contact each week per credit. LeBlanc's competency approach represents a major challenge to the traditional credit hour concept, and if successful, it is likely to be more widely adopted, especially by several of the large for-profit colleges. But so far, most of the online programs being offered by both nonprofit and for-profit accredited institutions are still providing the same amount of content per credit hour offered that they would otherwise have provided in a regular classroom.

In a presentation at Harvard University, LeBlanc (2012) listed the crucial elements that have led to SNHU's phenomenal success. His list includes the following:

- Understand who we serve and what they need.
- Build systems around those needs.

- Disaggregate functions and scale.
- Measure relentlessly.
- Communicate.

LeBlanc noted later in the presentation, "If you are not measuring, you are only practicing."

The college actively promotes its online programs. Its TV ads prominently mention that SNHU is a nonprofit university, a message LeBlanc says that he consistently stresses. He wants prospective students to know that his university is not beholden to stockholders.

Interestingly, Clayton Christensen, the guru of disruptive innovation, is on the SNHU board. LeBlanc and Christensen met while both were graduate students. LeBlanc's newest efforts are truly disruptive. They may well rearrange the fundamental ways in which the acquisition of higher learning, and the symbols of its attainment, is offered and judged.

A disruptive innovation is an innovation that creates a new market and way of valuing a product or service, ultimately partially or fully replacing the market model it is displacing. According to Christensen, as companies' products or services become too sophisticated or expensive, they open a space for lower-end companies to enter the market. Often they succeed by accepting lower gross margins than the top companies are willing to consider. Those companies do not realize that the space at the bottom of the market will expand for these disruptive innovators.

One of Christensen's examples is the growth of the community college sector. Many public four-year institutions were not interested in the low-tuition model of serving the less well-prepared or adult student market and ceded it to the community colleges. The community colleges then grew, not only by appealing to students the four-year colleges did not really want, but also by attracting large numbers of students who otherwise would have spent their first two years at the four-year institutions (Christensen & Eyring, 2011).

The SNHU model remains to be tested to see just how well it can work, but it is a giant step in the direction of breaking the nexus of inputs and reputational quality. For too long, higher education institutions and programs have been judged on the basis of how selective the admissions were, how published the faculty were, and how many faculty were in each subspecialty, among other input criteria.

This focus ignored the value added by the college, a concept that should never be ignored. If a wealthy and famous college attracts and admits top students, it should be no surprise if they earn high scores on graduate or licensure examinations, or get desired jobs. The important questions really are, Would they have done just as well or better at a less known college? What has a college added to what the student started with?

University of New England

UNE, in southern Maine, is another success story. Its president, Danielle N. Ripich, has taken bold moves to position the university as an important health professions institution, by adding a College of Pharmacy and a College of Dental Medicine to the university, to supplement its existing College of Osteopathic Medicine, Doctor of Physical Therapy program, myriad other health programs, and strong, science-oriented College of Arts and Sciences.

The university, which is ranked in the top 100 colleges in the North for 2013 by *U.S. News & World Report* (2014), began its collegiate life in 1952, as St. Francis College, a small Franciscan college for young men. It started to admit women in 1967. The school suffered from low enrollments and inadequate financial resources, and the Franciscans withdrew their support in 1974, turning the college over to a lay board. Several years later, in 1978, the College of Osteopathic Medicine was opened on the campus. Later, the name of the institution was changed to the University of New England.

When I came to UNE in 1995, it was still quite small, with about 1,700 students overall, and a budget of about $21 million. The following year UNE was merged with a much smaller school, Westbrook College in Portland, which had about 260 total students and was in real danger of closing down.

Following the merger, a dedicated board and a team of committed leaders pushed the university forward, raising salaries, building facilities, strengthening programs, and enhancing its academic reputation. Together, the combined campuses of the university have flourished. UNE now has more than 8,000 students and a budget of about $150 million.

Under Ripich's leadership, UNE has built several very strong online graduate degree programs in social work, education, and health. Ripich, like other successful presidents, stresses the need to focus on customer service. "The for-profits have forced us to recognize the need to be more student focused," she said. "If we don't serve our customers well, they won't keep coming." In addition, she stresses that all students, not just those enrolled in online programs, can benefit from the online experience. "I told a group of our students I was speaking to earlier today that in order to be educated in this century, they each need to take at least one online course here." She noted, "Our present model of in-class teaching is shifting. Higher education is moving to a more distributed method of delivery." She added, "We are fundamentally different from the for-profit companies. Their goal is to make dollars for their investors. Our goal is to use any surplus to help our students."

UNE was a pioneer in offering online programs, though its early models required some on-campus time. Like the models that Christensen has suggested create disruptive innovation, UNE's early graduate programs in education, although lauded by the graduate students who took them, required adjustments to refine them. Now UNE's online Master of Science in Education program is ranked among the top 70 in the nation (*U.S. News & World Report*, 2013b).

Now UNE offers a well-respected master's of social work degree online, along with education, public health policy, and medical leadership graduate degrees, among others. It is also ranked among the fastest growing private master's-level colleges in the nation, at number nine (Almanac of Higher Education, 2013).

Liberty University, SNHU, and UNE all fit the generic description of upstart challengers that Christensen and others posit as disruptive innovators. None of them was well known a decade ago, although UNE has been seen as a "comer" in New England for the last dozen years, and Liberty initially had church support. Still, none of them had the kind of academic reputations that made more prestigious schools worry about them as competition. Now all three institutions are growing, not just in numbers, but in their academic reputations as well.

Other Bold Online Institutions

The State University of New York (SUNY) also has decided to develop online programs. In 2013, the system's board of trustees approved moving into new models of course offerings, from a palette of options, especially the system-wide expansion of the type of prior-learning assessment and acceptance of credits earned elsewhere partially pioneered by one of the SUNY colleges, Empire State College.

The chancellor of SUNY has announced that OpenSUNY, the system's online program, is planning to add 100,000 new students online as well as to make it possible for at least one quarter of them to earn a degree from SUNY in three years (Kolowich, 2013). The idea is to have students finish in less time and at lower cost. The SUNY system expects to add the extra 100,000 students by opening its processes to competency-based credit systems and online presentations.

SUNY, with 468,000 students, could become a very big player in the online market. The fundamental questions that will decide how successful it will be are: What will it do differently than all the other aspirants eager to enter the same market? and How will it shorten the time it takes to earn a degree?

SUNY's pioneer online provider, Empire State College, was designed as an adult, working-student college that could offer flexible programs of study for people who already had some college or appropriate experiential knowledge, giving them a way to demonstrate their academic competence while providing faculty mentoring and support. Empire State was one of the first colleges in the nation to allow students to receive academic credit for prior learning.

In recent years, Empire has partnered with StraighterLine and other companies accepting or awarding credit yet maintaining academic standards. On its website, Empire states that undergraduates can choose to learn through "guided independent study, online courses, study groups and residency-based studies, or blend a combination of approaches. [They] also may take courses at other colleges and universities, as long as the courses are determined to be relevant to [their] degree program plan" (SUNY Empire State College, 2014).

The SUNY board wants to build on and expand the Empire model using prior-learning assessment, competency-based programs and massive open online courses (MOOCs). SUNY will be joining Coursera but has not yet decided whether it will use Coursera or some other platform for the bulk of its new offerings.

In Florida, a number of the public colleges offer part of some introductory classes online. This does not save much in personnel costs, but it does save teaching space. Colleges can quite successfully "stretch" their classroom space by having some sessions delivered online, instead of on-site.

The state also offers a Florida Virtual Campus that allows potential students to explore a list of all distance education courses available at public colleges in the state, as well as private colleges that have opted to join in the listings. Adult education, college preparatory, continuing education, and college credit courses are covered.

The Florida legislature has given the University of Florida, which is ranked number 17 in the nation by *U.S. News & World Report* (2013a), $15 million to start a series of online bachelor's degree programs in science, technology, engineering, and math (Straumsheim, 2013). The university plans to offer 20 or more of these degrees. The cost of the expanded online programs the university will be offering is expected to be only about 62% of the cost of on-campus programs.

In the fall 2013 semester, 5,296 courses were being offered through the Florida Virtual Campus. Although the actual number of different courses was considerably smaller, because three or four colleges often were offering the same online course, the presence of the Virtual Campus site facilitates the use of these programs by allowing students to review the courses that are available and register for them online.

Other states and other colleges are also developing online courses and degree programs. The colleges likely to be most successful in these efforts are those that were early adopters of online offerings, and those with deep enough pockets to underwrite the necessary investments in technology and develop measurements of competencies necessary to document the successes of their graduates.

Blended Programs

Perhaps one of the best ways to use online course delivery is to blend it with traditional classroom experiences. There are a number of models for how this can be done. The easiest model of all is to offer a blended course in which two hours of classes are presented face-to-face with a professor and one hour is online. This enables a student to raise questions or engage in classroom discussion about material presented online. Another easy way to use a hybrid style is to provide classroom instructors/aides who are available for an hour or more a week in a classroom or seminar setting to offer assistance. Some models could offer an online program with call-in support, or alternating online and face-to-face classes.

San Jose State University has developed two pilot programs using blended approaches. One is used for students who need remedial work in areas such as mathematics. This program, which partnered with Udacity to offer students low-cost fully online minicourses with online mentors available 24 hours a day, was not successful and was discontinued in late 2013. Its other pilot program aims to help students achieve acceptable grades in one of its engineering courses, a course that about 40% of its students must retake or else change their major. Initial results showed that with the blended class, 91% of the students passed, versus just 59% in the regular class (Lewin, 2013b).

Pace University in New York City was named as having the best online bachelor's degree program for 2013 by *U.S. News & World Report* (2013a). The rating was based on factors such as graduation rates and academic and career support services offered to students. Although Pace's program is not advertised as blended, one of the reasons it does well is that most of the students in its online program live within 100 miles of the school and are able to see a professor when they must.

One excellent technique involving video presentations to a class, coupled with online access, is used at a Michigan State University College of Osteopathic Medicine branch campus housed in a Detroit hospital. Many of the lectures are delivered to the medical students from professors at the East Lansing campus. They are viewed in classrooms at the hospital on large monitors, or they can be viewed online at home or wherever the students wish.

The advantage for the students of coming to the Detroit classrooms is that teachers on-site facilitate back-and-forth discussions, answer questions, are available for consultation, and provide a lot of feedback. When I visited the program as part of an accreditation team, the medical students indicated to me that they loved the setup.

Challenges and Opportunities

Online classes are increasingly necessary, especially as a means of providing access to college classes for students who want to enroll but find that there are not enough spaces available for them to be admitted to nonprofit colleges in their communities.

In the spring of 2013, community college enrollments in California were the lowest in 20 years. This drop was not due to flagging demand. Because of budget cuts, not enough teachers could be hired by the community colleges. This meant that fewer courses were offered, and fewer students were admitted. According to a study by the Public Policy Institute of California, if enrollment rates had remained "at 2008–09 levels the community college system would today be serving an additional 600,000 students" (Bohn, Reyes, & Johnson, 2013, p. 2).

In addition to access issues are concerns about mismatches between what colleges teach their students in some fields such as business and education and what employers say they are looking for in their workplaces. The move under way, from course completions to competency demonstrations, may bring the worlds of preparation and execution closer together.

Right now almost half of all employed U.S. college graduates are working in jobs that do not require a bachelor's degree, according to a study based on Bureau of Labor statistics. Furthermore, 37% are in jobs that require only a high school diploma. The study states that the combination of rising college costs and "perceived declines in economic benefits may well lead to declining enrollments and market share for traditional schools and the development of new methods of certifying occupation competence" (Vedder, Denhart, & Robe, 2013).

Some positions require licenses that are contingent on degree attainment, but the vast majority of jobs do not. Many employers prefer to hire college graduates because they believe that the attainment of a degree attests to good work habits and dependability.

However, the shift from traditional to online learning should lead to more reliance on demonstrable competencies rather than simply degree attainment. That is because of the ability of online courses to enrich learning through linkages that expand upon course material and allow students to access working examples of what they are engaged in studying.

As traditional colleges try to redesign their programs to move more of them online, they will run into numerous problems. They will need to either hire people who understand how to build platforms or partner with firms that can provide platforms to deliver online courses. They will also need technicians who can manage their systems, and people who can teach faculty how to use the systems. In addition, they will need faculty who are willing and able to present their work online, and they will need legal support to ensure that they are complying with different state and regulatory requirements, as well as to protect their contractual interests in partnerships and other presentation arrangements.

Early adopters have a clear advantage, says Paul LeBlanc, who points out some of the reasons. "It is harder to get online market space now than it was five years ago. The space is more crowded, so you have to spend a lot more money to be effective." In addition, lead generation and lead acquisition have gotten more costly to purchase. Leads are names and addresses of potential students, including their e-mail addresses. Many are purchased through online sites that attract potential online students. Leads can also be attained by paying such sites to provide their viewers with online links to your application materials. Some sources are more productive than others. According to LeBlanc, "You need to know how to leverage your investments in this area." He adds, "You also need to be on top of regulatory issues, when your online programs are taken by students in different states. We have three full-time people, including one attorney, working on getting and maintaining our state authorizations. We spend over $500,000 a year for this."

On the same day that LeBlanc told me about the need to be on top of regulatory issues, a news article by Tamar Lewin (2013a) appeared in the *New York Times* indicating that a group of higher education leaders was seeking to make the process of getting state authorizations for online programs simpler and less cumbersome. According to Lewin, the group, the Commission on the Regulation of Postsecondary Distance Education, issued a report titled *Access through Regulatory Reform: Findings, Principles, and Recommendations for the State Authorization Reciprocity Agreement (SARA)* (Commission on the Regulation of Postsecondary Distance Education, 2013). The report proposed a plan for voluntary interstate reciprocity, which would reduce the costs and time involved in gaining approvals. The newspaper article discussed the high fees it could cost colleges to apply for authorization in each state in which an online student enrolled, and quoted one commission member who noted that his college and others choose not to enroll in certain states in order to avoid the authorization costs. It could cost a public university system "about $5.5 million to comply with 49 states, not counting administrative expenses" (Lewin, 2013a, p. A13).

As more colleges jump on the online bandwagon, there will be increased pressure to reduce barriers, and it is reasonable to assume that they will become easier to surmount. Still, for those players who arrived early to the party of building online programs, the parking lots had more open spaces from which to choose and offered more room to drive around and explore the room there. Others can and will play catch-up, of course, but fewer places will be open, and the costs of entry will rise for the latecomers, just like the costs of units in a new condominium building rise when they become a much desired place to live.

For many of the small independent colleges, the costs of entry will be more than they can pay. Already strapped for dollars to sustain their present programs, and fighting losing battles to retain present enrollment numbers, they lack the money to hire or hold creative employees who could help them design programs, as well as the means to make serious investments in quality online offerings.

For some of the early entrants, building online capacity meant postponing returns on their investments. While the market for their programs was still small, they learned how to evaluate and improve their offerings. For new entrants now, the quality barriers are positioned much higher. When few colleges had online programs, yours did not have to compete with well-researched, well-marketed, already established products.

Now, to enter the market successfully, a college will have to outperform its competitors along some dimensions: better outreach, better mentoring, or clearer or more entertaining presentations. They will need metrics in place to demonstrate why and how their courses are superior to others, or cheaper than others, or lead to better outcomes in the world of work. It will be a daunting task. Not undoable, but not for the faint of heart, or the dilettantes who want to offer a few trial courses.

The colleges that will succeed in entering this new system of higher education delivery will be those whose leaders have a clear vision of where they want to go, how they want to add value to programs, and how they will measure and continually improve them. Most of all, they will commit to hiring and training talented people who share a passion for delivering quality education, and they will have a long-term plan, approved by their board, to make the necessary investments to build programs with integrity.

At SNHU, Paul LeBlanc is working on keeping his college ahead of where potential new entrants to the market will try to position themselves. He has hired a vice president for SNHU's Innovation Lab, whose job is to "focus over the horizon." LeBlanc says, "We are also bringing in game designers." He plans to keep his university at the cutting edge.

Even though he is committed to educating students through competency development, which he admits is more related to the world of work than to traditional college program offerings, LeBlanc worries that some "ineffable quality, such as in the humanities, may be squeezed out," like what occurred as a result of the No Child Left Behind federal program. Its focus on test results, some say, has produced students who can answer the test questions but have more difficulty with reasoning and building compelling positions. In fact, many students in my own classes in recent years have demonstrated this problem. Although they spell correctly, and their essays are largely grammatically correct (a pleasant change from the papers I received in earlier classes years ago), fewer know how to make a convincing argument.

There are other challenges coming with technology, some that we can imagine and some that we have not yet thought of. Of those we can imagine, several leap readily to mind. Even with a superstar presenter, a student may not stay tuned in or learn the material. One professor offering an online course has said that fewer than 10% of students who sign up for his online course finish it (Leuty, 2013). To do well in online courses, students need to be disciplined and committed. Not everyone will stick it out.

The faculty union at the University of California at Santa Cruz signaled another problem when it demanded laws to guarantee that professors would own the intellectual property rights to classes and lecture materials they offer. The union claimed that proposed waivers for professors offering courses on Coursera would irrevocably grant the university absolute rights to use the materials (Rivard, 2013).

In addition, MOOCs are costly to put up and administer and still have not earned money. If they do become successful, they too will face their own competition.

One leader of a for-profit college corporation confided that he believes MOOCs are unlikely to be as successful as their advocates claim. He said that they have not yet developed a viable business model for financing their offerings. Furthermore, the executive pointed out that as the MOOCs get courses accredited, the for-profits are likely to offer credit to their students for taking them. "We are already looking at this issue," he said. "If a course is available and legitimate, why would we not give credit for it?"

As more students take classes online, we may experience a further breakdown in socialization, which is already taking place and has been much written about and discussed. For example, in his brilliant article "Bowling Alone," Robert Putnam (1995) argues that we have become increasingly disconnected from friends and family, and the organizations people in America used to join. The example he uses about bowling comes from his data showing that although more people in our country are bowling more than ever before they are not bowling in leagues.

The Internet has allowed people to live life far more vicariously than was possible for most of them in the past. People have virtual friends and virtual experiences. One relative of mine recently argued with me about some of her online friends. Even though most had never met her, they cared about her, she assured me, offering what she claimed were examples of their concern for her well-being.

How much farther down the rabbit hole of living virtually instead of actually will many students go if they take all or almost all of their learning activities online? They may pass examinations more easily, especially if the training modules pinpoint and adjust to their learning styles and needs. But will they be able to synthesize what they know and use it in real-world activities, which increasingly rely on teamwork in the workplace?

Another issue that will potentially confront online education models will be the rise of superstar presenters. Much like gifted writers or talented athletes, they may "freelance" their offerings to the highest online college bidders. We may soon see a day when the best online teachers receive compensation based on the number of "hits" their classes receive, much like advertisers pay for hits on sites that feature their ads.

Already StraighterLine has a program that lets professors decide how much they want to charge for a course they offer. The program is called Professor Direct. A professor offering a course through the program sets a price to charge for the course. Of that charge, a base amount goes to StraighterLine, and the rest goes to the instructor. Of course, competition determines whether or not one professor can charge more than others do for similar courses, but after all, there are a lot of different prices for all kinds of goods and services in the marketplace.

Finally, what will be the social cost of further fractionation of our citizenry? When I was young, we all read the same one or two major newspapers in our town. We watched the same three or four television stations for news. We may not have received all the news that was fit to print or speak about, but we all read and heard much the same slants on the news.

Today newspapers are having a hard time surviving. Technology is rendering them obsolete, not because they are not needed, but because their business model is no longer working. Not enough people are reading them to induce enough advertisers to spend enough money for newspapers to support their missions.

The same thing is happening across the major television news outlets, as more move from expensive news gathering to less expensive opinion presenting. More and more people read, listen to, or watch only those papers or shows that agree with the opinions the readers and listeners already have.

More people than ever go online for their news now but frequently select only that which reifies what they already believe. Moreover, many cannot adequately separate fact from fiction, and thus rumors take on active lives online. This can be destructive to the fabric of our communities and our citizenship.

It is not all negative, though. It is certainly wonderful to be able to do online searches of all kinds. The web is used so much precisely because it provides so much value. But the loss of formative socialization experiences must not be taken lightly. Although many students in the past never had a residential college experience, even those who commuted to their classes or were loners still had shared time in the classroom or the cafeteria or on walks across their campuses. The loss of these kinds of shared experiences could be devastating for the students and the nation.

References

Almanac of Higher Education 2013. (2013.) Fastest growing campuses. In *The Chronicle of Higher Education, 59*(46), 27.

Bohn, B., Reyes, B., & Johnson, H. (2013, March). *The impact of budget cuts on California's community colleges.* San Francisco, CA: Public Policy Institute of California.

Christensen, C., & Eyring, H. J. (2011). *The innovative university: Changing the DNA of higher education from the inside out.* San Francisco, CA: Jossey-Bass.

Commission on Osteopathic College Accreditation. (2013, November 18). *Colleges of osteopathic medicine.* Retrieved from http://www.osteopathic.org/inside-aoa/accreditation/predoctoral%20accreditation/Documents/current-list-of-colleges-of-osteopathic-medicine.pdf

Commission on the Regulation of Postsecondary Distance Education. (2013, April). *Advancing access through regulatory reform: Findings, principles, and recommendations for the state authorization reciprocity agreement (SARA).* Retrieved from http://www.sheeo.org/sites/default/files/publications/Commission%20on%20Regulation%20of%20Postsecondary%20Distance%20Education%20Draft%20Recommendations%20FINAL%20April%20_0.pdf

Kolowich, S. (2013, March 20). SUNY signals major push toward MOOCs and other new educational models. *The Chronicle of Higher Education.* Retrieved from http://chronicle.com/blogs/wiredcampus/suny-signals-major-push-toward-moocs-and-other-new-educational-models/43079

LeBlanc, P. (2012, November). *Confronting crisis: SNHU rethinks higher education.* Presentation at Harvard University, Cambridge, MA.

Leuty, R. (2013, February 1). Big MOOCs on campus. *San Francisco Business Times.* Retrieved from http://www.bizjournals.com/sanfrancisco/print-edition/2013/02/01/big-moocs-on-campus.html?page=all

Lewin, T. (2013a, April 12). Proposal addresses out-of-state web courses. *New York Times,* p. A13.

Lewin, T. (2013b, April 30). Colleges adapt online courses to ease burden. *New York Times*, p. A1.

Liberty University. (2013a). *Consolidated financial statements and supplementary information years ended June 2013 and 2012.* Retrieved from http://www.dacbond.com/dacContent/doc.jsp?id=0900bbc78011c8c2

Liberty University. (2013b). *Liberty University quick facts.* Retrieved from http://www.liberty.edu/index.cfm?PID=6925

Liberty University. (2013c). *Notice of nondiscrimination.* Retrieved from http://www.liberty.edu/law/index.cfm?PID=8533

Powell, J. (2008). What sort of e-business is post-compulsory education? In J. Boys & P. Ford (Eds.), *The e-revolution and post-compulsory education: Using e-business models to deliver quality education* (pp. 49–67). New York, NY: Routledge.

Putnam, R. D. (1995). Bowling alone: America's declining social capital. *Journal of Democracy, 6*(1), 65–78.

Rivard, R. (2013, March 19). Who owns a MOOC? *Inside Higher Ed.* Retrieved from http://www.insidehighered.com/news/2013/03/19/u-california-faculty-union-says-moocs-undermine-professors-intellectual-property#ixzz2O2J1AT00

Straumsheim, C. (2013, October 1). How to build a university in 7 months. *Inside Higher Ed.* Retrieved from http://www.insidehighered.com/news/2013/10/01/u-florida-races-create-online-campus-jan-1-opening-date-approaches

SUNY Empire State College. (2014). *Ways to study.* Retrieved from https://www.esc.edu/degrees-programs/ways-to-study/

U.S. News & World Report. (2013a). *Best online bachelor's programs.* Retrieved from http://www.usnews.com/education/online-education/bachelors/

U.S. News & World Report. (2013b). *Online degree search: Graduate education programs.* Retrieved from http://www.usnews.com/education/online-education/education/search?name=university+of+new+england

U.S. News & World Report. (2013c). *Southern New Hampshire University.* Retrieved from http://colleges.usnews.rankingsandreviews.com/best-colleges/southern-new-hampshire-university-2580

U.S. News & World Report. (2014). *Regional university North rankings.* Retrieved from http://colleges.usnews.rankingsandreviews.com/best-colleges/liberty-university-10392

Vedder, R., Denhart, C., & Robe, J. (2013, January). *Why are recent college graduates underemployed? University enrollments and labor-market realities.* Washington, DC: Center for College Affordability and Productivity. Retrieved from http://centerforcollegeaffordability.org/research/studies/underemployment-of-college-graduates

7 Prescriptions for Higher Education

Yogi Berra, the Yankees baseball star, famously said, "When you come to a fork in the road, take it." Higher education has come to its fork in the road, and it is a very portentous fork. On one side lies the path to doing more of the same old thing, a road to decline for all but the strongest, wealthiest, most selective independent colleges and well-funded state colleges. On the other side is the route to improved opportunities through technological innovations and managerial shifts that will enable America's nonprofit colleges to remain viable and strong.

Technology is providing many potential tools to do this. For example, the state of California has opened a path to reduce textbook costs for students. The state passed two bills in late 2012 to provide free, open-source textbooks for 50 of the most widely taken introductory courses offered by colleges in the three state college systems: the University of California, the California State University, and the California Community College systems.

This will potentially save hundreds of dollars a year for each student in California's public colleges. It is a great way for the state to ensure that its funding is of direct benefit to the students attending the state schools. It is a fine example of the use of technology to lower the costs to several hundred thousand students. It is also a harbinger of the opportunities that the use of technology may enable.

Other states can and should follow suit. They owe it to their students to invest in reducing the costs for them to receive the college education they will need to become productive and appropriately employed adults.

In thinking about the future of higher education, it is easy to assume that what we have always known will continue, and that colleges will remain what they have been, with a little tweaking to make them more effective and responsive. But that comfortable scenario is unlikely to hold, even though most educators still are betting on it. In fact, they are betting so heavily that most colleges have only tangentially altered their programs or financial models to add a handful of online courses in some cases, or to find ways to tighten their belts in others. This is partly because most higher education leaders frankly do not know what to do, or how to confront a rapidly changing future, especially if their institutions lack deep pockets.

Higher education is all about learning, so it is reasonable to ask what our traditional colleges are learning now about changes they must make. Certainly corporate educational entities are trying to learn as much as they possibly can that will be useful to them from the nonprofit sector. They are trying to learn it and apply what they feel is valid and reasonable for their colleges as quickly as possible.

What For-Profits Have Learned From Nonprofits

For-profit colleges have a lot at stake, and they are trying to learn as much as they can to enhance their productivity and success. To do this, they are looking at the nonprofits to see what they can learn from them. One of the easiest ways to do this is to hire leaders from the nonprofit sector, and many of the for-profit colleges are doing just that.

These leaders bring with them the knowledge of what does and does not work well in traditional higher education institutions. The for-profits that want to adapt what works in the nonprofit sector have not been shy about copying good programs and strategies.

Increasing Retention and Graduation

First and most important, for-profit colleges know that they must improve their retention and graduation rates. This means that they must be able to have a higher proportion of their students complete their present coursework and stay in the college until they have completed the degree program for which they enrolled.

The main reason they need improvement in this area is that retention and graduation rates for many for-profit colleges are too low for them to maintain accreditation, which threatens federal aid availability for their potential enrollees. A second reason is that low retention is economically costly and therefore bad business practice. It costs a lot more to recruit a new student than to retain an existing one.

The leaders of these colleges know, from the myriad studies of retention in higher education, that there is a strong relationship between the selectivity of a college and its retention and graduation rates. Students with higher grade point averages (GPAs) and higher college entrance examination scores are more likely to persist in their studies. So are students who have come from high schools and preparatory schools that are known for their academic rigor.

By and large, those are not the students who apply to for-profit colleges. Their students' average SAT college entrance examination scores have been more than 200 points below the average for all high school seniors. Only 54% had GPAs that were a B or above, compared with 83% of all seniors. In addition, 71% came from families where neither parent had graduated from college, and far more of them came from households whose income before taxes was $40,000 or less (Kantrowitz, 2009, p. 3).

Students who enter college with fewer advantages can persist in college and do well. Some community colleges and four-year institutions have developed programs to help less well-prepared students be successful in their academic programs. The key to doing this is to build strong academic advising programs and learning support centers.

Advising helps students to understand the academic programs in which they are most likely to enjoy success, and the courses they will need to take to receive a degree in one of those programs. Learning centers help students to learn good study habits, as well as to identify their own best learning styles. Learning centers also generally offer tutoring services.

Providing Institutional Financial Aid

Some for-profit colleges are already tinkering with various discounting methods gleaned from the independent colleges. However, they are applying them in more businesslike models that resemble "buy-one-get-one-free" sales offers and frequent-flyer point programs.

Even if for-profits go down the discount war road, they are unlikely to fall into the economic muddle that some independents now face because their economic models require budgets that are expected to yield returns on investments.

Providing Personalized Student Services

As the for-profit college sector grows, it is likely to enhance its student services, starting with the advising and learning center type of services, but expanding to other arenas, especially tutoring. In particular, for-profit colleges with mostly online programs that want to rise to the top will need to find ways to augment their online offerings with some face-to-face tutoring and learning services.

Interestingly, one of the best examples of the advantage of face-to-face personalized service is offered not by a nonprofit college, but by one of the world's most successful and profitable companies: Apple. There are a lot of reasons why Apple is a great company, starting with its creativity and the quality of its products. But a significant reason that people buy and use Apple products is the personal tutoring and product services that Apple provides, through its Apple retail stores and its AppleCare telephone services.

If you have a problem with Microsoft, good luck. You can send the company an e-mail, but most likely you will not get an immediate response, or the response may not be clear or help to resolve the problem. But if you get an AppleCare warranty, you receive several years of eligible call-in support, with generally quick resolution of your issues.

If you have either hardware or software problems, your Apple retail store staff are available to walk you through your issues. Apple products frequently cost more than the competition's, but the quality of the products and the quality of the services make them worth more.

People who transfer to Apple from another operating system have to learn new methods of managing their computing needs. Although Apple is easy to use, the transition to Apple's system may not be easy for first-time users. Apple knows this and makes it easier to learn to use their products by offering hands-on, in-store classes for $99 a year, which allows a purchaser to take as many in-store, face-to-face classes as he or she wants for the one low price.

For-profit colleges could learn a lot from Apple. In conjunction with their online classes, large educational corporations should look at setting up small tutoring centers across the nation where online students can drop in to get face-to-face help with their classes when they need that extra support.

What Nonprofits Can Learn From For-Profits

Robert Reich, the former U.S. secretary of labor under President Clinton, has offered a succinct prescription for what nonprofit higher education needs to do. In an article written for college trustees, his response to a question about what colleges should do to make sure they remain competitive and responsive to the needs of their students was that they should

- Expand online learning, along with evening, weekend, and summer classes.
- Develop three-year bachelor of technology programs combining the last year of high school with the first two years of college.
- "Reduce amenities unrelated to learning" (p. 40).
- "Run more large-scale lecture classes combined with small, intensive seminars" (Reich, 2013, p. 40).

Although profit-seeking colleges may not yet be doing a nearly good enough job, they will improve. To meet the competition that the for-profits offer, nonprofit colleges will have to make some important changes. The easiest ways for for-profits to determine the kinds of changes that are necessary are to look at where the for-profits are and are not putting their resources, followed by examining the for-profit college sector's successes and failures.

This does not mean that public and independent colleges should copy what the for-profit sector is doing. There would be no need for nonprofit colleges if the marketplace could perfectly provide the mix, the quality, and the ethical commitments to the life of the mind and spirit that the nonprofit schools, at their best, provide. But if we want to have great nonprofit colleges and universities available in the future for people other than the richest or smartest or most extraordinarily talented, then major alterations have to take place in the usual ways that nonprofit colleges conduct their programs and manage their educational institutions.

This book has proposed nine strategies that can help nonprofit colleges survive and flourish. The adoption of each of these strategies will help to enable our nonprofit colleges to lower their costs, reduce or hold down their tuition levels, and compete effectively for students. The nine strategies are as follows:

1. Focus on outcomes.
2. Strengthen customer service.
3. Develop and market a brand.
4. Rent more and build less.
5. Phase out tenure.
6. Reduce administrative bloat.
7. Eliminate intercollegiate athletics.
8. Outsource noneducational services.
9. Use technology to enhance academic programs.

Focus on Outcomes

American colleges spend their resources largely on inputs. They want large applicant pools and low acceptance rates in order to show how desirable they are. They try to build newer and better facilities and to hire faculty who are well known in their own fields. Of course outputs such as retention and graduation rates matter, but the expectation is that if you put in the right mix of inputs, you will get the desired outputs. What all colleges need to do instead is to focus on the outcomes they want their graduates to be able to achieve, and then design and test the programs they need to offer to see if they yield the desired results.

Regional accrediting agencies are now requiring colleges they accredit to better demonstrate the processes they use to determine appropriate outcomes for their graduates, and to show how those outcomes are being met. Specialized accreditation needs to do the same thing. Although many of the specialized accrediting agencies now stress outcomes, most still stress inputs far too much. "Bean counting" of the number of professors in the program, the credentials of program chairs, the number of books in the specialized library, the GPA of the entering class, and similar inputs still weigh far too heavily in evaluations. What should and must matter are the competencies that the graduates can master, the ability of the graduates to be hired for the jobs for which they were trained, and the satisfaction of both employers and graduates with the education that was provided.

Strengthen Customer Service

Improving customer service requires training personnel to respond rapidly to applicant and student requests. While a traditional college is putting together its acceptance lists, its competitors have already admitted the students on those lists. Academic offices are often slow to respond to prospective students' questions. Academic staff at all levels need to understand that the college's enrollments, and hence their jobs, depend on potential students' perceptions of their responsiveness.

Responding to customer needs includes scheduling more classes at times that are convenient not only for the students who live on campus, but for those who commute or must work. The for-profit colleges have grown even their on-site campuses by offering classes in the evenings and on weekends, when working students are able to attend.

Customer service also means listening carefully to what students complain about. This does not mean offering gut courses, or dumbing down the curriculum. It does mean making tough decisions about faculty who are regularly criticized as poor teachers. Some smart colleges have centers to assist faculty in learning to be better teachers. All colleges need them.

Develop and Market a Brand

Every college needs to think about and develop its own brand, based on whom it wishes to serve and how it wants to structure and offer its own set of programs. For-profit colleges excel at building market awareness for their institutional brands.

A brand tells potential students who an institution is and what it offers, and how it offers it in ways that are different from those of other colleges in which an applicant might enroll. The college must then market itself aggressively.

Rent More and Build Less

Putting money into building new facilities ties up funds. Those funds could otherwise be invested immediately in strengthening existing programs or building exciting new ones. Colleges should rent needed additional facilities rather than building them wherever feasible.

For-profit colleges spend very little of their resources on facilities they own except when they buy an extant college campus. Instead, they use their funds up front, developing their content, their advertising, and their admissions efforts.

Phase Out Tenure

Colleges can gain a lot of additional flexibility without eliminating tenure just by phasing it out for all new hires. While this is a long-term fix, it can work only if no exceptions are made. That means that instead of hiring part-time and contingent faculty to avoid granting tenure, full-time people are hired on multiyear contracts, with reasonable expectations of contract renewals.

Many colleges invested in the wholesale use of contingent faculty still offer tenure, of course, but they reserve it for occasional faculty stars. Making the commitment to phase out tenure is a more ethical way to achieve faculty staffing flexibility while ensuring that students have full-time faculty teaching their classes, so that the faculty are invested in their students and fully available to them, after class as well as in class.

Reduce Administrative Bloat

Staff growth in the nonprofit higher education sector has far outpaced faculty growth, adding costs and unnecessary layers of administration. This bloat increases the levels of command; ensures costly redundancies in decision making; and makes it harder, rather than easier, to make rapid changes.

Reducing the bureaucracies that have been built up in many colleges and universities is one of the easiest fixes that institutions can undertake. It takes the will and determination of boards and presidents and requires that they ask remaining staff to take on additional, reasonable responsibilities. They can often do this by just reducing the numbers of approvals that members of the college community need to get, for even simple tasks and expenditures, and by reducing the number of intermediate levels of administration.

Eliminate Intercollegiate Athletics

Colleges need to stop pouring their scarce resources into intercollegiate athletics. The money lost on competitive sports can be far better used to improve academic programs, support services, and technological expansions.

Intercollegiate athletics benefits only a small number of students at large, athletically competitive schools, such as those in the football bowl league. Of course, many other students at those colleges, especially resident students, do strongly support their teams, in particular men's football and basketball teams. The costs, however, add to the tuition burdens of every student at colleges with large competitive sports budgets because only a handful of colleges break even on their athletic expenditures, let alone make a profit.

The cost of athletics is one major expense that most for-profit colleges never budget for. They recognize that intercollegiate athletics is not the major recruitment tool that traditional colleges have assumed it is. The fact that you do not need to spend your money on athletics to attract or hold students could be one of the most valuable lessons that public and independent colleges could learn from those in the for-profit sector. The convenience and ease of entry of your programs means more to the bulk of prospective students than supporting athletic programs does.

Outsource Noneducational Services

Colleges of the future are going to concentrate their efforts on delivery of educational programs and services. Smart ones will do what modern businesses have been doing for a long time: outsourcing the work that is not central to what they do. In particular, they need to outsource work that others do better or can provide more efficiently or less expensively at desired quality standards.

Use Technology to Enhance Academic Programs

Nonprofit colleges need to use technology to build new content delivery models, thereby enhancing their academic programs. A lot of different models of content delivery are being offered by the for-profit sector. Many of the programs being provided, even by the largest for-profit colleges, still utilize old-fashioned classrooms and chalkboards with the teacher lecturing in front of the class.

The come-on has often been the lure of e-learning, but the reality translated into the same old comfortable models, just offered at more convenient times and places and schedules. For-profits, as well as some forward-looking nonprofit colleges, have been moving heavily into online courses, and now online degree programs. This is where higher education is heading, and all the resistance in the world is not going to make it recede.

Those colleges that want to jump on the bandwagon, building online competence, need to develop more than just online courses to offer. They also need to build an infrastructure of support personnel, including information technology staff, committed faculty, Internet resources, website builders, and technical and legal experts. Building online delivery capacity will enable colleges to enhance learning opportunities and, if done well, eventually lower delivery costs.

The commitment must extend beyond staff and into a culture that values and seeks new opportunities and is willing to determine appropriate outcomes for its programs. The commitment must also include openly measuring and documenting not only the institutional successes, but the failures as well. Colleges will also need to demonstrate how they have learned from their failures, and what they are doing to mitigate those problems.

Nonprofit colleges may never be able to lower their costs per student as much as for-profits do. The reason is that the states (in the case of public colleges) and boards and constituencies (in the case of independent colleges) may have expensive requirements or preferences. For state colleges, some high-overhead programs may be necessary to offer, such as dentistry or aeronautical engineering.

Some independent colleges with costly but high-quality specialized programs, such as a doctoral program in physics or an undergraduate program in mining engineering, may determine that their institutional mission or ethos justifies such expenditures. In fact, for most nonprofit colleges, both public and independent, offering a wide array of academic degree programs is a cornerstone of what they believe is their responsibility if they are to provide students with an education the colleges can be proud of.

Some nonprofit colleges have learned some things from the for-profits already, according to Paul LeBlanc. He says of his college,

> We borrowed their approach to strong customer service. We have learned to speed up the processing of applications. We log calls in with our admissions representatives. We search for people with strong skills in this area, and then train them on our processes. Our approach is very disciplined. We ask ourselves, what underserved market can we serve? What are they buying from us? How can we best serve them? We build a business model to serve their needs.

As LeBlanc has shown, colleges that want to compete successfully in the college education marketplace of the future must develop standards and measurement processes that will yield metrics to document their effectiveness.

How Accrediting Agencies Can Support Reform

Across the political spectrum, there is a lot of criticism about our accrediting agencies. It is particularly strong among some conservative factions, who see accreditation as costly and rigid, standing in the path of exciting new ways of delivering content. Others acknowledge that accreditation can protect students from low-quality programs but argue that these organizations substantially serve as gatekeepers for their present members, raising barriers to entry, which protect the inefficient and potentially raise costs for users of the services.

The Heritage Foundation states:

> The accreditation system has morphed into a powerful and rigid system whereby a few large regional and national accrediting agencies have a tremendous amount of power over higher education. This system, in turn, creates massive and expensive headaches for existing colleges and universities; crowds out new higher education start-ups; and creates an inflexible and questionable college experience for students who, in order to be eligible for federal student aid, have little choice but to attend accredited institutions. (as cited in Burke & Butler, 2012)

Critics on the other side see regional accreditation as too complacent and opaque. They want tougher standards applied, to prevent colleges that are marginal from operating at the expense of their students, who remain uninformed that their school may have been threatened with loss of accreditation more than a few times.

Others see accrediting agencies as too soft on for-profit colleges and letting standards get diluted. When ITT bought financially troubled but still accredited Webster College in New England, a spokesman for the American Association of Collegiate Registrars & Admissions Officers said that the regional accrediting bodies "bestow the valuable credential with scant scrutiny of the buyers' backgrounds" ("ITT 'Buying Accreditation' Strategy," 2010).

Accreditation agencies are accused of being too protective and not protective enough, or of being averse to change. However, some of the agencies are forthrightly supporting new ways of looking at student achievement if a college presents strong proposals and is a "trusted player," as one agency president put it.

Some academic leaders suggest that having geographical bounded areas for regional accreditation might no longer be appropriate, given the rise of national for-profit colleges and the e-learning networks with national and international reach. Shirley M. Tilghman, president of Princeton University, said that it might be more useful to have accrediting agencies relate to the types of institutions, such as their Carnegie classifications, rather than their regions (Lederman, 2011).

As someone with experience on both regional and specialized accrediting bodies, I know how committed members of these commissions are, and how hard they work. And having had to go through accreditation reviews at five different institutions, I believe that the process of institutional self-analysis strengthens colleges and is more than worth the dollar investment. Accreditation helps an institution hold a mirror up to itself and observe what others see. Smart institutions use the process to strengthen themselves. In fact, a recent study by the American Council on Education reported that a majority of presidents at both public (59%) and private (54%) institutions indicated that assessment of and accountability for student learning is emerging as the most important driver of change at their own institutions (American Council on Education, 2012).

There are two crucial changes that accrediting agencies need to make. The first is to pare back the high costs of accreditation. "Accreditation needs to become more streamlined," according to Judith Eaton, president of the Council for Higher Education Accreditation (CHEA). "We can drill down and rethink what levels of detail we really need." The second change is to shift from an accreditation focus still heavily focused on inputs to one substantially looking at outcomes. Although outcome assessment is now a major driver for some agencies, all of them need to reduce the long-term emphasis on inputs that has led to increased costs and undermined creativity in program delivery.

How Government Can Support Reform

Higher education is free or very low cost in some nations, and it was free in some American cities and states in the past. If technology and the rise of for-profit colleges had not changed the playing field so much, a good argument could be made for having our national government underwrite college tuition as a public good, similar to welfare programs and Medicare. It could be means tested, but it would be available to everyone, enabling the poor to fairly compete economically for college seats.

This is very unlikely to happen today, partly because of the state of the American economy and partly because public organizations are not generally efficient providers of services. Inefficiency thrives when no one's pocketbook is directly impacted by an incompetent employee, an outmoded work custom, or too many paid holidays.

Although the public sector can be more equitable in distributing opportunities than the for-profit sector, higher education is still relatively stratified in the United States. According to one critic, "Higher education has become a type of market for career advancement that is drifting out of the reach of those in lower socioeconomic classes" (Strong, 2007, p. 52).

What government policies should do is facilitate the widest possible access to higher education across all income groups. What they should not do is dictate the content of academic programs, nor the method by which they are delivered. Such academic decisions should be made only by faculty within disciplines that a college offers and approved by the appropriate regional and specialized accrediting agencies. But government can offer financial carrots or withhold monetary benefits from academic institutions that fail to meet certain public goals.

What States Can Do

States need to model good behavior for their colleges if they want their colleges to perform efficiently and at high quality. The most important single action that states can take to show how serious they are about quality and cost control at their colleges is to empower their system offices and not do legislative end runs around them.

At the same time, system offices need to demonstrate that they run with lean, highly professional staffs that can and do make hard decisions to rationalize what the colleges offer and the budget allocations to them. All colleges need to offer certain basic general education courses, but system boards should significantly limit duplication of specialized, expensive, or low-enrollment programs.

System offices should be responsible for assembling building and maintenance requests, as well as prioritizing them. Deferred maintenance on heavily utilized facilities should normally have priority over the building of any new facilities unless they are crucial to the provision of educational services on a campus.

Colleges need to be freed from the cost and time involved in having to support lobbying efforts. Many colleges hire lobbyists not just to help them get more resources at the public trough, but more frequently to prevent takeaways, or poaching efforts by their sister colleges.

For public colleges to give up their lobbying effort and expenditures, governors and legislative leaders need to agree to support systems, rather than individual colleges, including their land-grant universities, except in the most extraordinary circumstances. It ought to be seen as a mark of dishonor for a college leader, or a legislator, to try to get around system agreed-to recommendations.

States also need to demand more accountability from their colleges. This does not mean cutting budgets, but rather rewarding accomplishments, even if the dollars are redirected from the same pool.

When I was at the University of Minnesota Duluth in the early 1990s, it was well known that some of the professors and advisors were encouraging their majors to take just 12 credits a semester, especially in their first year or two. The *light loads*, as they were termed, were recommended so that the students would not be overburdened and would do well in all their classes. At that rate, in eight semesters, they would earn just 96 credits. They needed 120 credits to graduate. As a result, the four-year graduation rate was dismal. Most advisors and professors, there and elsewhere, no longer encourage light loads except for students having academic problems or needing a lot of support to become acculturated to college-level academic expectations.

Most students who take light loads today do so at their own behest, though. Some need to work and cannot fit a full load of classes into their schedules. Others drop courses when they are not doing well in them, have missed too many classes, or are behind in turning in assignments. For too long, colleges have been lax in allowing generous dropout policies with no academic or other penalties.

The state of Florida has toughened up its penalties for students using its Bright Futures scholarships, creating disincentives for noncompletion of courses. Students who withdraw from or do not complete courses will have to reimburse the program for dollars they received to pay for those courses.

Public universities in Florida made improvements between 2007 and 2012, even though state funding for the University of Florida system fell from $2.6 billion to $1.7 billion. Its full-time equivalent student funding fell from $7,656 to $4,387. In spite of the cuts to the budgets, the system's universities increased their overall enrollment by 12% between 2006 and 2011, and their combined six-year graduation rate increased to 66%, placing them in the top 10 nationally (American Council of Trustees and Alumni, 2013, pp. 1–2).

States can reward colleges for improved graduation rates. They should give rewards for graduating students who start as freshmen in four years, as well as those who transfer into a college in their junior year and graduate within two years. A reward for the latter metric could do a lot to finally make the concept of seamless transfers a reality because colleges would push their faculty to remove the barriers that require so many transfer students to have to spend an extra semester or year in the transfer institution due to protectionist policies that often require needless repetition of courses already taken, or additional requirements in the major taken at the new college.

Performance-based funding is growing in several states. Tennessee and New Mexico are giving extra support to colleges that graduate high numbers of older students and low-income students. Missouri is tying funding to graduation rates and licensure-passage rates (Education Commission of the States e-Clips, 2013).

States need to take a harder line on the overbuilding of facilities at their public colleges. Again, this does not mean refusing to fund necessary facilities, but rather raising hard questions about needs, and respecting the prioritization of building projects proposed by system offices.

States can also urge their colleges to work on three-year bachelor's degree programs and reward them for students who successfully complete such programs. The reward should not be given for programs that simply force the students to go to school year-round.

Athletics is a difficult area to ask state governments to deal with. On the one hand, state officials do not want to be embarrassed by athletic scandals. On the other hand, they love it when tourists and the media come to their communities when they have winning teams.

It is hard to know how much support for diminishing the presence of intercollegiate athletics any college leader will get from local and state officials and politicians. After all, these are the people who assess low- and middle-income taxpayers in order to build athletic stadiums for privately owned, for-profit professional athletic teams whose owners are multimillionaires.

The biggest thing that states can do for their public colleges is to give them more financial support in return for the colleges keeping tuition levels low. Then the states must monitor compliance to be sure that the funds go where they are intended, to keep classes affordable.

What the Federal Government Can Do

The federal government could make a decision to fully fund higher education for all undergraduates in the nation. Other countries do this. But our republican system of governance has vested the primary responsibility for funding all levels of education with the states. At the moment, there is no serious discussion at the federal level of providing free higher education. Discussions remain limited to Pell Grants and other forms of aid, along with federal loans for higher education.

Even if the federal government were to fully fund students, most people would want the carrots of aid but not the sticks of control. Almost no one really wants the federal government to meddle too much in higher education because our government is an even more inefficient provider of services than the average university. However, there are a few things that our national government, fiddling around the edges, could accomplish.

The most important thing that the federal government could do for American colleges would be to reduce the onslaught of regulations to which colleges have been subjected. Most of the regulations have little to do with education itself, except for the reporting on IPEDS. IPEDS is the Integrated Postsecondary Education Data System, a set of surveys that colleges participating in federal student financial aid programs are required to fill out each year.

Colleges must provide information on their enrollments, program completions, graduation rates, faculty and staff, finances, institutional prices, and student financial aid to the U.S. Department of Education National Center for Education Statistics (NCES). These data are then made available to the public.

It is reasonable to expect colleges to provide these data to prospective students and their families, as well as to other interested citizens. But this is far from the only set of regulations required of colleges. Most of the requirements, such as those under the Environmental Protection Agency (EPA), are there for good reasons. However, the sum total of all the regulatory compliance required is burdensome and costly.

Our government needs to carefully examine its hundreds of thousands of regulations, and not just for higher education. The list of federal regulations is so lengthy that the 2009 edition of the Code of Federal Regulations ran to just over 163,000 pages in 226 individual books (Office of the Federal Register, 2010).

Another area where government policy could make a difference, at least in leveling the nonprofit college competition playing field and slowing down the arms race, is in the tax treatment of endowments. Any policy changes here would be just as valid for nonprofit organizations outside of the academic arena.

There is nothing wrong with colleges and other organizations building endowments. In fact, well-managed organizations can and should raise funds and invest them. Endowments help organizations have rainy-day funds to tide them over during economic turndowns in donor support, or to cope with unforeseen emergencies. They also allow colleges to provide scholarship support, or to have the funds available to provide extra dollars for star-level visiting professors.

The issue, however, is not endowments, but the use of tax advantages to enable some organizations and colleges to build up far more dollars than they need, in funds that do not get spent on the organizations' goals and may never get spent. In the world of donors and fund-raising efforts, too often those who have are those who get.

Nonprofit institutions such as Harvard University could fund themselves for years just by spending down their endowments, without raising any additional dollars at all. In an article on Philanthropy Roundtable, Tom Riley (n.d.), noting that endowment funds at big nonprofits have "skyrocketed," asks, "Is it 'charitable' to fund programs at organizations that could just as easily fund these programs themselves?" He further asks, "How is it that those large nonprofits that are swimming in money are so successful at garnering more money?" The answer he provides is that they already have money and thus can hire the best fund-raisers.

Most nonprofits can never raise this kind of money. "There are not enough charitable resources in this country for every charity to stockpile funds worth several times their annual budgets, and operate using only the interest income generated by these funds," according to the American Institute of Philanthropy ("Large Asset Charity," 2009).

Service on several grant-making foundations taught me that the neediest and most worthy organizations sometimes could not write the best proposals. The communities they were serving might have had the greatest needs, however. Helping these smaller nonprofits step up to the next level could often yield a much greater return on the dollars granted than grants to more sophisticated organizations in terms of the differences they could make.

Because the federal government allows a tax deduction for charitable gifts such as those made to endowment funds of tax-exempt organizations, our government could tinker with the tax code to lessen the tendency of some nonprofits to hoard their endowment dollars while they continue to raise more and more funds. There are several ways this could be done. One way would be to continue the tax exemption for qualified nonprofits but have nonprofit organizations pay taxes scaled to the percentage of funds they hold in their endowment or as a surplus in their budget in excess of two years (or any other arbitrary amount) of operating funds.

A second option would be to require endowments that are more than twice the size of an organization's annual budget to spend a much higher percentage of the surplus above that amount or lose their tax deduction. Exceptions could be made for foundations that are set up for the primary purpose of giving out grants, though they also should have higher payout requirements. A third option would recognize consumer choice and allow the giver to make the decision by reducing the giver's level of tax deductibility for gifts to nonprofits with the kinds of excess fund capacity illustrated.

This is not an argument against endowments, which organizations must build, or against tax deductibility. Instead, it is an effort to recognize in public policy that when an organization accepts a tax exemption it becomes semipublic in that the rest of the tax-paying public is effectively subsidizing the exemption by needing to replace the funds that are taken from the public coffers through the exemption.

Through its federal financial aid programs, the federal government is the biggest player of all in higher education. The federal government funded 71% of all student aid and 41% of all grant aid to postsecondary students in 2012–13. (College Board, 2013, p. 3).

Pell Grants need to be more generous, though. They need to keep pace with inflation. Even though many critics say that federal aid allows colleges to raise their rates as students receive more support, there is no real evidence to support such a charge. Moreover, colleges vary widely in their pricing levels, so benefits to students cannot be translated directly into benefits to colleges.

Along with increasing the amount of grants, the federal government needs to better regulate college loan programs. Additional regulations on lenders are needed to protect students from repayment scams, which frequently offer students low repayment interest rates that escalate sharply if a student misses even one scheduled debt payment.

Finally, the government should offer more ways for students to have some of their repayment forgiven by working at needed public service jobs. This could accomplish two goals: reducing student debt loads, and providing valuable job experience on which graduates could build their resumes.

On to the Future

Although there are things that state governments and the federal government can do to help our nonprofit colleges be sustainable and thrive, no government actions in and of themselves will make a lot of difference if our colleges do not boldly face their own futures.

Colleges can act individually or together within consortiums of like-minded institutions. No college can prevent the tsunami of changes that technology is now enabling, nor can any college stop the onslaught of advertising and marketing that for-profit colleges are increasingly going to be mounting. The spigot of potential student profits has been turned on, and it is not likely to be turned off. In fact, investments in the profit sector are likely to grow.

The challenge for traditional colleges will be in finding ways to hold on to demonstrably valuable traditions that truly provide students with both quality education and quality of life benefits while shifting to a newer, more strategic and efficient combination of content and delivery of educational programs and cocurricular services.

Some colleges have already undertaken substantial moves to align what they are offering with future trends and needs. Others are tinkering at the edges of change but not making the major realignments of their resources that will be necessary for institutional success a decade from now.

There will always be some colleges that can avoid making changes and still thrive. For some of them, when the need for change overwhelms them, they may be able to dig into their deep pockets and buy the fixes that they will need. Most colleges will not be able to do this, though. They need to start investing in their futures now.

A recent article in *Forbes* argued that the next big bubble in the economy will not be caused by nonprofit colleges closing their doors. The promise of online learning is not as good as it seems, the article claims. Online learning could wipe out traditional approaches "if learning were truly the purpose of attending Princeton" (Tamny, 2013). The article argues that when parents "spend a fortune on their children's schooling, they're not buying education." Instead, they are buying access to the right contacts and friends and career opportunities (Tamny, 2013).

That may be true for the fortunate few, but most Americans will not be able to afford to purchase those contacts and opportunities. For them, for the colleges that will need to serve them, and for a more egalitarian society, there need to be affordable options within the nonprofit higher education sector. To ensure access and some kind of decent campus life, we need to work on keeping our nonprofit colleges healthy and stable.

Higher education has enabled wonderful growth in the United States. At the age of 10, my father set out for America with his younger sister and arrived here two years later. After high school, by working at odd jobs, he was able to pay to bring the rest of his family here and put himself and his younger brother through pharmacy school.

My father died when I was a teenager, but I was able to attend an Ivy League university on a full scholarship. (I did pay full tuition when I returned to my alma mater for graduate school.) My life has been made meaningful through my long involvement in higher education, on many levels: as a faculty member, a faculty leader, an administrator, a trustee, an advocate, and now a critic. All the criticisms that are made here have been invoked in an effort to protect and improve one of the greatest assets of our nation, our nonprofit colleges and universities. They need to succeed.

References

American Council of Trustees and Alumni with the James Madison Institute. (2013, June). *Florida rising: An assessment of public universities in the sunshine state.* Executive Summary. Washington, DC: Author.

American Council on Education. (2012). *The American College President 2012.* Washington, DC: Author.

Burke, L., & Butler, S. M. (2012, September 21). *Accreditation: Removing the barrier to higher education reform.* Backgrounder #2728 on Education. Retrieved from http://www.heritage.org/research/reports/2012/09/accreditation-removing-the-barrier-to-higher-education-reform

College Board. (2013). Trends in college pricing. In *Trends in Higher Education.* Retrieved from https://trends.collegeboard.org/sites/default/files/college-pricing-2012-full-report_0.pdf

Education Commission of the States e-Clips. (2013, July 8). *A daily bite of top state education news.* Retrieved from http://view.exacttarget.com/?j=fe5910757466 05757c1c&m=febe15787c660074&ls=fdf710757c600c7e74177177&l=fe58 167572650d7f7c10&s=fe1d107770620d7f721c72&jb=ffcf14&ju=fe2f16797-4640c7f721671&r=0

ITT "buying accreditation" strategy makes critics uneasy. (2010, March 22). *Bloomberg News.* Retrieved from http://www.ibj.com/itt-strategy-of-buying-accreditation-makes-critics-uneasy-/PARAMS/article/18816

Kantrowitz, M. (2009, December 22). *Characteristics of students enrolling at for-profit colleges.* Retrieved from http://www.finaid.org/educators/20091222for-profit-colleges.pdf

Large asset charity threatens to close hospitals. (2009, August). *Charity Rating Guide & Watchdog Report.* Retrieved from charitywatch.org/articles/Shriners_Threatens _to_close_hospitals.html

Lederman, D. (2011, February 7). Policy making by Post-it Notes. *Inside Higher Ed.* Retrieved from http://www.insidehighered.com/news/2011/02/07/federal government_panel_begins_plotting_a_future_for_accreditation

Office of the Federal Register. (2010, July 15). *Federal register facts.* Retrieved from http://federalregister.gov/uploads/2011/01/fr_facts.pdf

Reich, R. (2013, March/April). How will education today affect the economy tomorrow? *Trusteeship,* 21(2), 40.

Riley, T. (n.d.). Them as has, gets: The problem of the profitable nonprofit. *Philanthropy Roundtable.* Retrieved from http://www.philanthropyroundtable.org/ topic/excellence_in_philanthropy/them_as_has_gets

Strong, A. B. (2007). Educating for power: How higher education contributes to the stratification of social class. *The Vermont Connection, 28,* 51–59.

Tamny, J. (2013, June 9). Online education will be the next 'bubble' to pop, not traditional university learning. *Forbes.* Retrieved from http://www.forbes.com/sites/ johntamny/2013/06/09/online-education-will-be-the-next-bubble-to-pop-not-traditional-university-learning/

Sandra Featherman is president emeritus of the University of New England. She was the president from 1995 through July 2006.

Dr. Featherman has vast experience in higher education standards and accreditation. She has worked at both public and private institutions, both Research I and community colleges, as a faculty member, administrator, or trustee. She has chaired the board of the Community College of Philadelphia and now serves on the board of Florida Polytechnic University, a new member institution in the State University System of Florida. She previously held positions at the University of Minnesota Duluth as vice chancellor for academic affairs, and at Temple University as assistant to the president and as president of the faculty senate.

Her many awards include Champion of Economic Development, Maine Development Foundation; Distinguished Daughter of Pennsylvania, Governor of Pennsylvania; Woman of Distinction, International Women's Forum; Woman of Distinction, Girl Scouts of Maine; City of Philadelphia Community Service Award; Brooks Graves Award, Pennsylvania Political Science Association; and Administrator of the Year, Minnesota Women in Higher Education.

Sandra's leadership roles have included service as vice chair of the Commission on Osteopathic College Accreditation (American Osteopathic Association), president of the Maine Independent Colleges Association, and president of the Greater Portland Alliance of Colleges and Universities. She has served on the Commission on Institutions of Higher Education (New England Association of Schools and Colleges), the Committee on Public Policy (National Association of Independent Colleges and Universities), and the Commission on Women in Higher Education (American Council on Education).

Dr. Featherman has chaired numerous state commissions including the State of Maine Governor's Blue Ribbon Commission on Health Care, the Maine Judicial Compensation Commission, the Maine Presiding Officers' Advisory Committee on Legislative Ethics, and the Maine Commission on the State Ceiling on Tax-Exempt Bonds. She also served on the Maine Task

Force on Pre-K through Grade 16, Pennsylvania Commission on the Arts, and the University of Maine System New Challenges/New Directions Task Force.

She has also served on the boards of numerous state and national organizations, including the Maine Community Foundation, the Samuel Fels Fund, the Girl Scouts of Maine, the American Association of University Women Education Foundation, the Maine Women's Forum, the Virginia Gildersleeve International Fund, Women and Foundations/Corporate Philanthropy, and the United Way of Pennsylvania.

Her BA, MA, and PhD are from the University of Pennsylvania. Her more than 50 academic publications include: "Higher Education in the United States: Changing Markets and Evolving Values" (University Press of America, 1998); *Race and Politics at the Millennium: The 1999 Mayoral Race in Philadelphia* (American Jewish Committee, 2000); and "The Status of Women in Higher Education Administration in the United States and Canada" (UNESCO, 1993), which was published in English, French, and Spanish.

of University of New England,
194–95
online graduate degree programs,
194–95
online lectures, 37
OpenCourseWare Consortium, 37
OpenSUNY (online program), 195
operating costs, of facilities, 107–11
Oregon, 67
OSHA. *See* Occupational Safety and
Health Administration
outcome focus, 166–67, 209–10
out-of-state students, 165–66
outsourcing
for-profit colleges, 155–56
nonprofit college's nonacademic and,
178–79, 212

Pace University, 197
Pattenaude, Richard L., 144, 152
Pell Grants, 103, 142, 221
pension plan policies, 135–36
personalized student services, 207–8
pharmacists, 22
PhD programs, 122, 177
physical therapy, 23, 92
Pilati, Michelle, 39
political lobbyists, 134–35, 216
politics, 20
population growth, 11
Potter, Claire, 17
Powell, J., 187
price lowering, 62–63
price point, 47, 98, 100
private colleges, 6–7
borrowing funds by, 106–7
closing of, 7
pension plan policies of, 135–36
problems confronting, 10
rising costs of, 26
state government funds assisting, 28
student numbers struggle of, 9
productivity gains, 82
Professor Direct, 202
professors, 37

proprietary colleges, 141
public bonds, 106
public colleges
economic issues faced by, 79–81
enrollment technology needed in,
180
finding right balance in, 77
Florida searches for, 150
legislative pressure on, 128–29
local boards governing, 133–34
pension plan policies of, 135–36
political influence on, 20
political lobbyists hired by, 134–35,
216
state government funds assisting, 28
state requirements for programs in,
58
state support declining for, 63
subsidies decreasing to, 132
unionized faculty at, 135
veterinary medicine programs at,
131–32
public funding, 4
public officials, 132
public school closings, 4
Purcell, Jim, 73
Putnam, Robert, 201

radiology residents, 21
rapid response time, 144–46
real-world activities, 202
recruitment
independent college focus on, 85–86
intentions, 85
student enrollment commissions for,
142
reforms, 213–15
regulations, 218
college costs complying with,
111–12
compliance with, 219
federal government's loan, 221
nonprofit colleges compliance with,
78–79
Reich, Robert, 208

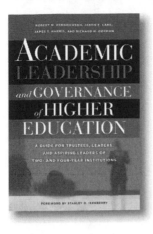

Academic Leadership and Governance of Higher
Education
*A Guide for Trustees, Leaders, and Aspiring Leaders of Two- and
Four-Year Institutions*
Robert M. Hendrickson , Jason E. Lane , James T. Harris III,
and Richard H. Dorman
Foreword by Stanley O. Ikenberry

"The book is content rich for those looking for detailed background information on a wide range of topics. The list is far too long to repeat here, but suffice it to say that this is a comprehensive work that addresses issues related to organizational dynamics, policy frameworks, government interests, academic programs, faculty responsibilities, trusteeship, global education, legal matters, strategic planning, and, of course, student success. If there is one comprehensive text you are prepared to study about higher education, make it this one."

—*Mark L. Putnam*,
President of Central College, in The Department Chair

"Enabling our colleges and universities to reach their highest academic and economic potential requires a commitment to the core values of higher education and to cultivating the partnerships in community, business, and government that allow us to bring those values to scale. *Academic Leadership and Governance of Higher Education* is a mindful handbook that leaders will find themselves referring back to often as the mission of higher education continues to evolve."

—*Nancy L. Zimpher*,
Chancellor, State University of New York

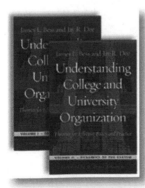

Understanding College and University Organization
Theories for Effective Policy and Practice
James L. Bess and Jay R. Dee
Foreword by D. Bruce Johnstone

Volume I: The State of the System
Volume II: Dynamics of the System

Now available in paperback, this two-volume work is intended to help readers develop powerful new ways of thinking about organizational principles, and apply them to policy-making and management in colleges and universities.

"Quite simply a tour de force. Not only have the authors written by far the broadest and deepest theoretical analysis of college and university organization I've seen, but they have clearly organized a complex topic, and written it engagingly. This will be seen as a landmark work in the field. It should be required reading for all who claim to understand higher education institutions and the behavior that goes on inside and around them."

*—**David W. Leslie**,*
Chancellor Professor of Education, The College of William and Mary

Paperback, also available at a Set price

Sty/us

22883 Quicksilver Drive
Sterling, VA 20166-2102   Subscribe to our e-mail alerts: www.Styluspub.com